# Voting from Abroad

*The International IDEA Handbook*

INSTITUTO FEDERAL ELECTORAL

# Voting from Abroad

*The International IDEA Handbook*

**Lead Writers**

Andrew Ellis
Carlos Navarro
Isabel Morales
Maria Gratschew
Nadja Braun

**Contributors**

Alan Wall
Arlinda Chantre
Brett Lacy
Catinca Slavu
Dieter Nohlen
Epp Maaten
Florian Grotz
Graham Hassall
Jacobo Hernández Cruz
Jeff Fischer
Jon Fraenkel
Judy Thompson
Kåre Vollan
Leticia Calderón
Linda Edgeworth

Luis Arias Núñez
Manuel Carrillo
Marina Costa Lobo
Nada Hadzimehic
Nuias Silva
Nydia Restrepo de Acosta
Ozias Tungwarara
Pasquale Lupoli
Patrick Molutsi
Phil Green
Reginald Austin
Richard Vengroff
Simon-Pierre Nanitelamio
Stina Larserud

**Handbook Series**

The International IDEA Handbook Series seeks to present comparative analysis, information and insights on a range of democratic institutions and processes. Handbooks are aimed primarily at policy makers, politicians, civil society actors and practitioners in the field. They are also of interest to academia, the democracy assistance community and other bodies.

Views expressed in this publication do not necessarily represent the view of International IDEA, the Federal Electoral Institute of Mexico, or their respective executive boards, governing bodies, and/or member states. This Handbook is independent of specific national or political interests. It is the result of a collaborative effort by these institutions and the work of prominent experts in the field of elections.

© International Institute for Democracy and Electoral Assistance 2007
© The Federal Electoral Institute of Mexico 2007

Applications for permission to reproduce or translate all or any part of this publication should be made to:

International IDEA
S-103 34 Stockholm
Sweden

Federal Electoral Institute of Mexico
Viaducto Tlalpan No. 100, Arenal Tepepan
14610 Mexico City
Mexico

Cover Illustration: Helena Lunding
Map: Kristina Schollin-Borg
Graphic Design: Trydells Form
Printed by: Trydells tryckeri AB, Sweden

ISBN: 978-91-85391-66-0

# Foreword

## Enabling displaced and expatriate people to vote and the role of the international community

Almost 150 years after the US state of Wisconsin passed the first law enabling external or 'out-of-country' voting, enfranchising its soldiers fighting in the American Civil War, many democracies offer the option of external voting to their nationals residing abroad. Responding to the consequences of advancing worldwide democratization and massive economic, social and cultural globalization, an increasing number of less developed countries are today also seeking to offer external voting to their citizens, of whom a significant proportion often reside abroad. Furthermore, in post-conflict societies, with large numbers of refugees and displaced persons, external voting operations are being organized on a massive scale to allow for the inclusion of these people in the electoral and political processes at home that are designed to lead to national reconciliation and lasting peace. At the same time, technological progress (including but not limited to e-voting) can sometimes provide increasingly effective and efficient means for elections to be free and fair, even if a large proportion of the voters are outside their country of origin. The International Institute for Democracy and Electoral Assistance (International IDEA) has played an important and timely role in bringing together this practical Handbook on external voting. Various international organizations, including IFES (formerly the International Foundation for Electoral Systems), the Organization for Security and Co-operation in Europe (OSCE), the Council of Europe, the United Nations Electoral Assistance Division (UNEAD), the European Parliament and the International Organization for Migration (IOM), have been at the forefront of including migrant populations in democratic electoral processes in their countries of origin. In the case of the IOM, the mandate to promote humane and orderly migration as a means to benefit both migrants and society has allowed for external voting operations to promote conditions conducive to the return of refugees and other displaced persons, notably in Bosnia and Herzegovina, Kosovo (Serbia and Montenegro), East Timor, Afghanistan and, most recently, Iraq.

However, external voting operations are complex and pose considerable challenges. In democracies holding regular elections in peacetime, provisions for external voting can be included in the electoral legislation and implemented at each electoral event, using well planned and practical timetables and deadlines. In most transitional situations, however, external voting programmes have to be set up from scratch, with neither staff nor structures in place where they are needed to enable multiple activities to happen in parallel and at great speed. Since all planning steps and operational benchmarks lead up to the ultimate deadline of election day, the deadlines for each step are usually tight and inflexible. Planning for sufficient resources to be mobilized quickly is crucial, while at the same time the political sensitivities of any electoral process—often heightened in post-conflict situations—have to be balanced. It is therefore justified in such situations to treat external voting operations as emergency operations, and those involved have to be prepared not only for the long working hours but also for having to take 'short cuts' with established standard procedures. However, the basic operational and electoral rules and regulations have to be followed so that the short cuts do not endanger the overall security and accountability of the electoral process.

From my personal experience of external voting, working under high stress levels, with hundreds or even thousands of temporary staff, often in remote geographic locations spread around the globe and in different social and cultural environments, is extremely challenging, but can at the same time be very rewarding. A high level of flexibility and creativity is indispensable in order to make external voting operations a success but, as experience has shown, good preparation based on expert knowledge goes a long way in securing the success of any emergency operation.

When judging the results of any election, other decisive factors such as the general political climate, the existence of equal opportunities in the run-up to an election, the turnout on election day, and of course the vote-counting itself, cannot be excluded, since all of them directly impact on the actual outcome. However, by providing the means for nationals overseas to participate, the international community undoubtedly contributes to promoting the individual's right to vote, and enhances democratic participation and peaceful development.

The IOM and others who have implemented external voting operations on a global scale will find their cumulative experiences summarized in this Handbook. I therefore trust that all those who are, or will be, involved in external voting processes will find the insights contained in this Handbook useful.

Pasquale Lupoli

Director, Operations Support Department
of the International Organization for Migration (IOM)

# Preface

The ability of people who are outside their home country when an election takes place to exercise their right to vote has long been an issue in electoral design and management. As the number of countries holding democratic elections has increased, however, it has become much more salient. It is not only that many more people are travelling and working around the globe. As elections take place in countries in transition after authoritarian rule, and even more so after violent conflict, the rights of refugees and people living outside a country to participate in building its future are increasingly important. At the same time, questions of principle have emerged: exactly who has the right to be represented, and how?

External voting is not always easy to design and implement. It raises issues of cost and of practical administration alongside the political considerations and considerations of representation. Many approaches have been adopted. Where they have resulted in success, this has often made a contribution to the credibility and the legitimacy of electoral events.

International IDEA and the Federal Electoral Institute of Mexico (Instituto Federal Electoral, IFE) have come together to produce this Handbook, one of the series on electoral design topics which IDEA has pioneered. This partnership combines IDEA's experience in producing global knowledge on electoral matters in a practical form for democracy builders on the ground, and the ground-breaking work of the IFE in the course of the introduction of external voting in Mexican presidential elections. This Handbook maps, explains and compares external voting provisions worldwide. It is a unique comparative product for anyone involved in improving present electoral structures, planning for external voting processes, or participating in debate.

In addition to the authors of this Handbook, we would like to express our thanks to many other people who have helped in the course of its assembly and production, and in particular those listed in the Acknowledgements.

Vidar Helgesen
Secretary-General
International IDEA

Dr Luis Carlos Ugalde
President Councilor
IFE, Mexico

# Acknowledgements

Many individuals and organizations have been involved in the production of this Handbook and we owe them several debts of gratitude. The idea of a Handbook on external voting was first raised in 1998, when the project first took shape, under the direction of Professor Reginald Austin, then head of the Rules and Guidelines Division at International IDEA, and Vijay Patidar, then deputy head of the division. Since then many people have been involved in contributing ideas and concrete work. Under the direction of Andrew Ellis, the then head of the IDEA Electoral Processes Team, the Handbook took shape in 2004 and 2005.

This is a joint publication, produced in partnership with the Federal Electoral Institute of Mexico (Instituto Federal Electoral, IFE). Under the systematic direction of Manuel Carillo and the International Department of the IFE, the Handbook further develops an overview of external voting systems and practices studied by Dr Carlos Navarro Fierro of the IFE's International Department. His colleague Isabel Morales has also given invaluable help in the research and data collection. We would also like to extend our grateful thanks to the IFE and colleagues there for their kindness and the well-prepared meetings of the editorial group. The TEPJF kindly provided their expertise for this project, under the generous guidance of Eloy Fuentes, Fernando Ojesto, and Leonel Castillo.

The responsible project managers for the Handbook were Maria Gratschew of International IDEA's Design of Democratic Institutions and Processes Team, and Carlos Navarro. It is our hope that their dedication in bringing this Handbook to fruition has resulted in a user-friendly product that contains both a theoretical discussion and practical advice for those involved in the work and debate on external voting.

The lead writers and editorial group for this Handbook were Isabel Morales, Carlos Navarro Fierro, Nadja Braun, Maria Gratschew and Andrew Ellis.

We are particularly grateful to the Federal Chancellery of Switzerland, Section of Political Rights, headed by Hans-Urs Willi, for their generosity in providing the outstanding expertise of Nadja Braun, on secondment to International IDEA during 2004. Nor can we neglect the early contributions by several individuals when the project was being managed by Programme Officer Bruce Henry at International IDEA. Daniela Capaccio, Marc Douville, Jeff Labovitz, Shawn O'Brien, Renata Tardioli and Amare Tekle were early contributors of ideas, suggestions and work on external voting issues. Data and information were also provided by Peter Erben, Giff Johnson, Kristina Lemon, Gerald Mitchell, Joram Rukambe, Domenico Tuccinardi and Vadim Zhdanovich. We thank Hanna Bertheim, Linda Ederberg, Samuel Jones, and Johan Lindroth for providing detailed research for the comparative overview, as well as suggestions for other content; and Stina Larserud for continuing the work temporarily in 2005. We extend our appreciation for her efforts to Atty Kabaitan R. Guinhawa-Valmonte of the Commission on Elections of the Republic of the Philippines; and special thanks go to Erin Thiessen for her most helpful input on turnout among external voters. Brett Lacy for excellent research assistance, and Thomas Buchsbaum for research on external voting for European Parliament elections.

Additional thanks go to Per Ahlström, Magalí Amieva, Ayman Ayoub, Allassoum Bedoum, Francesca Binda, Åsa Björklund, Anthony Bowyer, Theofilus Dowetin, Naomi Effah, the Electoral Office and the Electoral Enrolment Centre of New Zealand, Mileydi Fougstedt, Malin Frick, Lourdes González, Margot Gould, Jeremy Grace, Ossama Kamel, Domingos Magalhaes, Zoe Mills, Stephan de Mul, Rushdi Nackerdien, Simon-Pierre Nanitelamio, Konrad Olszewski, Therese Laanela Pearce, Miguel Pinto, Antonio Spinelli, Martin Tete and Emad Yousef.

Finally, we wish to thank Nadia Handal Zander, Florencia Enghel, Lisa Hagman and Anh Dung Nguyen of the International IDEA Publications Team and José-Luis Escutia of the IFE International Department for their patient work, as well as the editor Eve Johansson for her meticulous attention to detail.

# Contents

**Foreword** .................................................................................................................III
**Preface** .....................................................................................................................V
**Acknowledgements** ................................................................................................VI
**Acronyms and abbreviations** ................................................................................XIV

## Introduction ............................................................................................................1
Nadja Braun and Maria Gratschew
    1. Background ......................................................................................................1
    2. In which types of election does external voting apply? ..................................4
    3. Categories of external electors: who is entitled to an external vote? ............4
        3.1. Restrictions ................................................................................................5
    4. Ways of voting from abroad: what are the procedures for casting an external vote? ..........6
    5. Looking ahead..................................................................................................7
    6. Terminology .....................................................................................................8

## Chapter 1. External voting: a comparative overview .......................................11
Carlos Navarro, Isabel Morales and Maria Gratschew
    1. Introduction.....................................................................................................11
    2. The countries which have current provisions for external voting.................12
        2.1. Countries where provisions for external voting exist
        but are still to be implemented ................................................................13
    3. Types of elections to which external voting applies ......................................15
    4. Persons eligible to vote from abroad ............................................................18
    5. Voting procedures in use for external voting ................................................22
    6. Political representation for external voters...................................................28
    7. External voting and participation...................................................................30
        7.1. A sample of the information available on turnout by external voters ......31
        7.2. The reasons for lower turnout by external voters ...................................32
        7.3. Problems arising from lower turnout by external voters..........................34

**Table 1.1**: Countries and territories with current provisions for external voting..........12
**Table 1.2**: Countries where provisions for external voting exist but are still to be implemented............13
**Table 1.3**: Types of election for which external voting applies ....................................17
**Table 1.4**: Countries and territories which restricted entitlement to an external
    vote according to activity abroad (14) ..........................................................19
**Table 1.5**: Some examples of countries and territories which restrict entitlement
    to an external vote according to length of stay abroad ...............................20
**Table 1.6**: External voting procedures ........................................................................23
**Table 1.7**: Countries with mixed procedures for external voting .................................26
**Table 1.8**: Political representation in national legislatures for external voters............28

**Case study**
    **Botswana**: disappointing results of external voting ........................................36
    Patrick Molutsi

## Chapter 2. The history and politics of external voting .................................................. 41
Andrew Ellis

    1. A survey of the history of external voting ................................................................. 41
    2. External voting in democratic transitions ................................................................. 44
    3. External voting and electoral system design............................................................. 45
        3.1. Personal voting and electoral system design............................................... 46
        3.2. External voting and electoral system design ............................................... 47
        3.3. Proxy voting and electoral system design.................................................... 47
        3.4. Timing issues ................................................................................................. 48

**Case studies**

    **The Cook Islands:** seat for overseas voters abolished ............................................. 50
    Graham Hassall

    **Indonesia:** a long-established system for external voting at diplomatic missions .................. 53
    Alan Wall

    **Zimbabwe:** highly restrictive provisions ................................................................. 56
    Ozias Tungwarara

    **Mozambique:** a system that is too subjective? ....................................................... 59
    Simon-Pierre Nanitelamio

## Chapter 3. The legal framework and an overview of electoral legislation .................. 65
Dieter Nohlen and Florian Grotz

    1. External voting: a challenge for democracies in the 21st century?........................ 65
    2. The concept and provisions of external voting: basic features and institutional choices ..67
        2.1. The concept of external voting.................................................................... 67
        2.2. Legal sources for external voting ................................................................. 67
        2.3. Entitlement to an external vote and requirements for registration
        as an external elector ........................................................................................ 68
        2.4. The procedures for external voting .............................................................. 68
        2.5. The assignment of external votes to electoral districts............................... 69
    3. Three structural problems of external voting ........................................................... 71
        3.1. External voting: the problem of representation .......................................... 71
        3.2. External voting: the challenge of electoral organization ........................... 73
        3.3. External voting and electoral dispute resolution......................................... 74
        3.4. A preliminary summary of the structural problems .................................... 74
    4. Conclusions ................................................................................................................. 74

**Table 3.1:** Overview of the arguments for and against the introduction of external voting ..................... 75

**Case studies**

    **Colombia:** representation of emigrants in the Congress .................................................. 78
    Nydia Restrepo de Acosta

    **Portugal:** extended voting rights and decreasing participation ................................. 83
    Marina Costa Lobo

## Chapter 4. Entitlement to vote .................................................................................................. 89
Phil Green

    1. Introduction ........................................................................................................................ 89
    2. Types of election ................................................................................................................ 90
    3. Conditions for entitlement to vote externally ................................................................. 90
        3.1. Citizenship ............................................................................................................. 91
        3.2. Place of residence ................................................................................................. 93
        3.3. Compulsory voting and external voting ............................................................. 96
    4. Qualification to stand as a candidate in elections ........................................................ 96
    5. Registration of external electors ...................................................................................... 97
    6. Examples of qualifications for external voting ............................................................... 98
    7. Conclusions ..................................................................................................................... 101

**Box 4.1:** Examples of qualifications for external voting ........................................................ 99

**Case studies**

    **Senegal:** a significant external electorate ......................................................................... 104
    Richard Vengroff

    **The Marshall Islands:** a high proportion of external voters ........................................ 108
    Jon Fraenkel

## Chapter 5. The implementation of external voting ............................................................. 113
Judy Thompson

    1. Introduction ..................................................................................................................... 113
    2. The procedures for external voting ................................................................................ 114
    3. Timelines .......................................................................................................................... 115
    4. Costing and budgeting .................................................................................................... 118
    5. Logistics ............................................................................................................................ 121
    6. The security of election materials .................................................................................. 122
    7. Voter registration ............................................................................................................. 123
    8. External voting and the secret ballot ............................................................................. 124
    9. Contracting out external voting ..................................................................................... 126
    10. Conclusions ................................................................................................................... 126

**Table 5.1:** Advantages and disadvantages of external voting procedures ........................ 115

**Table 5.2:** Examples of election timelines for external and in-country voting ..................116
**Table 5.3:** Examples of the cost of external voting programmes ..................................119
**Figure 5.1:** Envelopes used for external voting ..............................................................125
**Case studies**
    **Brazil:** compulsory voting and renewed interest among external voters ...............128
    Leticia Calderón-Chelius

    **Honduras:** a decision based on political calculations ............................................132
    Jacobo Hernández Cruz

## Chapter 6. Host country issues ....................................................................................137
Brett Lacy
    1. Negotiating with host countries .............................................................................138
    2. The roles and responsibilities of host countries ....................................................139
    3. Host country agreements ......................................................................................144
        3.1. The role of third parties ..................................................................................145
        3.2. General guidelines for host country agreements ............................................145
        3.3. External voting in consulates, in embassies or by post ..................................146
    4. Costs .......................................................................................................................146
    5. Conclusions ............................................................................................................148

## Chapter 7. The political rights of refugees and displaced persons: enfranchisement and participation ..............................................................................151
Jeff Fischer
    1. Introduction ............................................................................................................151
        1.1. Who is a 'refugee'? .........................................................................................151
    2. Obstacles to refugee enfranchisement ..................................................................153
    3. The regulatory framework .....................................................................................154
        3.1. Entitlement ......................................................................................................154
        3.2. The election cycle ...........................................................................................155
        3.3. Systems of representation ..............................................................................155
        3.4. Security ............................................................................................................155
    4. Special political and logistical requirements .........................................................156
        4.1. Country and organizational constellations .....................................................156
        4.2. Information ......................................................................................................157
        4.3. The politics of displacement ...........................................................................157
    5. Conclusions ............................................................................................................157

**Table 7.1:** Refugee populations and electoral events ......................................................153

**Case studies**

    **Afghanistan's 2004 presidential election:** external voting for a large displaced population 158
    Catinca Slavu

    **Bosnia and Herzegovina:** post-war trends in external voting ...................................................163
    Linda Edgeworth and Nada Hadzimehic

    **Iraq:** a large diaspora and security concerns ................................................................................168
    Judy Thompson

## Chapter 8. The political rights of migrant workers and external voting ...... 173
Carlos Navarro Fierro

    1. Introduction ................................................................................................................................. 173
    2. Awareness of migrant workers' political rights ................................................................. 174
    3. The challenges of designing an external voting mechanism that
    includes migrant workers ........................................................................................................ 175
    4. Alternatives for design and implementation ..................................................................... 179
    5. Concluding comments ............................................................................................................ 181

**Case studies**

    **The Dominican Republic:** political agreement in response to demands for
    the right to vote from abroad ...................................................................................................184
    Luis Arias Núñez

    **Mexico:** safeguarding the integrity of the electoral process .......................................... 189
    Carlos Navarro Fierro and Manuel Carillo

    **The Philippines:** the first experience of external voting ................................................. 193
    Philippines Committee on Overseas Absentee Voting

    **Cape Verde:** a large diaspora and low turnout by external voters ................................. 200
    Nuias Silva and Arlinda Chantre

## Chapter 9. Observation of external voting ...... 205
Kåre Vollan

    1. Observing elections: general background ......................................................................... 205
    2. Types of observation and their purpose ............................................................................. 206
    3. The assessment prior to observation .................................................................................. 207
    4. When should external voting be observed? ....................................................................... 207
    5. External voting: controlled and uncontrolled environments ........................................ 208
    6. Data collection ......................................................................................................................... 209
    7. The observation process: possibilities and limitations .................................................. 210
        7.1. The political environment ............................................................................................. 211
        7.2. Personal voting in a controlled environment ........................................................... 211

  7.3. Postal voting .................................................................................................. 212
  7.4. Electronic voting ............................................................................................ 212
 8. Conclusions .............................................................................................................. 213

## Chapter 10. E-voting and external voting ............................................................. 217
Nadja Braun

 1. Introduction ............................................................................................................. 217
 2. Remote e-voting and external voting ................................................................... 218
 3. Arguments in favour of and against remote e-voting for external voters ......... 221
  3.1. In favour .......................................................................................................... 221
  3.2. Against ............................................................................................................ 221
 4. Some security challenges for remote e-voting and possible solutions ............. 222
 5. Other support through new information and communication technologies ... 224
 6. Conclusion ............................................................................................................... 225

**Table 10.1:** Security challenges for remote voting and possible solutions ................ 223

**Case studies**
 **Estonia:** more options for external voting ................................................... 226
 Epp Maaten

 **Switzerland:** external voting in a federal state with direct democracy ........ 230
 Nadja Braun

**Annex A.** External voting: a world survey of 214 countries and territories ................ 234
**Annex B.** Glossary of terms ........................................................................................... 246
**Annex C.** References and further reading .................................................................... 252
**Annex D.** The cost of external voting: some examples ............................................... 262
**Annex E.** About the contributors .................................................................................. 267

**About International IDEA** ............................................................................................. 276
**About the Federal Electoral Institute of Mexico** ........................................................ 278
**Map of the 214 countries and territories**

# Acronyms and abbreviations

| | |
|---|---|
| **AU** | African Union |
| **BiH** | Bosnia and Herzegovina |
| **BPRAS** | Bundesgesetz über die politischen Rechte der Auslandschweizer (Switzerland) |
| **CEB** | Central Electoral Board (Dominican Republic) |
| **CIP** | Cook Islands Party |
| **COAV** | Committee on Overseas Absentee Voting (Philippines) |
| **COMELEC** | Commission on Elections (Philippines) |
| **CSFE** | Conseil supérieur des Français de l'étranger (Council of French Citizens Abroad) |
| **DFA** | Department of Foreign Affairs (Philippines) |
| **DFA-OAVS** | Overseas Absentee Voting Secretariat, Department of Foreign Affairs (Philippines) |
| **DP** | Democratic Party (Cook Islands) |
| **DPD** | Regional Representatives Council (Indonesia) |
| **DPR** | People's Representative Council (Indonesia) |
| **DFA** | Department of Foreign Affairs (Philippines) |
| **DPR** | People's Representative Council (Indonesia) |
| **DPRD** | Regional Representative Council (Indonesia) |
| **EMB** | electoral management body |
| **ERAO** | Electoral Registry Abroad Office (Dominican Republic) |
| **ERB** | Election Registration Board (Philippines) |
| **EU** | European Union |
| **Frelimo** | Frente de Libertação de Moçambique (Mozambican Liberation Front) |
| **FPTP** | First Past The Post (electoral system) |
| **FRY** | Federal Republic of Yugoslavia |
| **ID** | identification document |
| **IDEA** | International Institute for Democracy and Electoral Assistance |
| **IDP** | internally displaced person |
| **IEC** | Independent Electoral Commission (Botswana) |
| **IECI** | Independent Electoral Commission of Iraq |
| **IFE** | Instituto Federal Electoral (Federal Electoral Institute) (Mexico) |
| **IFES** | International Foundation for Election Systems |
| **IOM** | International Organization for Migration |
| **JEMB** | Joint Electoral Management Body (Afghanistan) |
| **JRT** | Joint Registration Taskforce (Kosovo) |
| **KPU** | National Election Commission (Indonesia) |
| **LCO** | Logistic Coordination Office (Dominican Republic) |
| **MECO** | Manila Economic and Cultural Office (Philippines) |
| **MMP** | Mixed Member Proportional (electoral system) |
| **MOU** | memorandum of understanding |
| **MP** | member of parliament |
| **NEC** | National Electoral Commission (Mozambique) |

| | |
|---|---|
| **NEC** | National Electoral Council (Colombia) |
| **NGO** | non-governmental organization |
| **NRCS** | National Registry of the Civil State (Registraduria Nacional del Estado Civil) (Colombia) |
| **NZD** | New Zealand dollar |
| **OAV** | overseas absentee voter (Philippines) |
| **OCV** | out-of-country voting (Iraq) |
| **ODIHR** | Office for Democratic Institutions and Human Rights |
| **ONEL** | Observatoire National des Elections (Senegal) |
| **OSCE** | Organization for Security and Co-operation in Europe |
| **PC** | personal computer |
| **PDA** | personal digital assistant |
| **PHP** | Philippines peso |
| **PPLN** | overseas voting committee (Indonesia) |
| **PR** | proportional representation |
| **Renamo** | Resistência Nacional Moçambicana (Mozambican National Resistance) |
| **RESG** | Refugee Elections Steering Group (for the 1996 elections in Bosnia and Herzegovina) |
| **RS** | Republika Srpska (Serb Republic) (Bosnia and Herzegovina) |
| **SADC** | Southern African Development Community |
| **SBEI** | Special Board of Election Inspectors (Philippines) |
| **SNTV** | Single Non-Transferable Vote (electoral system) |
| **TAL** | Law of Administration for the State of Iraq for the Transitional Period |
| **TRS** | Two-Round System (electoral system) |
| **TSE** | Tribunal Electoral Superior (Superior Electoral Tribunal) (Brazil) |
| **UK** | United Kingdom |
| **UN** | United Nations |
| **UNAMA** | UN Assistance Mission in Afghanistan |
| **UNDP** | United Nations Development Programme |
| **UNEAD** | United Nations Electoral Assistance Division |
| **UNHCR** | United Nations High Commissioner for Refugees |
| **USD** | US dollar |

# Introduction

# Introduction

Nadja Braun and Maria Gratschew

## 1. Background

The globalization of political, personal and professional life, the spread of democracy throughout the world and an increase in migration for many different reasons have all contributed to an increasing interest in voting rights for refugees, diplomats, members of the armed forces serving overseas and other people who are temporarily or permanently absent from their own country. While the constitutions of many countries guarantee the right to vote for all citizens, in reality voters who are outside their home country when elections take place are often disenfranchised because of a lack of procedures enabling them to exercise that right. The following chapters examine the theoretical and practical issues surrounding external voting, map existing provisions worldwide, and contain examples of how external voting is implemented in different countries.

International IDEA is well suited to take on the task of producing this Handbook. Being the source for global and comparative electoral and institutional knowledge, tools and materials, IDEA has in this long-awaited Handbook sought to bring together existing knowledge and experience of external voting and to make them available to stakeholders of the electoral process who could benefit from knowing more about whether and how their decisions will affect and have implications for external and internal voters. Theoretical and practical approaches meet in this Handbook. Stakeholders such as legislators, election administrators, politicians, government officials, academics, the media, election observers and others appointed to evaluate or design external voting processes have access to very few or only inadequate resources to guide them in their work. As there is currently no likelihood of general, global common electoral standards or guidelines being developed, the gathering of existing knowledge and the sharing of resources and experience between electoral management bodies (EMBs) becomes key to the enhancement of future external voting activities.

The aim is that this Handbook will engage stakeholders in debate and further discussion on the topic in order to improve present structures, future readiness and practice in external voting. On both theoretical and practical levels it aims to contribute to the discussion of the basic principle of representation and how to operationalize and balance criteria such as inclusiveness and effectiveness. IDEA hopes that it will also create greater general understanding of electoral and institutional design issues on the part of legislators, EMBs, political parties and other participants debating change. Providing good external voting practices is a future challenge to democracy and to the perception of democracy—among migrant voters in particular.

In 2000 there were 175 million international migrants in the world, that is, one out of every 35 persons in the world was an international migrant. This total represented a more than twofold increase from 76 million in 1960. By comparison, the world population only doubled from 3 billion in 1960 to 6 billion in 2000. Interestingly, statistics show an increased concentration of migrants in the developed world and in a small number of countries. Trends also show that there has been a shift of labour migration to East and South-East Asia, and migration has also been responsible for the increase in population growth in receiving countries where fertility levels have been low.

Although exact statistics on migration are difficult to collect, estimates show that the total number of migrants in the world may have reached 190 million in early 2005. The number has more than doubled since the 1970s. The collapse of the Soviet Union produced a high proportion of these migrants during the late 1980s and early 1990s. The number of migrants living in developed countries is higher than the number living in developing countries, and has increased since the 1970s. It has increased mainly in North America and in the territory of the former Soviet Union, while it has decreased particularly in Asia, Latin America and the Caribbean. In 2000 the number of countries where migrants accounted for 10 per cent of the population was 70. There are six countries or areas in the world where migrants constitute more than 60 per cent of the population.

Professional groups, students, tourists and other potential external voters have also increased in numbers since World War II. Not only have the numbers of potential external voters increased over the world; they are also more mobile and move or travel faster, which increases the demand for external voting practices to function in different circumstances.

Furthermore, the past decade has seen a number of instances of the international community assisting in the organization of elections as an important element of agreements designed to end major intra-state conflicts. In each of these elections, including those in Cambodia, Bosnia and Herzegovina (see the case study), Croatia, Mozambique (see the case study), Angola and Haiti, the participation of refugees and/or other citizens residing outside the country at the time of the election has been a major issue of concern to the parties. In some cases, the large populations displaced by the conflict have been able to vote; in others their participation has not been ensured. While each case raises its own special issues, there are common circumstances which need to be analysed for the lessons they can provide for the resolution of future similar conflicts.

It is also the case that international migrants are a potentially important political force whose votes can in many cases significantly affect election results. Political parties, sitting governments and oppositions are therefore likely to have different views on participation in the elections. If large groups of citizens have left the country for political reasons, it can be assumed that the ruling party will not favour extending voting rights to these groups.

Less controversial are the special provisions enacted by a number of countries to enable voting by diplomats and members of the armed forces outside the country. Even less controversial are provisions that allow all a country's citizens living abroad to vote from abroad. Voting rights for such people must also be considered in conjunction with mechanisms to facilitate voting by those who are normally resident in the country but are temporarily absent, such as tourists, students or those travelling on business.

External voting is now on the political agenda in many countries. Historically, it is quite a recent phenomenon. There are exceptions, as a small number of countries have practised this for many years—for example, Iceland allowed sailors and fishermen an external vote as early as the beginning of the 20th century—but even in some long-established democracies citizens who were resident in other countries were not granted the right to vote until the 1980s or the 1990s. External voting was recently introduced in Mexico (see case study), where it was extended to all voters abroad for the first time in the July 2006 presidential election, and in Ghana, where it will be applied for the first time in the 2008 national elections, as well as in Panama. *Andrew Ellis* outlines the history of other early introductions of external voting in chapter 2, and *Dieter Nohlen and Florian Grotz* point out in chapter 3 that its sudden relevance in different regions of the world clearly derives from the worldwide political changes of the 1990s.

External voting is currently allowed by 115 countries and territories in the world. Of those countries, some two-thirds allow all their citizens a vote from abroad, and one-third partially restrict the right to an external vote. One hundred and fifteen countries, or more than 50 per cent of the world's democracies, if for this purpose we take the criterion for being a democracy to be the 'lowest common denominator' of the holding of multiparty elections and the guarantee of universal suffrage, allow external voting. Twenty-eight African countries and 16 countries in the Americas have external voting. A fairly high number of European countries (41) allow it, as well as ten in Oceania and 20 in Asia (see table 1.1 for a complete overview).

The simple presence or absence of external voting provisions is, however, far too simplistic a measure. It is more constructive to analyse the external voting provisions in detail, since there is a variety of systems in use. There is great variation when it comes to which groups of people are allowed to vote from abroad, and under what circumstances, what is required from them, how and where votes can be cast and how they are counted. Some countries, for example, allow external voting only for certain groups abroad or if a certain minimum number of voters register in one country; others allow external voting only for certain elections or only in very few countries abroad.

Five countries have provisions for allowing external voting but have not yet implemented them, for different reasons. These are Angola, Bolivia, Greece, Nicaragua and Panama. One example until recently was Mozambique, where provisions to allow external voting were introduced in the early 1990s but not implemented at an election until December 2004. The reasons for having provisions for external voting in place but not implementing it in practice differ and may be political, financial, administrative or logistical. In the case of Mozambique (see the case study), for each individual election, external voting cannot be held until the country's EMB deems that certain necessary conditions, material and organizational, are satisfied. External voting was first implemented in Mozambique in 2004 some ten years after the law on external voting was written.

Table 1.1 and annex A list 115 countries that have provisions for external voting and the 100 countries and territories that do not allow it. Table 1.2 lists countries that have external voting arrangements in place but have not so far applied them because their implementation mechanisms are pending for different reasons.

The practical implementation of external voting is complicated by factors such as the number of voters, their locations, the distances involved, the cost of external voting and the complexity of the voting system. As *Judy Thompson* writes in chapter 5, external voting makes election planning more complex. Planning for external voting processes also needs to take into account issues of preventing double voting, such as voters casting a vote both from their home country and from abroad.

## 2. In which types of election does external voting apply?

External voting can be applied at national or local elections or both. It can also be used for referendums and sub-national elections. It is most common for countries to allow external voting for national elections only, that is, for presidential or legislative elections. Some countries, such as Ireland and Russia, allow external voting for all these types of election, including referendums and sub-national elections. Table 1.3 and annex A give details of the types of election for which external voting applies in the countries which allow external voting.

## 3. Categories of external elector: who is entitled to an external vote?

There are several categories of external electors in the world and different approaches to categorizing them. Social, political, cultural or ethnic circumstances all lead to migration and also, therefore, produce groups of potential external voters. This Handbook suggests that there are four main groups of people staying or residing abroad who are entitled to vote. These are (a) migrant workers, (b) refugees and, for the purposes of this Handbook, internally displaced persons (IDPs), (c) individuals in certain professional groups, such as military personnel, public officials or diplomatic staff (and their families) and (d) all a country's citizens living or staying abroad, temporarily or permanently (sometimes subject to restrictions: see section 3.1). *Phil Green* discusses these groups and their entitlements in more detail in chapter 4.

- The first group is *migrant workers*. Of the 190 million people mentioned above, at least 50 per cent are migrant workers. A high proportion, or about 30–40 million, of these are illegal workers, without the proper documentation, which both makes it difficult for them to register and vote as external electors and leads to feelings of insecurity as they fear being penalized if they do. *Carlos Navarro* writes about these issues in chapter 8 and highlights the large numbers of Mexican migrant workers in the United States.

- In addition to the international migrant workers, the International organization for Migration (IOM) suggests that approximately 8.5 million people are *refugees* in the world and about 24 million people are *IDPs*. Refugees are those who have migrated to a second country because of political, social or cultural circumstances, and can therefore clearly qualify as external electors. IDPs may be regarded as migrants or refugees within their own country, but they are considered together with refugees in this Handbook because they present similar problems and can constitute a large group whose right to vote is threatened. Organizing external voting for IDPs or refugees may be very complicated, as a great deal of information is needed before such activities can take place. As *Jeff Fischer* indicates in chapter 7, several issues must be taken into account, including the fact that the country holding elections needs to know where its electors are located, the fact that there may be security problems in organizing elections in a certain area or country, and the question whether agreements need to be reached with the host country. In addition, these elections may involve high costs, and careful and timely planning may be crucial to the electoral process. Lessons learned tell us, however, that time is often the one resource which is lacking. The enfranchisement of refugees might have some difficult political implications, but at the same time it can also help to resolve conflicts, since the political motives for displacing people would be reduced if refugee populations produced by 'rogue' regimes did not lose their political rights but continued to have a voice and to vote regardless of their temporary dislocation. The organization of external voting for refugees usually involves collaboration with international organizations.

- The members of a *professional group* are those that are resident in a country other than that of their franchise by virtue of their work, usually in some form of state service. Some countries, for example, India, Zimbabwe and several other countries of all regions, allow only certain groups to register and vote from abroad (see chapter 1). *Dieter Nohlen* and *Florian Grotz* discuss in chapter 3 whether voting should be regarded as a fundamental right for all, regardless of their location, or whether it should be restricted and tied to citizenship, or to residency or location.

- The final category is *all a country's citizens abroad*. Austria, Russia and Sweden, for example, allow external voting by all their electors abroad.

### 3.1. Restrictions

As chapter 3 by *Dieter Nohlen* and *Florian Grotz* also indicates, there are some restrictions on the entitlement to vote externally that certain countries apply. Restrictions are normally related to the time spent abroad or the activity carried out abroad. About 30 countries in the world have restrictions in place for external electors.

For practical reasons, a country may limit the availability of external voting to citizens living or staying in certain (in some cases neighbouring) countries. Some countries, such as Senegal (see the case study), make the option of external voting available only when a minimum number of external electors are registered in a host country.

Entitlement to vote from abroad is sometimes restricted to a specific type of election or referendum (see section 2 above).

The entitlement to vote from abroad is sometimes restricted to voters who are assumed to have a connection with their home country. They may have to show an intent to return to their country of origin, as in the case of the Philippines (see the case study).

Sometimes there are additional requirements, for example, that voters must not be abroad for longer than a specified number of years. This is the case, for example, in the United Kingdom (see chapter 1).

## 4. Ways of voting from abroad: what are the procedures for casting an external vote?

There are several ways in which electors can cast their vote from abroad. Some countries, for example the Cook Islands (see the case study), Indonesia (see the case study), India and Slovenia offer alternative methods for voting from abroad, while other countries limit their options to one, for logistical or financial reasons. Some options are more costly than others, while some offer a more secure or faster voting channel. The four main voting options (also the subject of chapters 1 and 5) are the following.

• *Personal voting*. The voter must go to a specific place and cast his or her vote there in person. This can be a diplomatic mission or a polling place specially set up abroad. This is the procedure most widely used for casting an external vote and is found as the single voting method in for example Afghanistan (see the case study), Argentina, Hungary and South Africa.

• *Postal voting*. The voter fills out the ballot paper at a place he or she chooses and the vote is then transmitted by ordinary post to the home country. Sometimes witnesses are required to confirm the identity of the voter and witness that he or she has filled in the ballot paper freely and without interference. Postal voting is the single voting method in for example Canada, Jersey, Norway, Mexico (see the case study) and Switzerland (see the case study).

• The *proxy vote*. A citizen living or staying abroad may be enabled to vote by choosing a proxy who casts the vote for the voter at a polling place in the home country, or abroad. All but four countries that provide this method provide it in combination with personal voting or postal voting.

- *Electronic means*. The voter may use the Internet, personal digital assistants (PDAs), telephones or a mobile phone to cast his or her vote. This type of electronic voting is most often referred to as remote electronic voting, or e-voting and may become more common in future. The case study on Estonia and chapter 10 discuss the piloting of this kind of option.

There are also other methods. Two countries—Australia and New Zealand—allow their external voters to vote by fax, in certain circumstances and if specially required.

Tables 1.6 and 1.7 and annex A list the procedures used in different countries or mixed voting procedures. The most common option, made available by most countries that practise external voting, is personal voting. Voting often takes place in diplomatic missions or other official facilities. This option is used by 55 countries. The main advantages of this option are that it ensures the secrecy of the vote, and that the voter's choice is guaranteed to end up on the ballot paper. The second most common single option is postal voting. The advantages of this option include that it can be practised from most countries in the world, while the disadvantages may include high costs and slow postal services. However, mixed systems, which offer external voters more than one voting option, are not uncommon and are found in 27 countries. Mixed systems can for example offer personal voting and postal voting, or proxy voting and postal voting.

Very few countries have started using electronic voting for their external voters, although several tests are being carried out, and systems are being piloted. Only Estonia, France and the Netherlands have so far offered this option to its external voters. The recent spread of new information and communication technologies, especially the Internet and mobile phones, may provide new voting channels that could facilitate external voting in particular in the near future. As *Nadja Braun* highlights in chapter 10, the security issues involved with electronic voting, and especially with remote e-voting, pose some challenges that should be resolved before this new voting channel can be introduced. Cost is another issue of concern that should be addressed before moving into a wide use of e-voting. While e-voting has only been tested and implemented on a few occasions, more experience is available when it comes to using electronic means for facilitating parts of the external voting process, such as the provision of information on the parties and candidates and voter registration.

## 5. Looking ahead

In many countries the right of citizens who are resident abroad, or of tourists or travelling businessmen who are temporarily or permanently abroad on election day, to participate in elections is a fairly recent development, and it is not yet universal in any part of the world. Universal—that is, unrestricted and unconditional—external voting is, however, regarded by many as part of the citizen's rights in a world where living or staying abroad forms part of the life of millions of people and where the exercise of rights and the enforcement of laws are becoming more transnational every day. With respect to political rights and duties, it is also interesting to discuss whether countries should or should not allow non-national residents to vote for institutions in the home country, such as the national legislature, in referendums or for the presidency. If they do not and there is no provision for external voting in the home country, this represents a significant loss of political rights for those who are abroad. Some countries, for example Sweden, allow it at local or regional level. Chapter 3 broaches this issue.

Some countries will review their provisions to allow external voting, and in the process may decide to abolish or continue it. The main reason for abolishing external voting seems to be its high cost, especially the cost per voter, but the principles of the equal right to participate and equal opportunity to participate argues against applying criteria of cost-effectiveness to such a fundamental political right. Discussions about the introduction of external voting are ongoing in several Latin American countries, while the possibility of abolishing it is also being discussed in some other countries.

This Handbook also presents examples of the cost of external voting; rough estimates as well as actual cost (see case studies and Annex D). Most countries with provisions for external voting organise it through their administrative settings, with assistance of mail services, the Ministry for Foreign Affairs etc. However, a smaller number of countries, typically those that have recently come out of a conflict, organise it with the assistance of international organisations, other countries or partners. Assistance of international partners may be necessary in some cases for a variety of reasons, including issues relating to trust, security or organisational settings. However, as suggested by appendix D and certain case studies, working on external voting through international partners can be extremely costly.

Finally, this Handbook brings up examples of disappointing participation rates among external electors, for example, in Botswana and Mexico (see the case studies and chapter 1). There are several reasons for potential external electors not to register or vote. They may relate to a person's fear of being located at a place where he or she is not expected to be, for work or political reasons. Other reasons may include that a person has become distanced from the political issues in their own country, or the sometimes complex or costly logistical efforts that have to be gone through in order first to register and then to vote. The final section of chapter 1 discusses the importance of participation and considers why some countries do not allow external voting, or are planning to abolish it.

## 6. Terminology

For the purposes of this Handbook, external voting means procedures which enable some or all electors of a country who are temporarily or permanently abroad to exercise their voting rights from outside the national territory. The term used throughout the Handbook is 'external voting'. Expressions such 'absent voting', 'absentee voting' or 'out-of-country voting' which are commonly found mean the same thing. Annex B provides a glossary of other terms used in this Handbook.

# CHAPTER 1

# 1. External voting: a comparative overview

Carlos Navarro Fierro, Isabel Morales and Maria Gratschew*

## 1. Introduction

This chapter presents a comparative overview of external voting practices worldwide. It is based on 214 countries and related territories. They include all UN member states as well as territories which, although they have a different juridical status, share a common feature: they elect their own authorities and are not represented in a parliament or legislative body of the state to which they belong. A full list of countries and territories and the external voting provisions in each of them is presented at annex A of this Handbook.

The research shows that 115 states and territories have legal provisions which allow their electors to cast a vote from abroad (as of May 2007). This figure includes five which have legal provisions in place to allow external voting but, for different reasons, it has not yet been implemented.

Annex A and the information provided in this chapter only include reference to countries and territories where external voting provisions exist for national elections or national referendums. Countries and territories where provisions for external voting exist only at local level have not been included.

A small number of countries have had legal provisions on external voting but only applied them exceptionally at one time in their history. There are cases where external voting has been used at one time in the history of a country or territory but where it is no longer continued or provided for in the legal framework. Eritrea and East Timor are examples of such cases. External voting was allowed in the referendums related to their independence, in 1993 and 1999, respectively. Another example of earlier use of external

---

*Brett Lacy assisted with research for this comparative overview and for Annex A.

voting, on a very restrictive basis, is Cambodia, where external voting was allowed for elections to its Constituent Assembly in 1993, but only if voters had first travelled to Cambodia to register. Tokelau also falls into this category: here external voting was only used on a limited basis in its independence referendum in 2006.

This overview attempts to map out the different practices in external voting, and to describe and group some of them. It should be noted that the process of categorizing these builds on 115 cases of external voting and, while it aims to describe all practices, some may seem simplified or may not be represented at any great length. Annex A provides more detailed information country by country.

## 2. The countries which have current provisions for external voting

As table 1.1 shows, external voting provisions are widespread throughout the world. External voting is most common in Europe, but is found in every region of the globe. All regions have in common that a majority of the countries and territories have external voting.

Examination of the types of countries that have external voting also shows that they are very different in the level of socio-economic development: they include both Organisation for Economic Co-operation and Development (OECD) member countries and countries from the less developed regions of the world. While there is no obvious correlation between external voting provisions and socio-economic or political features, these factors remain important in the debates and decision making related to external voting provisions and practices, and are often reflected in the challenges or complexities faced. The countries also differ in the length of time for which their democracies have been established, their roots, and the stability and consolidation of their institutions and democratic practices. They include well-established democracies along with the emerging or restored ones, and even some countries that can only doubtfully be classified as democratic.

Table 1.1: Countries and territories with current provisions for external voting

| Region | Country |
| --- | --- |
| **Africa (28)** | Algeria, Angola, Benin, Botswana, Cape Verde, Central African Republic, Chad, Côte d'Ivoire, Djibouti, Equatorial Guinea, Gabon, Ghana, Guinea, Guinea-Bissau, Lesotho, Mali, Mauritius, Mozambique, Namibia, Niger, Rwanda, São Tomé and Principe, Senegal, South Africa, Sudan, Togo, Tunisia, Zimbabwe |
| **Americas (16)** | Argentina, Bolivia, Brazil, Canada, Colombia, Dominican Republic, Ecuador, Falkland Islands, Guyana, Honduras, Mexico, Nicaragua, Panama, Peru, United States, Venezuela |
| **Asia (20)** | Afghanistan, Bangladesh, India, Indonesia, Iran, Iraq, Israel, Japan, Kazakhstan, Kyrgyzstan, Laos, Malaysia, Oman, Philippines, Singapore, Syria, Tajikistan, Thailand, Uzbekistan, Yemen |

| Region | Country |
|---|---|
| **Western, Central and Eastern Europe (41)** | Austria, Azerbaijan, Belarus, Belgium, Bosnia and Herzegovina, Bulgaria, Croatia, Czech Republic, Denmark, Estonia, Finland, France, Georgia, Germany, Gibraltar, Greece, Guernsey, Hungary, Iceland, Ireland, Italy, Jersey, Latvia, Liechtenstein, Lithuania, Luxembourg, Isle of Man, Moldova, Netherlands, Norway, Poland, Portugal, Romania, Russia, Slovenia, Spain, Sweden, Switzerland, Turkey, Ukraine, United Kingdom |
| **Pacific (10)** | Australia, Cook Islands, Fiji, Marshall Islands, Micronesia, Nauru, New Zealand, Palau, Pitcairn Islands, Vanuatu |
| **Total 115** | |

## 2.1. Countries where provisions for external voting exist but are still to be implemented

There are five known cases (see table 1.2) where, despite there being some kind of constitutional or legal provisions making voting from abroad possible, it has not materialized due to the lack of the political, legislative, financial or administrative agreement required for it to be regulated or organized (with the exception of Ghana, where external voting is scheduled to be extended to all voters abroad in the elections of 2008). This provides evidence of the increasing relevance of external voting on the political and electoral agenda in several regions of the world, as well as of the polemics involved in debates on its relevance and feasibility and the varied complexities of decision making.

## Table 1.2: Countries where external voting provisions exist but are still to be implemented

| Country | Situation |
|---|---|
| Angola | The electoral legislation from 1992 authorizes citizens living abroad to take part in elections to the legislature, and provides for an electoral register to be established in every diplomatic mission where votes will be cast in person. The law also states that the community abroad will be considered as an electoral district, from which three representatives will be elected to the National Assembly. Its application depends on the presence of the required material conditions and a decision of the National Electoral Commission, which has not yet been made. |
| Bolivia | From 1991 the electoral legislation provides for a regulation (currently article 97) that establishes that Bolivian citizens living abroad who are eligible to vote will be able to vote for the president and vice-president, and specifies that this right will be regulated by a specific law. A law was passed in the lower chamber of the parliament in December 2005. It is now being discussed in the upper chamber of the parliament. No regulation has been enacted yet. |
| Greece | The constitution provides the possibility of voting from abroad for national elections by post or 'any other appropriate way', but the law required to apply this provision has still not been passed. |

| Country | Situation |
|---|---|
| Nicaragua | The electoral law enacted in 2000 provides (as the previous electoral law from 1996 did) for the possibility for citizens who are temporarily out of the country or living abroad to vote in presidential and legislative elections. This possibility is restricted by the facts that (a) 'the same conditions of integrity, equality, transparency, safety, control, oversight and verification as those pertaining within the national territory' must exist (article 122), and (b) the electoral authority should decide six months prior to the beginning of the electoral process if it is possible for these requirements to be met, and act accordingly, after consulting the political parties. There is no evidence that the electoral authority is going to use it for forthcoming elections, nor is there or concrete plan to do so. |
| Panama | Introduced external voting by law in 2007. It will be implemented at the next upcoming presidential election in 2008. |

The case of Ecuador is here as representative as it is paradoxical. In late 2002 the Congress finally approved the legislation for external voting to be applied during the presidential elections of 2006; however, years before, in April 1987, the Congress had resolved to withdraw from the constitution dispositions on this matter that had been approved three months earlier on the grounds that they were unconstitutional. External voting will be implemented in Panama for the first time in 2008 after some recent legislation and debate passed in 2007.

There are other countries, such as Chile, El Salvador and Guatemala in Latin America, where, although no legal provision has been approved, the issue is so relevant that external voting has entered the agenda of political and legislative debate or been advocated as a priority topic on that agenda. In Chile it has been suggested that external voting be applied to presidential elections and referendum instruments. Regional organizations have pointed out the importance of external voting in relation to earlier elections in Guatemala. The lower chamber of the Costa Rican Parliament has received a draft new electoral law which includes provisions for external voting. Parliamentary committees in Panama have discussed draft bills to provide for external voting and potential methods. A decision has been taken by the Congress in 2006 and by the Electoral Tribunal in 2007 to allow external voting, scheduled to be implemented in 2008.

As to other regions of the world, there is for example a draft reform of the electoral code before the Congress of the Comoros article 4 of which would introduce the possibility of voting in referendums from abroad. Some countries, for example Egypt, consider the introduction of external voting to be a purely administrative measure which will soon be in place. Discussions in Nigeria have also led to an increased interest in external voting.

Several countries that have existing provisions for external voting and in some cases a long history of implementing it are considering extending or improving the external voting process. This can be done by extending the voting rights to additional types of election or to a larger group of voters or by offering additional voting methods to the existing external voters. One example is that Estonian voters have been able to try and vote through electronic voting (e-voting) from abroad, in addition to personal and postal voting.

Armenia is a recent example of a country deciding to abolish external voting. The new electoral law which came into force in January 2007 in the context of allowing dual citizenship has no provisions for external voting. It was argued that Armenians abroad should not have any major say in deciding on the leadership and fate of Armenia, and that this should be the exclusive right of Armenians living in Armenia. Interestingly, despite the large size of the Armenian diaspora, very few use their external voting rights. Turnout among external voters has been very low and there are no signs that those voters could have had a significant influence over earlier election outcomes.

The following sections of this overview focus on three main issues. These are:

- the types of election to which external voting applies;
- the entitlement to external voting; and
- the voting methods for voting from abroad.

These sections cover only the 115 countries that have current provisions on external voting. The world map accompanying this Handbook shows in detail how the 115 countries and territories are distributed, distinguishing both the type of election and the procedure for voting (see below). The map also shows the five countries where external voting has been used in the past and the five countries where it has been enacted but not yet implemented.

The overview does not discuss the detailed aspects of these themes: they are the subjects of chapters 2–10 of this Handbook.

The chapter concludes with a brief description of eleven countries where the recognition of the political rights of citizens residing abroad has reached the point of seats being reserved in the national legislature or parliament in order to guarantee a quota of political representation.

## 3. Types of election to which external voting applies

The decision as to the kinds of election for which external voting will apply is important. It relates not only to political and institutional considerations (which institutions and which levels of government should be influenced by the votes of electors abroad?) but also to technical and logistical considerations, mostly linked to the type of system used to elect the legislature or the president and to the procedures that will be used for external voting (see table 1.6).

The overview shows us that external voting can apply to four different types of elections:

- legislative elections;
- presidential elections;
- referendums; and
- sub-national elections.

It can apply to one type of election only or to a mix of several kinds of elections. The first two kinds are related to the election and renewal of organs of national representation such as legislative bodies and the presidency. The third group is referendums. We consider these only at national level, although in some federal states the constituent entities have the right to adopt their own instruments of direct democracy at local level.

The group of sub-national elections includes all elections to legislative or executive bodies at political–administrative levels of government lower than national level; however, this may vary from country to country according to the particular form of state or government. The key criterion is that representatives are chosen by popular vote. This group has only been studied in combination with other types of election for the purposes of this Handbook.

The question of external voting for supranational representative bodies should not be forgotten. However, so far, there is only one instance of external voting for a supranational institution—the elections to the European Parliament.

In some cases citizens of one European Union (EU) or Council of Europe member state who reside temporarily or permanently in another EU or Council of Europe member state are able to vote in the sub-national elections of their country of residence.

The 115 national cases where external voting is established can be grouped according to the different types of election or combinations of elections to which it applies (see table 1.3).

Where external voting is only allowed for one type of election, the most common practice is to allow it for legislative elections, which is the case in 31 countries. Fourteen countries allow external voting for presidential elections only. There are no known cases of external voting being allowed for referendums only.

Some countries which hold both legislative and presidential elections do not allow external voting for both. For example, Afghanistan applied external voting for its presidential elections in 2004, but it was not applied for the legislative elections in 2005. Azerbaijan allows external voting for legislative elections only, even though the president is directly elected.

## Table 1.3: Types of election for which external voting applies

| Type of election | No. of cases | Countries |
| --- | --- | --- |
| **Legislative elections only** | 31 | Angola, Australia, Azerbaijan, Bangladesh, Belgium, Botswana, Czech Republic, Fiji, Germany, Gibraltar, Greece, Guernsey, Guinea-Bissau, Guyana, India, Iraq, Japan, Jersey, Laos, Lesotho, Luxembourg, Marshall Islands, Nauru, Netherlands, Oman, Pitcairn Islands, South Africa, Thailand, Turkey, United Kingdom, Zimbabwe |
| **Presidential elections only** | 14 | Afghanistan, Benin, Bolivia, Brazil, Central African Republic, Chad, Côte d'Ivoire, Dominican Republic, Ecuador, Honduras, Mexico, Panama, Tunisia, Venezuela (for presidential recall only) |
| **Legislative elections and presidential elections** | 20 | Argentina, Bulgaria, Cape Verde, Croatia, Djibouti, Equatorial Guinea, Georgia, Ghana, Guinea, Indonesia, Israel, Mozambique, Namibia, Nicaragua, Philippines, Romania, São Tomé and Principe, Senegal, Singapore, Syria |
| **Legislative elections, presidential election and referendums** | 11 | Austria, Colombia, Moldova, Peru, Poland, Portugal, Rwanda, Slovenia, Tajikistan, Ukraine, Uzbekistan |
| **Legislative elections, presidential elections, sub-national elections and referendums** | 6 | Algeria, Belarus, Ireland, Russia, Togo, United States |
| **Legislative elections and referendums** | 7 | Canada, Cook Islands, Estonia, Hungary, Italy, Latvia, Sweden |
| **Presidential elections and referendums** | 7 | France, Gabon, Kyrgyzstan, Lithuania, Mali, Niger, Yemen |
| **Other combinations** | 19 | Bosnia and Herzegovina, Denmark, Falkland Islands, Finland, Iceland, Iran, Isle of Man, Kazakhstan, Liechtenstein, Malaysia, Mauritius, Micronesia, New Zealand, Norway, Palau, Spain, Sudan, Switzerland, Vanuatu |
| **Referendums only** | 0 | — |
| **Total** | 115 | |

Forty-five of the 115 countries and territories with provisions for external voting apply it to only one type of election, but a number allow it for two or more types of elections. The most common practice is to allow it for two types of election—most frequently presidential elections and legislative elections, which is found in 21 countries. A little over 20 countries and territories use a combination of three types of elections or more. The numbers in table 1.3 do not, however, tell the whole story. To allow external voting for the largest number of types of election might at first glance seem to be the arrangement that was most inclusive of external electors. However, the real degree of coverage of external voting and its inclusiveness depend in part on the technical and administrative arrangements, which may impose real or effective restrictions. For example, some countries make only one type of voting method available in one or very few countries, which may not necessarily catch a large number of external electors (see also section 4).

From a different perspective, the available information allows us to establish whether the voter has the option to vote for the type of authority that carries out the duties of government, for instance, whether in a presidential system the external elector has the chance to vote for president, while in a parliamentary system the external voter has the chance to vote for members of parliament (MPs).

## 4. Persons eligible to vote from abroad

The first key indicator of the degree of coverage or inclusiveness of external voting is related to the requirements—for citizenship, residency, voter registration or other—that must be met before a person can be entitled to an external vote. These requirements may change significantly from one context to another. In many cases they do not merely reproduce the normal requirements for an individual to exercise his or her political rights within the country, but also include some special or additional requirements related to the situation of the potential voter abroad.

When there is no special or additional requirement linked to the circumstances or personal situation of the potential voter abroad, a guarantee of universal access can be assumed in the sense that external voting is accessible to all citizens whether, for example permanently or temporarily abroad. The most common and widespread requirement, although not the only one, is that of citizenship, although there are exceptions. New Zealand, for example, recognizes citizens of other countries as external electors if they are permanently resident in New Zealand: they do not need to be New Zealand citizens in order to qualify as external electors. From this perspective New Zealand would be considered the most inclusive case. Chapter 4 considers questions of citizenship and entitlement in more detail.

In a majority of the 115 countries and territories the legislation on external voting does not include any special or restrictive requirement for individuals to be eligible for an external vote. In others, there are formal limitations on eligibility for an external vote, mostly relating either to the circumstances of the stay abroad (activity-related restrictions) or to the length of time for which the citizen has been out of the country (length of stay abroad restriction).

The first type of requirement is found in 14 countries (see table 1.4). South Africa belongs to this group but has very particular features: it introduced external voting for its diaspora overseas for its historic elections of 1994 in very comprehensive terms, but since then has been restricting external voting in a systematic way. For the general elections of April 2004 it restricted external voting to members of the diplomatic corps and voters who were already registered in the country and would be abroad only temporarily. Interestingly, the law does not specify what temporary absence from South Africa involves, but it does give the parameters of when and how to register and apply for an external vote. Restricting external voting to diplomatic staff or to those employed by the government is a fairly common type of activity-related restriction: it is found, for example, in Bangladesh, Ireland, Israel, Laos and Zimbabwe. It also common to allow those who are in the armed forces, students or citizens involved in other official or international work to vote from abroad. External voting will most likely be extended in Ghana in the next upcoming elections in 2008 to include all voters residing abroad.

Table 1.4: Countries and territories which restricted entitlement to an external vote according to activity abroad (14)

| Country/territory | Voters |
| --- | --- |
| Bangladesh | Only government officers on official duty |
| Fiji | Only citizens abroad who are carrying out an official or military function, working for an international organization to which the country belongs, studying, or working for a company that it is registered in Fiji |
| Ghana | Only diplomats, employees of the United Nations and other international organizations, police and military personnel on peacekeeping missions, and students on government scholarships |
| Guyana | Only employees of the government or any public corporation on duty abroad and students engaged in full-time courses in any foreign educational institution |
| India | Only members of the armed forces and government servants deployed abroad |
| Ireland | Only citizens carrying out official missions abroad of a diplomatic or military nature |
| Israel | Only citizens carrying out official missions abroad of a diplomatic or military nature |
| Laos | Only for those employed by the state |
| Lesotho | Only citizens carrying out official missions abroad of a diplomatic or military nature |
| Malaysia | Only diplomatic officers and students abroad |
| Mauritius | Only diplomatic staff |
| Singapore | Only for those employed by the government on fixed contracts |
| South Africa | Only diplomatic staff and registered voters who are temporarily abroad |
| Zimbabwe | Only citizens carrying out official missions abroad of a diplomatic or military nature |

Table 1.5 lists some examples of the second type of restriction, concerning the length of stay abroad. This restriction can also take different forms. In most of these countries there is an upper limit to the time the voter can stay abroad before they lose their voting rights. The maximum time abroad in Guinea, for example, is 19 years, while Australia's limit is six years, although an extension can be requested in this case. The Falkland

Islands allows voters abroad to vote only if they are abroad temporarily, and only if they are residing in the United Kingdom (UK) and nowhere else. The governor of the Falkland Islands has to make a series of administrative arrangements for conducting the ballot abroad. The maximum length of stay abroad for Germans is 25 years, for the UK 15 years, for Canada five years and for Turkey six months.

The length of stay abroad restriction can also work the opposite way, meaning that a voter needs to be away from his or her country for a certain period of time in order to be able to vote from abroad. This is the case for voters from Chad, for example, who need to register in a consular registry at least six months before the election. External electors from Mozambique need to have been resident abroad for at least one year before the electoral registration process begins in there. Unless the voter has been abroad for at least six months and registered at a diplomatic mission, he or she can only vote if appointing a proxy. Gibraltar, Guernsey, the Isle of Man and Jersey allow external voting only for a provisional stay abroad, and registration for elections can only take place within the territory. Senegalese voters need to reside abroad for at least six months to have external voting rights, and external voting and registration can only take place in countries where Senegal has a diplomatic mission.

Table 1.5: Some examples of countries and territories which restrict entitlement to an external vote according to length of stay abroad

| Country | Requirements for length of stay abroad |
|---|---|
| Australia | A maximum of six years resident abroad (an extension can be requested) |
| Canada | A maximum of five years resident abroad |
| Chad | The elector must be enrolled in the consular registry six months before the beginning of the electoral process |
| Cook Islands | A maximum of four years resident abroad, with the exception of periods abroad for medical reasons or studies |
| Falkland Islands | Only a temporary stay in the United Kingdom is allowed for external electors |
| Gibraltar | Only a provisional stay abroad |
| Guernsey | Only a provisional stay abroad |
| Guinea | A maximum of 19 years resident abroad |
| Isle of Man | Only a provisional stay abroad |
| Jersey | Only a provisional stay abroad |
| Mozambique | At least one year abroad before beginning registration as a voter abroad |
| New Zealand | A maximum of three years resident abroad |
| Senegal | At least six months of residence in the jurisdiction of a diplomatic representation abroad |
| United Kingdom | A maximum of 15 years resident abroad |

Cases where external voting is legally or practically restricted to voters who are only temporarily out of the national territory are in the minority. More often because of technical or administrative limitations than for strictly legal reasons, it is most common for external voting not to be provided for people who are only out of their country on a temporary basis, whether for work, for business, for study, or for medical or recreational reasons. Australia, Canada, Denmark, New Zealand and Norway are among the few countries that offer facilities to voters who are in transit travelling or provisionally abroad. Either their electors are not required to register specifically as voters abroad, or they can ask to register as such up to a few days before the period stipulated for voting.

However, there are also some other forms of restriction on external voting. Even for the approximately 80 countries and territories that do not specifically restrict the entitlement to an external vote, there is no guarantee that all eligible voters will be entitled to vote. Their exercise of this right can be hindered or limited by other kinds of legal requirement, such as those necessary before a person can register as a voter, or by technical, administrative or operational provisions related to electoral registration or voting itself. Administrative obstacles may, for example, involve difficulties in accessing or posting ballot papers. Some other restrictions are discussed below.

The Philippines case deserves particular attention because it is the only country where there are special requirements for the eligibility and entitlement to vote of certain categories of citizens abroad, although these requirements do not apply for ordinary citizens abroad. There are special requirements for natural-born Filipinos who became naturalized citizens of another country but wish to re-acquire their Philippine citizenship according to the 2003 Act on Citizenship Retention and Re-acquisition, including a one-year residency in the country. In addition, there are special requirements for Filipinos abroad who are recognized as immigrants or permanent residents by another country. Such individuals are required to sign an affidavit of intention to return and resume actual residence in the Philippines no later than three years from approval of their application for registration as 'overseas' voters.

There are other administrative and technical requirements or conditions which, even though they do not formally restrict entitlement to an external vote, can have a considerable and even decisive influence on the ability or opportunity to exercise the right to vote from abroad. The requirements and conditions for proof of identity to register as an external elector are particularly important in this context (see also chapter 4). The more rigorous the requirements for verifying identity and registering as a voter abroad, and the more difficult this is to do or the shorter the time period allowed for doing so, the more restricted the coverage of the potential external electorate will be. For example, when the United Nations Transitional Authority in Cambodia (UNTAC) allowed external voting for the elections to the Constituent Assembly in Cambodia in 1993 it made it conditional on a voter having registered previously within the country, and finally set up polling centres only in Paris, New York and Sydney, which drastically reduced its inclusiveness.

The documents needed to prove that a person satisfies the eligibility requirements, and therefore can register as an external elector, can be especially important for those potential voters who because of their migratory status or the length of their stay in the host country might not have them or might face difficulties in obtaining them (see in particular chapters 7 and 8). For its first application of voting from abroad in 2006, Mexico allowed only those citizens who were provided with a voting card issued (free) by the electoral authority, but only within the country, to vote externally. Some countries require external electors to show a valid visa before they are allowed to vote.

In similar vein, if the procedure for registering as an external elector has to be carried out at an embassy or consulate, the extent and geographical distribution of the country's network of diplomatic missions overseas and the distance between the diplomatic missions and the regions or zones where the potential electorate resides and/or works could have a negative influence on the coverage of the mechanism for external voting.

By contrast, if the requirements for verifying the voter's eligibility and for registering as an external elector are reasonable for any citizen, and if the citizen has ample material facilities or time in which to register (for example, to request, replace or update the required documents at the home country's diplomatic missions abroad or by post, or possibly by electronic means), this will undoubtedly favour an increase in the participation of external voting in many cases.

Registration for the Afghan presidential election of 2004 provided an interesting case. External voting was conducted only in the two neighbouring countries where most of the Afghan refugees were located—Iran and Pakistan. A large number of Afghan voters residing in Iran were not registered by the representatives of the Afghan electoral authorities, but were eligible to vote by reference to their Iranian refugee registration document (see the case study).

## 5. Voting procedures in use for external voting

Countries that allow external voting need to ensure that it is conducted in such a way as to meet the requirements of security, transparency and secrecy. It is also desirable that as far as possible all electors have the same opportunity to vote. However, countries and territories also need to make adjustments and innovations to cope with the challenges that are particular to external voting, such as the geographical location of voters, security in transporting ballot papers, the high costs of external voting and other administrative issues mentioned above.. It is therefore interesting—if perhaps not surprising—to see that in general the procedures for voting from abroad are equivalent to those that apply within the national territory. Nor it is surprising that in some cases exceptional procedures are adopted, especially to bring a wide range of facilities within the reach of all external electors in order for them to be able to exercise their right to vote from far-off or inaccessible places. Every voting procedure when applied abroad has implications in terms of the coverage of potential voters and their opportunity to cast a vote. Chapter 5 discusses these aspects and the different procedures such as postal, personal and proxy voting, and their advantages and disadvantages, in greater depth.

There are five different voting methods in use for external voting throughout the world. These are:

- personal voting at diplomatic missions or other designated places;
- postal voting;
- voting by proxy;
- e-voting; and
- voting by fax.

Table 1.6 shows the procedures for external voting grouped into four broad categories: personal voting, postal voting, voting by proxy and mixed methods. Table 1.7 then gives a further breakdown of the countries that have mixed voting procedures.

In 83 cases, only one voting method is available to the external voter. Of these, 54 countries opt to use conventional personal voting at a polling station that is specially set up, for example, at a diplomatic mission or other designated place. This is by far the most common procedure for external voting. Twenty-five countries use postal voting only. Voting by proxy is the sole voting method in four countries. In the remaining 27 cases, a mix of two or more voting methods are in place, including the exceptional use of voting by fax and e-voting.

## Table 1.6: External voting procedures

| Procedures | No. of cases | Countries |
|---|---|---|
| **Personal voting only** | 54 | Afghanistan, Angola, Argentina, Azerbaijan, Belarus, Botswana, Brazil, Bulgaria, Cape Verde, Central African Republic, Colombia, Côte d'Ivoire, Croatia, Czech Republic, Djibouti, Dominican Republic, Ecuador, Equatorial Guinea, Finland, Georgia, Ghana, Guinea-Bissau, Guyana, Honduras, Hungary, Iceland, Iran, Iraq, Israel, Kazakhstan, Kyrgyzstan, Laos, Moldova, Mozambique, Namibia, Niger, Peru, Pitcairn Islands, Poland, Romania, Russia, Rwanda, São Tomé and Principe, Senegal, Singapore, South Africa, Sudan, Syria, Tunisia, Turkey, Ukraine, Uzbekistan, Venezuela, Yemen |
| **Postal voting only** | 25 | Austria, Bangladesh, Bosnia and Herzegovina, Canada, Denmark, Falkland Islands, Fiji, Germany, Gibraltar, Guernsey, Ireland, Italy, Jersey, Lesotho, Liechtenstein, Luxembourg, Malaysia, Isle of Man, Marshall Islands, Mexico, Norway, Panama, Switzerland, Tajikistan, Zimbabwe |
| **Proxy voting only** | 4 | Mauritius, Nauru, Togo, Vanuatu |

| Procedures | No. of cases | Countries |
|---|---|---|
| Mixed procedures | 27 | Algeria, Australia, Belgium, Benin, Chad, Cook Islands, Estonia, France, Gabon, Guinea, India, Indonesia, Japan, Latvia, Lithuania, Mali, Micronesia, Netherlands, New Zealand, Palau, Philippines, Portugal, Slovenia, Spain, Sweden, Thailand, United Kingdom |
| Not yet implemented or not available | 4 | Bolivia, Greece, Nicaragua, Oman |
| Total | 114 | |

Note: The United States is not included in this table since the procedures for external voting vary by state.

When personal voting is used, it would be easy to imagine that the participation of external voters depends on the extent or range of the home country's diplomatic or consular networks around the world. The differences between countries in this respect are considerable. For example, Russia has diplomatic or consular missions in more than 140 countries or territories, whereas Peru only has effective diplomatic representations (that is, not considering honorary consulates) in about 55 countries, Gabon in a little over 30 countries, Azerbaijan in about 20 countries and the Central African Republic in some 10 countries. However, the correlation between the number of official representations overseas and the coverage of potential external voters is not a linear one, since the geographical distribution of potential voters abroad is also important. Specific legal provisions are sometimes made to install polling stations abroad on the basis of technical or logistical considerations, such as the estimated number and concentration of potential external voters, or the number actually registered in a certain jurisdiction.

For financial or logistical reasons, it is not unusual for countries that have external voting to limit the arrangements for registering and voting to a particular group of jurisdictions overseas where it is believed that higher numbers of potential voters reside. The Dominican Republic chose a group of cities located in five countries (Canada, Spain, Puerto Rico, the United States and Venezuela) to conduct external voting for the presidential elections of 2004 (its first experience of external voting). Mozambique restricted its first external voting operation, during the presidential and legislative elections of 2004, to nine countries, of which seven were in Africa and two in Europe (Germany and Portugal). The coverage of Senegal's external voting operation for its elections in 2000 was a little wider since it was applied in 15 countries, including from outside the region four European countries, Canada and the United States.

The independence referendum held by Tokelau in 2006 might be the most extreme case of this practice, and was controversial for this reason. Initial proposals limited external voting to Tokelauans in Samoa. However, objections raised by the larger number of Tokelauans in Australia and New Zealand led to the vote, initially scheduled for late 2005, being postponed. The restrictions in the cases of Afghanistan and Honduras have been also very considerable. For its pioneering external voting operation in its 2002 presidential elections, Honduras decided to restrict the registration of external electors and external voting to a small group of six cities in the United States where it has consular representation, and it maintained the same coverage for the presidential elections held in 2006. As is mentioned above, Afghanistan only conducted external voting for its 2004 presidential elections in the two neighbouring countries where most of its displaced people where located—Iran and Pakistan.

To take a related example, there are countries which initially considered allowing external voting in all countries where they had official representations, but made the actual installation of polling stations conditional on the existence of a minimum number of registered voters. The required threshold differs substantially: while Bulgaria demands a minimum of 20 registered voters, and Brazil a minimum of 30, Senegal's threshold is very high, at a minimum of 500 registered voters. In certain cases, such provisions may also govern the establishment of polling stations on ships at sea.

Votes can also be cast abroad in polling stations installed in the head offices or premises of international or regional organizations, or in places specially set up or hired in the host country, such as sports facilities or schools. During post-conflict transitions where the international community plays a key role, such as those of Afghanistan and Iraq in 2004, or, as in Cambodia, Eritrea, East Timor or Bosnia and Herzegovina in the 1990s, external voting operations may be assisted or even conducted by international organizations, as the case studies in this Handbook illustrate.

The other main procedure for external voting that can be used in an exclusive way is postal voting. Twenty-five countries use only this method of external voting. It is most commonly found in Western Europe. Postal voting can be an efficient and low-cost method if the postal services operate well, efficiently and safely. However, postal services which do not live up to these standards can do damage to the electoral process for external voters.

As is mentioned above, 27 countries have a mixed system using two or more different voting procedures for external voting. This does not necessarily imply that the voter has the option of choosing freely the procedure he or she finds most comfortable or suitable; different methods may be available to external voters depending on where in the world they reside and what the reliable voting channels are from that location. The 27 countries can be grouped according to five combinations of voting methods (see table 1.7). The mix of personal and postal voting is the predominant one, being used by 12 of the 27 countries. A combination of procedures may be chosen to encourage electoral participation or to compensate for limitations or inadequacies that may arise from the use of only one system, in terms of coverage, certainty or reliability. For example, personal voting better fulfils the principles and imperatives of security, confidentiality and reliability in the casting and transmission of the vote, but its coverage of the potential electorate can be far more limited than that of postal voting. There is no doubt that, at least in a strictly geographical sense, the availability of a wider range of alternatives implies better potential coverage of voters abroad. Nevertheless, take-up will still depend to a great extent on the nature and features of the options available, such as the precise geographical location of the voter.

In some cases the elector will be able to freely select the method that best suits him or her; in others, the elector's geographical location may effectively restrict access to one procedure only.

Table 1.7: Countries with mixed procedures for external voting

| Mixed voting procedures | No. of cases | Countries |
| --- | --- | --- |
| Personal voting and postal voting | 12 | Cook Islands, Indonesia, Japan, Latvia, Lithuania, Micronesia, Palau, Philippines, Portugal, Slovenia, Spain, Thailand |
| Personal voting and voting by proxy | 7 | Algeria, Benin, Chad, France, Gabon, Guinea, Mali |
| Postal voting and voting by proxy | 2 | India, United Kingdom |
| Personal voting, postal voting and voting by proxy | 2 | Belgium, Sweden |
| Other methods in addition to any of the above | 4 | Australia (personal, postal, fax), Estonia (personal, postal, e-voting), Netherlands (postal, proxy, e-voting), New Zealand (personal, postal, fax) |

Six countries—Australia, Belgium, Estonia, the Netherlands, New Zealand and Sweden—stand apart from the rest since they offer the voter abroad three or more alternative ways of casting a vote. This—in combination with the fact that these countries impose no additional requirements, such as a voter having to spend a set period of time abroad or a set number of voters having to be abroad at the same time—clearly shows their intention of achieving the greatest possible coverage. However, their arrangements are very different.

Until recently, Belgium, with the reforms introduced in 2001—which expanded significantly the number of available options—and Sweden, with reforms introduced in 2002 which made postal voting, already available to some voters, accessible to all, were the only two countries to offer their voters abroad the possibility of choosing 'freely' between three procedures for external voting, although there are differences between them. Estonia and the Netherlands have since joined this group as well. In Belgium the following options are available: (a) personal voting at the diplomatic missions where the external elector has been registered, (b) voting through a representative or proxy at the same mission or in a national municipality (but only if the representative is resident within the area covered by the diplomatic mission or in the Belgian municipality, respectively), and (c) postal voting. In Sweden it is possible to vote by post from abroad or in person at diplomatic missions. (Postal voting was previously only available for Swedish voters residing in Germany and Switzerland: these countries did not allow external voting to take place at embassies on their territory. See the case study Switzerland for more information.) Sweden also has a unique procedure, called voting by messenger: the elector needs a special outer envelope which he/she can either obtain from the election administration or collect at any available voting place. Apart from the elector, a witness and a messenger are required to be present at the preparation of the vote. The elector prepares the vote in person, and the witness has to certify with his/her signature and personal identification number that the voting procedure was properly carried out. The messenger also has to sign the outer envelope, and transport and deliver the envelope with the documents and the vote to a diplomatic mission abroad or polling station within the country. The witness and the messenger cannot be the same person. This procedure is qualitatively different from that of the proxy vote, since the voter marks the ballot paper himself or herself.

Estonia and the Netherlands both offer postal voting, and in addition Estonia offers personal voting and the Netherlands voting by proxy. But what these two countries have in common as a third method is e-voting, which has only been implemented recently.

Australia and New Zealand make the personal vote and the postal vote generally available to overseas voters. In addition, voting by fax is possible for restricted groups of electors who otherwise could easily be deprived of the opportunity to cast their vote—those living in inhospitable areas or areas that are very difficult to reach, such as the polar zones. This facility gives priority to the principle of coverage and inclusion of voters over considerations of secrecy in the sending out and return of the ballot papers. Access by fax requires special application and is used only when absolutely necessary.

The United States, which is a federal and highly decentralized country where the different states have a great degree of autonomy in adopting and developing their own electoral laws and procedures, also offers up to three methods of casting an external vote. In addition to postal voting, which is allowed by all states, a few states open up the possibility of voting by fax or e-voting albeit in a very restrictive way since only a small number of electors abroad have access to these procedures. For its presidential elections of 2000, the United States was the first country to test, in a highly selective and very controlled way, a mechanism for external voting using e-voting, a method that is not only electronic but also genuinely remote or distant. Although there is no doubt that the implications of the use of new technologies for the transmission of votes will be very promising in the near future and several countries are already designing or testing pilot programmes for their use, their application to external voting is still essentially undergoing a test phase (see chapter 10).

For the group of 21 countries which allow two procedures for external voting, it is worth stressing that the potential coverage is related to the characteristics and conditions that regulate the application of each one of them and the precise ways in which they are combined. In Indonesia and Japan the external voter can choose between personal voting at diplomatic missions and the postal vote. In France and a number of countries in Francophone Africa, personal voting exists for those registered at embassies and consulates, often restricted to presidential elections and perhaps referendums, while proxy voting is used by those on temporary government or military service in professional missions abroad. The Philippines decided for its first implementation of external voting in 2004 that greater coverage of voters would be achieved by personal voting at diplomatic missions and other official premises, and this method was applied in 80 countries, while postal voting was only available for external electors located in three countries (Canada, Japan and the UK) because they had efficient and reliable postal services. The case of Portugal is also special, since external electors can only vote by post in parliamentary elections and have to vote in person in presidential elections.

## 6. Political representation for external voters

Eleven countries—four in Europe (Croatia, France, Italy and Portugal), four in Africa (Algeria, Angola, Cape Verde and Mozambique) and three in the Americas (Colombia, Ecuador and Panama)—not only allow their citizens abroad to participate actively in some electoral processes, but also enable them to elect their own representatives to the national legislature (see table 1.8). This was also formerly the case in the Cook Islands, but the 'external seat' there was abolished in 2003. This practice is clearly aimed at reinforcing external voters link with the national political community, enabling promotion of their own legislative agenda and direct intervention from an overseas viewpoint in the debates and processes of political decision making on topics of national interest. Each case has its own particular features.

Table 1.8: Political representation in national legislatures for external voters

| Country | Number of seats (percentage of total no. of seats in parliament, total no. of seats) |
|---|---|
| Algeria | 8 (2.0%, 389) |
| Angola | 3 (1.4%, 220). External voting has not yet been implemented. |
| Cape Verde | 6 (8.3%, 72). Two each from the Americas, Africa, and Europe and the rest of the world |
| Colombia | 1 (0.6%, 166) |
| Croatia | 6 (3.9%, 152). A maximum of 6 seats (see below) |
| Ecuador | 6 (4.6%, 130). |
| France | 12 (3.6%, 331). Senate only (elected through the Conseil Supérieur des Français de l'Etranger) |
| Italy | 12 (1.9%, 630). One constituency for Italians abroad representing four geographical groups; (a) Europe, including Russia and Turkey; (b) South America; (c) North and Central America; (d) Africa, Asia, Oceania and Antarctica |
| Mozambique | 2 (0.8%, 250). Two single-member constituencies, for Africa and the rest of the world |
| Panama | 6 (4.6%, 130). External voting has not yet been implemented. |
| Portugal | 4 (1.7%, 230) |

The constitution adopted by Cape Verde in 1992 provided for the creation of three districts abroad, with two representatives elected to the National Assembly in each of them—one district for voters residing in Africa, another for those residing in the Americas, and another for those living in Europe and the rest of the world. This rule was applied for the first time during the legislative elections of December 1995, and again in the elections of 2001 and in 2006. In Colombia, the constitution approved in 1991 provided for the creation of a special electoral district that would ensure the representation of political minorities, ethnic groups and citizens residing abroad. A decade later, the Congress approved a law for the creation of this special district, made up of five seats in the House of Representatives. It was decided that one of those seats would correspond to Colombians residing abroad, and this seat was occupied for the first time after the legislative elections of 2002 (see the respective case studies).

The law on parliamentary elections in Croatia adopted in 1995 created a special electoral district in the single-chamber parliament to represent the enormous Croatian diaspora (of whom it was estimated at the time that more than 400,000 persons were old enough to vote). Twelve seats were assigned to the district—the same number as to each of the ten multi-member districts into which the country is divided. As a result of criticism of the excessive number of seats assigned to Croatians abroad, the law was reformed. It now provides for a maximum of six seats, but states that the exact number will be determined after every election using a formula that takes into account the number of votes cast abroad and the average number of votes needed to obtain a seat in-country. For the elections of 2003, Croatians abroad were given only four seats.

In France, since 1948 citizens abroad have been provided with representation in the Senate, and since 1983 this has amounted to 12 seats. However, it is important to emphasize that these 12 senators are not chosen in any direct way by the French abroad; instead they are selected by a college made up of 150 elected members out of the 183 who make up the High Council of French Citizens Abroad (Conseil Supérieur des Français de l'Etranger, CSFE, also created in 1948), which represents before the French government some 2 million French citizens resident abroad. The 150 members of that council are directly elected by voters abroad.

Algeria has eight reserved seats in the parliament for voters abroad. This makes up 2 per cent of all MPs.

In addition to providing for the external vote for elections to the legislature and referendums, the constitutional reforms approved in Italy in 2000 stated that citizens abroad are provided with representation in both chambers of the parliament—12 seats in the House of Representatives and six in the Senate. These constitutional arrangements were regulated by a specific law enacted in early 2002, a few months after the May 2001 elections, and Italians abroad would gain political representation only after the subsequent legislative elections. For that purpose, the law foresaw the creation of four electoral districts abroad: one for Europe, another one for South America, the third for North America and Central America and the last to cover Africa, Asia, Oceania and

Antarctica, for both chambers. For every district a minimum of one deputy seat and one senator seat will be assigned, and the remaining ones will be distributed in accordance with the number of external voters. External voting took place for the first time in a referendum held in May 2003.

The constitution adopted by Mozambique in 1990 establishes, in addition to external voting for legislative elections, that two of the 250 seats that make up the Assembly of the Republic will correspond to the electoral districts constituted abroad—one for Africa and one for the rest of the world. Although consecutive electoral laws that have been approved since then have included some measures in this direction, it was only with the law and arrangements adopted by the electoral authority to regulate the general elections of December 2004 that these constitutional provisions finally materialized. The Mozambicans living in seven countries of the continent made up the electoral district for Africa, while those living in two European countries (Germany and Portugal) made up another district for which a representative was also elected (see the case study).

The Portuguese abroad have been represented in the House of Representatives since 1976. For this purpose, voters abroad also make up two electoral districts, one for Europe and the other for the rest of the world. Two deputies are elected in each of these districts, but only if a minimum of 55,000 electors cast a vote within the district. If fewer voters cast a vote, only one seat is assigned to the corresponding district. In the parliamentary elections of February 2005, both districts obtained their two seats.

Finally, Angola and Panama have not yet implemented external voting. Once and if this happens, three seats in parliament will be elected directly by, and represent, Angolans abroad according to the legislation on external voting.

## 7. External voting and participation[*]

Essentially, external voting is geared towards increasing political participation and thereby contributing to the legitimacy and accountability of democratic governments. As the chapters in this Handbook show, problematic as it can be from both the practical and the theoretical points of view, the right to an external vote can also be an essential part of the citizen's political rights; but the question of external voting does raise its own series of issues surrounding participation that need to be addressed.

To date, there has been far less focus on the levels of participation among external voters than on levels of voter participation in-country.

In most cases where external voting is permitted, external voters account for only a relatively small proportion of overall turnout. Nonetheless, an external voting population may have a considerable impact on election results. Examples include Italy's

---

[*] Erin Thiessen developed the writing of this section with the authors.

2006 legislative elections—the first held in which external voting was permitted. The election outcome was unknown until all the external votes were counted, giving this relatively small group considerable political impact due to the fact that the electoral system allows a bonus for the party or coalition with the highest number of votes. In some cases external votes have tipped the scales in an election; and they are often counted last. This effect may or may not be more pronounced in countries that have experienced massive population movements linked to conflict or the migration of labour. The 2004 elections in Afghanistan saw 10 per cent of the total electorate made up of external electors in Pakistan and Iran, due in part to extensive voter education campaigns and great interest in the country's first-ever democratic elections (see the case study). Another recent example of a country with a large population of eligible voters residing outside the national borders that could have potential impact on the outcome of elections is that of Iraq. Both Afghanistan and Iraq conducted large-scale external voting processes and voter education campaigns in their recent elections. One can only guess what the reactions would have been among the many external residents if external voting had not been organized for these groups. Turnout in the Iraqi January 2005 election was high (265,000 registered voters, although higher registration rates had been anticipated). Large numbers of Iraqis abroad are illegal refugees, and the risk of repatriation or expulsion to a war zone kept registration numbers low in some countries. Other reasons for low participation rates included security concerns, voter disinterest, difficult access to registration and voting facilities, and documentation issues. In the December election, when external voting was organised mainly by the IECI, 320,000 voters registered.

## 7.1. A sample of the information available on turnout by external voters

Where external voting is permitted, rates of registration and turnout among external voters are almost always lower than they are in-country. In several countries that have existing and well-functioning external voting practices, turnout has been low compared to turnout in-country. These include, for example, Brazil, Honduras, Italy, the Philippines, Senegal, Spain, Sweden and Venezuela. The turnout of Spanish external voters was below 30 per cent at the legislative election of 2004, compared to about 75 per cent among in-country voters. Even in Brazil, where voting is compulsory for citizens who are temporarily or permanently abroad, only about 50 per cent of eligible external electors participate. Mexico's newly launched external voting programme for its July 2006 elections saw an unexpectedly low registration rate considering the large number of Mexicans living in the United States. For the Afghan presidential elections in 2004, 80 per cent of the registered electorate in Pakistan participated in the polls, and approximately one-half of those in Iran.

Conversely, some countries have found that, despite the progressive decline in the numbers of people voting from abroad, the percentage of registered external electors who actually vote remains very high. In Bosnia and Herzegovina, for example, although the absolute number of external electors is dropping as more citizens return home, the turnout of registered external voters has remained at approximately 80 per cent since the early 2000s (see the case study).

In the elections to the European Parliament in 2004 only 8.9 per cent of the Finnish external electors residing abroad exercised their right to vote at the elections to the European Parliament. Women and men participated to almost the same extent in these elections as external voters. Low turnout among Finnish external voters has led to discussion about introducing postal voting from abroad so that external voters would not have to travel to a diplomatic mission in order to vote, and to the suggestion that reserved seats for external voters could be introduced to make external voting more meaningful.

Most countries that practise compulsory voting do not impose it on their external electors. Belgium, on the other hand, does impose this rule on external electors, but it is in effect an almost entirely theoretical rule as it is almost impossible to impose a sanction on a non-voter residing abroad. Turnout among Belgian external voters is lower than it is among Belgians residing in Belgium.

Namibia, which has personal voting only for external voters, organizes voting at 24 different polling places abroad and the roughly 1,900 voters who participated in the 2004 parliamentary and presidential elections averaged about 80 per polling station. Given the amount of preparation for and work involved during and after voting, much effort is put in for very few voters. Turnout among Namibian external voters is very low and represents only 0.09 per cent of the total turnout.

### 7.2. The reasons for lower turnout by external voters

The factors that influence lower turnout for external voters are political, administrative, institutional and financial. The reasons for low turnout vary among external voters just as they do among in-country voters, but some factors may be particular to external voting, such as the geographical location of polling stations, access to information, and the logistical arrangements for voter registration.

Locating polling stations only where embassies or consulates are available presents obstacles to voting for some external electors. For example, if polling stations are few in number or are difficult to access, this may contribute to low levels of participation. Conversely, Sweden set up fewer polling stations abroad in the 2006 parliamentary elections, but more votes were cast than when more polling stations had been available abroad. The opening hours of diplomatic missions may also affect the number of voters taking this opportunity.

The requirements for registering as a voter are also key to participation as this is in most cases the first step towards participation. One example of unfortunate arrangements is that of Mexico's attempt at external voting in 2006 which required would-be voters to obtain a photographic voting card which was available only by going in person to Mexico. While it is estimated that 4.2 million of the 11 million Mexicans abroad had a valid photographic voting card, only 40,665 of these ended up registering to vote. Similarly, in Cambodia's 1993 elections to the Constituent Assembly, external voting was possible at only very few locations in the United States and only if voters first travelled to Cambodia to register.

Requirements stating a minimum or maximum number of eligible voters may also work as a disincentive to participation or an obstacle to those who register as external electors but will not be included unless the numbers add up. Senegal, for instance, only organizes external voting if the total number of registered voters in one country is 500 or more. Other restrictions or preconditions, such as documentation requirements in the host country (Mexico) or stating an intention to return (the Philippines), can also make participation less attractive than it otherwise would be.

Depending on how, when and where the election campaign is organized, voters may feel more or less inclined to participate. In addition, only some candidates or parties may be represented in the campaign abroad, mainly for political or financial reasons. Some states (e.g. Mexico) have decided to provide a more level playing field between the participating political parties by simply not allowing any sort of campaign activity abroad, which has meant that the information made available to voters is not so dependent on the wherewithal of the parties to conduct international campaigns alongside their national campaigns. Furthermore, election and campaign information is not always readily available, thus putting the onus on the voter to inform himself or herself which may be more or less difficult depending on the circumstances. Even where large-scale media and advertisement campaigns are run—as was done within the USA, targeting the Mexican population, for the 2006 Mexican presidential elections—registration and turnout may still suffer.

The lack of sufficient cooperation by other states can make external voting difficult or even impossible due to legal and diplomatic issues. Liberia allowed external voting beginning in 1986, but abolished it in 2004 due to the inability of the electoral management body (EMB) to cope with refugees in the neighbouring countries, particularly as some of the neighbouring states objected to electioneering taking place within their territory. Another example of a country that used to restrict the options for voting methods for foreign voters is Switzerland, which until 1989 did not allow any voting in foreign elections to take place on its territory for sovereignty reasons.

Other reasons for low voter turnout can be attributed more directly to the voters themselves. Illegal migrants or those opposed to the regime in the home country may not be prepared to register to vote out of fear of reprisals. The Iraq elections showed that the sensitivity surrounding the registration and handling of personal information can dampen would-be electors' enthusiasm to register and vote if the political situation is precarious. External electors, particularly if they are permanent residents abroad and/or hold multiple citizenships, may feel detached or apathetic regarding political events in their home state. This may be exacerbated if the decisions made by that state have little or no impact on the everyday life of the voter or the voter's family.

On the other hand, several European countries have improved access to participation by external voters in elections to the European Parliament by allowing permanent residents with a foreign citizenship to vote in sub-national elections or elections to the European Parliament in their country of residence.

### 7.3. Problems arising from lower turnout by external voters

As is mentioned above, external voters may sometimes have a disproportionate influence on an electoral process. For example, nine countries have reserved seats in the legislature for external electoral districts (see section 6 above). Where this is the case, if external voter turnout is low, fewer votes will influence the outcome of the election for a parliamentary seat compared to internal constituencies, thus giving external votes disproportionate weight. Some countries weigh the number of external voters against the number of internal voters in order to decide how many seats can represent be allocated to represent external voters (e.g. Croatia).

Lower turnout by external voters also has to be seen in the light of the associated costs. External voting is often more expensive than organizing in-country voting (see annex D for some examples). Some may argue that participation is a right regardless of cost in monetary or political terms, while others may contend that the degree of political effort and financial cost must be justified by appropriate levels of participation by voters abroad. Botswana, for example, is considering abolishing its external voting provisions as a result of the low turnout rates among external electors and high costs associated with the arrangements. External voting for legislative elections was introduced in 1997 and was employed in the 1999 and 2004 elections but turnout has not been impressive, despite increasing the number of countries in which external voting is available as well as the number of polling stations. This has opened an ongoing debate about whether external voting should be abolished given the high cost per voter, particularly when compared to in-country elections (see the case study). In France, external voting is seen as very costly in terms of cost per voter.

Given examples such as these, a practical question must be asked whether the low turnout justifies the abolition of external voting or not introducing it in the first place, regardless of the more theoretical and normative counter-arguments surrounding citizenship. Levels of participation may influence decision-making processes regarding the introduction or abolition of external voting.

CASE STUDY: Botswana

# Botswana: disappointing results of external voting

Patrick Molutsi

External voting in Botswana was introduced fairly recently, as part of a package of constitutional and electoral reforms in 1997. The Constitutional Amendment Act of 1997, section 4, subsection (a) reduced the voting age from 21 to 18 years, while the Electoral Act section 5(3) amendment of 1997 permitted citizens resident outside the country to vote externally. Other major reforms made at the same time included the establishment of the Independent Electoral Commission (IEC) and the introduction of a limit to the term of office of the president to two terms of five years each. These substantive electoral reforms were the first of their kind since Botswana attained its independence from the United Kingdom (UK) in 1966. Previously, there had been occasional minor amendments to the electoral law, for instance, relating to the procedure for the counting of ballot papers, the type of ballot paper/discs, or adjustments to the campaign spending limits for candidates and political parties.

The reforms of 1997 took two forms. Because they involved changing some clauses of the constitution, those relating to the voting age and the establishment of the IEC were preceded by a national referendum, while those relating to the amendment of the electoral law were discussed and changed by the parliament without recourse to public consultation. However, all the final decisions were made by the parliament and acceded to by the president, thus becoming law.

These reforms were the result both of a long period of advocacy, mainly by the opposition parties and some sections of the civil society organizations, and of the rapid political changes of a similar nature taking place in Southern Africa during the late 1990s. In particular, changes made in Namibia in 1989, in Zambia in 1991, and in Malawi, Mozambique and South Africa in 1994 all introduced the concept of the independent electoral commission, made 18 years the voting age, introduced a limited term for the presidency, and introduced external voting, all as measures to extend democratic rights to wider sections of the population. As a long-established democracy in the region, Botswana would have appeared backward in the context of these changes taking place around it. However, the government was selective in aligning itself with the electoral reforms taking place in the region at the time. For example, the government and the ruling party did not agree with two other proposals, on the funding of political parties and change of the First Past The Post (FPTP) electoral system to the list proportional representation (PR) system which the opposition parties were advocating and which was being adopted by Namibia, Mozambique and South Africa at the time.

The external voting provisions permit all Botswanan citizens aged 18 years or above residing abroad to vote every five years. External voters may vote only for members of Parliament, not for local councillors. (Presidential elections are indirect in Botswana: the president is elected by Parliament.) External voting was introduced mainly because of the concerns raised by the opposition parties. It was felt that citizens outside Botswana were being denied their democratic right to vote for their own government. With the voting age being reduced to 18 years as opposed to 21, the external voting-age population was increased, hence a need to involve them in voting.

## External voting procedure

External voting procedure follows that which applies to registration and voting at home. Normally there are two main periods of concentrated registration, followed by a continuous registration until about six weeks or so before the election date. External voters register at Botswanan embassies and high commissions abroad and in major cities and centres in countries where there is expected to be an eligible voter population. So far only Australia, South Africa, the UK, the USA and Zimbabwe have had more than one polling station: the additional polling stations have been in cities and in institutions other than the official Botswanan diplomatic missions. External registration is normally administered by Botswanan mission staff under the supervision of the IEC. In the 2004 elections many students studying abroad were employed as registration and polling officers. The register of external voters is kept by the head of the mission, who updates it as people come to register.

Normally, external voting takes place two weeks before the general elections at home. The ballot papers are then brought to the IEC within a period of four days after the voting. Upon arrival they are counted and allocated to constituencies on the basis of the voters' choices in the presence of the candidates and political parties. This means that the results of external voting are known by stakeholders a few days before the main voting takes place, but they are never released before the rest of the results.

There is no postal voting for external voters. Where there are no polling stations, external voters are excluded from the right to vote. The argument is that the numbers involved are too small to justify the cost. However, residents abroad are free to go back to Botswana first to register and later to vote. Many who live in South Africa prefer to use this method.

## External voter participation

Botswanan citizens resident outside the country were given the opportunity to exercise their constitutional right to vote for the first time in the 1999 legislative and local elections. The second time they experienced external voting was in 2004. Botswana's experience with external voting is thus limited to the two most recent successive elections. When external voting was introduced in the 1997 reform, significant numbers of citizens were residing outside the country. Most were working people, migrant workers living in neighbouring South Africa and students studying abroad.

The numbers of eligible voters living abroad have fallen significantly since external voting was introduced. We estimate from the censuses of population that in 2004 a total of 25,450 citizens were living abroad (including those under the age of 18), compared to 38,606 in 1991. Between 1971 and 2004 we estimate that the expatriate population fell by over 20,000. This was a result of the reduced work opportunities in South African mines and other industries beginning from the early 1980s.

Participation in elections by citizens living abroad has not been impressive, as the table shows. In 1999, out of the 1,363 voters registered abroad, only some 23.3 per cent voted, compared to a 77.1 per cent turnout by in-country voters. At the time the IEC had restricted external voting to only six countries where there were sufficiently large concentrations of eligible voters—Namibia, South Africa, Swaziland, the UK, the USA and Zimbabwe—and to a total of 24 polling stations in these countries. In an attempt to increase participation, during the 2004 elections the number of countries covered by external voting was increased to 14. The number of polling stations—which were mainly in Botswanan embassies or high commissions abroad and major cities, and institutions of higher learning in the selected countries—also rose, from 24 in 1999 to 44 in 2004. However, the results of both registration and turnout were still below expectations. Out of 2,436 external voters registered, only 49.5 per cent voted. This was still far below the 76.2 per cent voter turnout recorded for the in-country voting population—although the very strong increase since 1999 is worth highlighting. However, with only 2,436 people registering to vote out of an estimated 25,450 citizens living abroad in 2004, the rate of registration may be an even bigger issue than turnout.

Table: External voter participation in the 1999 and 2004 Botswana elections

|  | 1999 | 2004 |
| --- | --- | --- |
| Number of external voters registered | 1,363 | 2,436 |
| Numbers who voted | 333 | 1,214 |
| Turnout | 23.30% | 49.54% |

Source: Independent Electoral Commission, *Report on the General Election* (Gaborone: Government Printer, 2004).

It is clear that the IEC has not been impressed by the level of external voter participation when it is set against the cost involved. The official reports on both the 1999 and the 2004 general elections recommended review of the relevant section of the law on external voting. External voting is likely not to last very long in Botswana, especially because its main advocates—the opposition parties—appear to have become lukewarm about its overall impact on the results. The concern expressed in the official report on the 1999 election was that, while provision for external voting was an important attempt to extend the democratic process, its value had proved disappointingly small that it would need careful review. The official report on the 2004 election expressed the same concern. The IEC feels that, given the scale of the logistical preparations involved, either the provision relating to external voting should be reviewed or more funds should be made available.

## The cost of external voting

The IEC does not have a separate budget for external voting. At the time of writing it was still waiting for embassies and high commissions to submit data on the costs of administering the voting in the respective countries. It was therefore not possible to disaggregate the costs of external voting from the total election costs. However, according to the IEC it is clear that its external travel budget and the costs of paying students and others to supervise elections abroad are very high. In the 2004 election the cost of external travel was 647,950 pula (BWP—161,460 US dollars (USD)). This excludes the costs of salaries, administration and supplies. However, the overall cost of the elections had increased only marginally, from 19 million BWP in 1999 to 21 million BWP in 2004.

## Conclusion

The prospects for external voting in Botswana are not bright. The IEC has recommended a review of the law in the past with a view to closing this window. The main concerns seem to be the high cost per voter and the low level of participation. The opposition parties, which were the drivers of the external voting process, also appear much less enthusiastic than before about defending the system.

# CHAPTER 2

# 2. The history and politics of external voting

Andrew Ellis

---

The case for external voting is usually presented as a question of principle, based on the universality of the right to vote. In reality, however, the introduction of external voting is enacted or enabled by legislation passed by elected politicians. Although there have been a variety of reasons for the enactment of external voting provisions, almost all have been the result of political impetus, and many have been controversial and even nakedly partisan.

## 1. A survey of the history of external voting

The first use of external voting appears to have been put in place by the Roman emperor Augustus, who is said to have invented a new kind of suffrage under which the members of the local senate in 28 newly established colonies cast votes for candidates for the city offices of Rome and sent them under seal to Rome for the day of the elections—an act which was undoubtedly based on political rather than democratic motives. In more recent times, the earliest known use of external voting took place in 1862, when Wisconsin became the first of a number of US states which enacted provisions to allow absentee voting by soldiers fighting in the Union army during the Civil War. (The franchise was defined at state level in the USA.) Political contention was from the beginning a major factor: Republicans backed external voting legislation as they believed that soldiers were likely to support Republican President Abraham Lincoln, while Democrats sympathetic to peace moves and the cause of the Confederacy opposed it. Outside the military context, New Zealand introduced absentee voting for seafarers in 1890, and Australia adopted it in 1902, although under operating arrangements which made its use outside Australia practically impossible.

Many more people were enlisted into armed forces during World War I (1914–8) than in previous conflicts. In the United Kingdom (UK), the political demand for a voice for those doing the fighting led in 1918 to the introduction of absentee voting for military personnel, conducted by proxy. New Zealand gave the vote to all military personnel, not just those over the then voting age of 21, during the period of the war.

Canada provides more early examples of the influence of political factors in the introduction and form of external voting. Postal voting for military electors on active service was agreed at federal level in 1915: the Unionist government believed that Canadians on active military service would be likely supporters. Before the federal election which followed in 1917, the military franchise was extended. In addition, the military voter could choose the electoral district where the vote would be counted— failing which the political party chosen by the voter could do so after the results of the civilian voting in-country were known!

Another Canadian example of the influence of political factors was seen in the province of British Columbia, which enabled military personnel overseas to vote in 1916 in referendums on women's suffrage and on the introduction of the prohibition of alcohol. While the referendum on the vote for women passed easily, the result of the referendum on prohibition was very close, and the votes of overseas soldiers were critical to the rejection of the proposition. Following allegations of malpractice by the supporters of prohibition, a legislative commission of inquiry recommended that most of the overseas votes be disallowed. This recommendation was subsequently passed into law, changing the result of the referendum, and prohibition was then enacted.

France introduced external voting in 1924 to cater to a different constituency: French administrators posted to the occupied Rhineland were enabled to vote by post. World War II (1939–45) produced further momentum for external voting by active servicemen. In addition to postal voting by military personnel, Canada introduced proxy voting on behalf of prisoners of war by their closest relatives for the 1945 general election, and extended postal voting to military families in 1955. Postal voting for military personnel, merchant seamen and others working overseas on matters of national importance took place in the UK in 1945, with a three-week delay between domestic polling and counting to allow for ballot papers to be returned. France introduced proxy voting for servicemen by 1946: by 1951, postal votes and/or proxy votes were available for voters in a range of specified categories, including those on government or military service or professional business away from their home.

A guarantee that US service personnel could register for a postal vote was passed in 1942, although this was reduced in 1944 to a recommendation to states (which are the registration authorities) to enable registration. The overseas postal vote was gradually extended to cover non-military personnel serving abroad (in 1955) and all US citizens abroad (in 1968). Finally, under political pressure from US citizens overseas, the registration provision became mandatory for states in 1975.

In common with many other aspects of electoral administrative tradition, external voting provisions often passed from the legislation of a colonial power to the legislation of a newly independent state. The existence and form of external voting in Malaysia followed its use in colonial Malaya, which had in turn derived it in the 1950s from the British legislation then in force. Postal votes were available for overseas service personnel, for overseas public servants and overseas students, and for their spouses. However, not all British colonies had introduced external voting before independence, and indeed some of the remaining British overseas territories and former colonies still do not have it.

Several French colonies retained the French proxy voting system at independence. France introduced personal voting in embassies and consulates in 1975 for presidential elections and referendums—an executive administrative initiative, because only one version of the ballot paper is required—and a number of former French colonies, for example Gabon and Guinea (Conakry), now have similar systems.

India enacted the core of its election legislation in 1950 and 1951, creating a model which was widely studied in other countries gaining independence. India at first specifically excluded proxy voting, and enfranchised its service personnel through postal voting. However, service personnel are now entitled to vote either by post or by proxy, and electors in government service outside India are entitled to vote by post.

Indonesia legislated in 1953 for its first democratic general elections. While some described the resulting law as over-complex and a search for democratic perfection, the principle of enfranchisement of all citizens, in particular migrant workers and students, led to the introduction of external voting in Indonesian embassies abroad—a mechanism that persisted through the elections of the years of authoritarianism and remained in use in the democratic era. A similar wide qualification was introduced by Colombia in 1961 (see case study).

The reasons for introducing external voting also differ according to the historical and political contexts. Thus, in several countries the introduction of the right to vote for overseas citizens was an acknowledgement of their active participation in World War I or World War II. In Spain, the introduction of external voting in 1978 had a symbolic character insofar as its inclusion in the democratic constitution meant the ex post facto acknowledgement of the republican emigration after the Civil War. In Argentina (1993) it reflected the government's political/pragmatic intention to maintain or strengthen the ties between emigrants and the mother country. In Austria the introduction of external voting (in 1990) followed a resolution of the Constitutional Court. The United States provides an example of those rare cases where external voting was finally enacted in response to the demands of citizens residing overseas (in 1975). While Swiss citizens had been able to travel back to Switzerland to vote for some years, the argument that Swiss sovereignty precluded foreigners from voting in Switzerland and therefore prevented the Swiss from seeking agreement for external voting was only finally overcome in 1989 (see the case study).

Political parties and actors can be the key players in introducing external voting. A provision in Honduras that had long been stalled was activated by a party which saw political advantage in doing so (see the case study). In the UK in the 1980s, the then

Conservative government saw advantage in the general enfranchisement of British citizens living overseas and enacted it, believing that many expatriates would be their supporters, but were disappointed by the very low take-up of overseas registration. Even an extension of the maximum period of overseas residence from five years to 25 did not bring the party the political benefits they anticipated.

However, communities of expatriates do often seek involvement in their country of origin, whether migrant workers seeking to retain links with their home, members of long-term diaspora communities opposed to a current or former regime, or expatriates remitting payments to relatives. Such communities can themselves be influential in lobbying for the introduction of external voting—as the Dominican Republic case study shows.

The fear of fraud in the operation of external voting provisions has sometimes been well-founded. France abolished postal voting in 1975 because of the incidence of fraud. French provisions for proxy voting before 1982 allowed proxies to be registered in any electoral district—which led in legislative elections to competition to register proxies in marginal electoral districts. Since 1982, proxies may only be registered in electoral districts with which the elector has a connection according to a list specified in the electoral law.

External voting provisions have not always proved to be sustainable. In the Cook Islands (see the case study), the undesirable effects of political party competition to fly voters overseas back for the poll led to the introduction of a separate electoral district for Cook Islanders resident overseas. Although Cook Islands elections have remained competitive, political support for the overseas seat declined and it was abolished for the 2004 election.

## 2. External voting in democratic transitions

The importance of political factors in the adoption and design of external voting provisions was accentuated during the democratic transitions of the 1990s. The inclusion of citizens abroad was often seen as a key element in the process of nation-building, for example, in Namibia in 1989 and South Africa in 1994.

Diaspora communities may be active in seeking a post-transition role, and may be particularly influential when they play a role in the domestic politics of major donor countries. However, such pressure is not always successful. The elections which took place in Palestine in 1996 were held under the terms of the Oslo Agreement of 1993 and the Israeli–Palestinian Interim Agreement of 1995. Under these agreements, the right of return of displaced Palestinians and their families was left for consideration in final-status negotiations. Although there was considerable pressure within the Palestinian diaspora for voting rights, no external voting provisions were introduced.

The international community frequently plays a leading or significant role in mediating transitions and even in implementing transitional elections. Transition agreements may therefore contain important and sometimes controversial external voting provisions. The General Framework Agreement for Peace signed at Dayton in 1995 led to the most complex use of external voting thus far attempted in the 1996 elections in Bosnia and Herzegovina. The issue at stake was the extent to which the 'ethnic cleansing' that had taken place during the conflict would be recognized in the elections. Would people who had been displaced or become refugees be able, both as a question of principle and in practice, to vote in the locality which they had left, or in a locality where they now were or where they intended to make a future home? The agreement provided for both options (see the case study). While the Organization for Security and Co-operation in Europe (OSCE) sought to implement the terms of the agreement, the political forces in Bosnia—many of which had been the major participants in the war—sought to encourage some versions of external voting, and to discourage others.

In a transitional context, the question of who implements external voting can be politically highly sensitive. The International Organization for Migration (IOM) organized external voting for Bosnia and Herzegovina in a variety of countries for several elections. When external voting for the 2004 elections in Afghanistan was being planned, Pakistan offered to organize the polling stations itself—politically a highly controversial proposal, which was not in the event accepted. The same arrangement may, however, be entirely acceptable in other circumstances. The electoral authority of the US territory of Guam organizes polling for the many citizens of the Federated States of Micronesia based in Guam, an arrangement which finds all-round support.

## 3. External voting and electoral system design

Political considerations are not only important in determining whether external voting takes place: they are also influential in defining its form. Many decisions relating to external voting are linked to electoral system design, another highly political aspect of democratic reform and democratic transition. Electoral system design is one of the most important elements in the institutional framework of a country, influencing as it does the political party system. Electoral system reform may be on the agenda as a result of vision or a motivation to improve democracy, or for more short-term, sectoral or even venal reasons on the part of some political participants. This is mirrored by external voting, which may be placed on the democratic agenda by those who believe strongly in the equal right of all citizens to participate—or by political forces which see potential advantage in it.

The desire to promote external voting may constrain the options for electoral system design. Conversely, the adoption of a particular electoral system may limit the options for external voting mechanisms. This can be illustrated by considering the three basic options for external voting—personal voting at an external polling site in a diplomatic mission, for example; remote voting by post, fax or some form of e-voting; and voting by proxy. Chapter 5 looks in more detail at the administrative and practical aspects of implementation; the discussion below looks at how these relate to aspects of principle in choice of external voting method.

### 3.1. Personal voting and electoral system design

Personal voting at a polling station in-country is easy: all voters at the polling station will normally be voting in the same electoral district in the same election or elections, and will thus need to receive the same ballot papers. Minor exceptions (such as the small number of members of the UK House of Lords, who may not vote in legislative elections but may vote in local elections) can be accommodated.

The same is not, however, necessarily true of a polling site in for example a diplomatic mission. The electors may originate from anywhere in the country that is holding the election. Where the same ballot paper is in use across the whole country, this is not a problem: for example, everyone receives the same ballot paper in a plurality or majority election for president. The same is true when electing legislators under a List proportional representation (List PR) system in which the whole country forms one electoral district, and even when closed List PR is used in smaller electoral districts using ballot papers which only carry party names and logos.

The position is very different when candidate-based systems or systems with smaller electoral districts are used to elect legislators, and ballot papers are not the same country-wide. First, the electoral authorities have to establish how many of each ballot paper to despatch to each diplomatic mission. Then, the mission staff have to issue the right ballot paper to each external voter.

Under plurality/majority systems, for example, First Past The Post, the Two-Round System, Alternative Vote, Block Vote and Single Non-Transferable Vote, polling site officials will need to know in which district a voter is entitled to vote. The same is true under Single Transferable Vote.

If open or free List PR are used, the individual candidate lists will be different in each district, even if the same selection of parties are contesting every district. With closed List PR, the same applies if it is thought that the voter has the right to know when voting the identity of the candidates on the list of each party. Mixed systems, whether Mixed Member Proportional (MMP) or Parallel, are the most problematic, posing the challenges of both of their components simultaneously. Problems are likely to be magnified further if a decision is taken to use external voting in regional and local elections.

The task of determining which ballot paper each voter should receive may not then be simple, especially if the voter has left the home country a considerable time before. Neither voters nor polling site officials might be expected to have detailed knowledge of precise electoral boundaries. It may be possible to use the registration process to determine the correct location of each elector and record it in a form that is accessible at polling sites, although this is a task that can consume considerable time and resources. Alternatively, electoral system designers can design versions of their chosen system in which a specific external district with reserved seats is created—as in Croatia. Another option is to allocate all external voters to a small number of electoral districts—as in Indonesia, where the external votes cast in Malaysia and Singapore are included in one of the two electoral districts in the capital, Jakarta, and all other external votes to the second Jakarta district (see the case study on Indonesia).

Even when the most recent place of residence in the home country of each elector is known, logistical challenges remain. The polling site needs to receive ballot papers for every district from the central electoral administration, and the polling site officials then need to ensure that the correct ballot paper is issued to each voter. There may be considerable potential for error and confusion. The values of electoral inclusion, electoral system sustainability and electoral integrity may pull in different directions, and a balance must be achieved.

## 3.2. Remote voting and electoral system design

While the electoral system design challenges for external voting using remote mechanisms are perhaps not as difficult as those using personal voting mechanisms, there are still substantial issues. While the packaging and despatch of correct ballot papers may be conducted under less time pressure, and the central election administration staff involved probably better trained and less likely to make mistakes than the officials at out-of-country polling sites, the possibility of error and confusion remains. The reliability of postal services in some parts of the world is clearly also an issue.

In addition, the electoral timetable can become a relevant factor. Ballot papers cannot be printed and despatched until nominations are closed and verified: time is then needed for international postal services to function in both directions. If the closing date for return of external postal ballot papers is set for polling day, this may not be consistent with the length of the campaign period. If it is set later than polling day, problems of the credibility of partial results may arise, especially in close elections where the external vote may be decisive. Timetable issues will be particularly difficult where a Two-Round System is in use, as the ballot papers for the second round can only be printed and despatched when the result of the first round is known.

## 3.3. Proxy voting and electoral system resign

Of the three approaches to external voting mechanisms, proxy votes cause the least problems to electoral system designers. The problems of allocating external voters to electoral districts remain, but if this can be achieved, the proxies can be considered just as the voters themselves would be. Voters will presumably choose proxies who are in-country and able to vote at the same polling stations as they themselves would. In any event, the choice of proxy is the voter's responsibility. A proxy voting system may, however, have other disadvantages, not least the issues that it can raise about electoral integrity.

### 3.4. Timing issues

External voting may be complex, and is always relatively time-consuming. However, where new electoral arrangements are being created, it is well known from experience that political actors will take all the time available for negotiating the form of a new election law. It is after all established negotiating practice to get maximum value for concessions by making them only when there is pressure of time to reach an agreement. This means that electoral administrators are almost certain to be operating without sufficient time to produce the ideal—or even a desirable—election. When corners need to be cut, simple systems which will work satisfactorily under pressure are therefore valuable. This may affect the choice of external voting method adopted.

CASE STUDY: The Cook Islands

# The Cook Islands: seat for overseas voters abolished

Graham Hassall*

The Cook Islands is a self-governing state which established free association with New Zealand in 1965. The suffrage in relation to Cook Islanders living outside the Cook Islands has been an important issue in Cook Islands electoral politics.

In 1965, when the constitution and electoral laws were drafted, external voting was not an issue and was not thought of. Some Cook Islanders lived abroad, mainly in New Zealand and Tahiti, but there was no international air service, shipping was irregular and expensive, and the Cook Islands principle of 'rangatira ki te ara' implied that those who had gone away should not interfere in what went on at home. In 1974, however an international airport was built, regular and relatively cheap international flights were introduced, and at the same time party political competition was intensifying.

The Cook Islands electoral system had provision for an external seat from 1981 until 2003, and an overseas member was thus elected at general elections in 1983, 1989, 1994 and 1999 (see Hassall 2001; and Crocombe 1979). The Legislative Assembly had 22 members in 1965, the number of seats being subsequently increased to 24 in 1981 (with the constitutional amendment the Assembly was renamed 'Parliament') and to 25 in 1991.

External voting was established in 1981 through an amendment to the Electoral Act 1966 (Constitution Amendment (No. 9) Act) so that an 'overseas constituency' became one of the legislature's 24 seats. The Electoral Act of 1966, with amendments as of 6 May 1989, Part II Constituencies, 5 (x), reads: 'The Overseas Constituency, being the islands comprising New Zealand and all other Areas outside the Cook Islands'. This means the whole world except the Cook Islands. At that time the great majority of overseas Cook Islanders were in New Zealand.

Article 28C of the constitution provided for the election of a member for the overseas constituency who was residing 'in New Zealand or elsewhere outside the Cook Islands', who was a Cook Islands citizen and who was enrolled as an elector in the overseas

---

* The author expresses his thanks to Emeritus Professor Ron Crocombe for providing essential information for this case study.

constituency. Article 28 (b) provided for the election of a member by 'postal vote, special vote, or by vote cast at one or more polling places situated outside the Cook Islands'. Voting was not compulsory, but registration was, and failure to register was an offence liable to a fine not exceeding 100 New Zealand dollars (NZD) (the currency used in the Cook Islands) on a first conviction (although there is no evidence that this fine was ever imposed).

The seat was established in the context of the growing number of Cook Islanders living abroad but the specific voting provisions restricted the number of islanders eligible to vote, since it only applied to those who had lived abroad for less than three years and who intended to return home to live permanently. This amounted to a small fraction of the total number of overseas Cook Islanders. It was the result of a move by the Democratic Party (DP) then in power to restrict the future influence of those whom they regarded as mostly loyal to the Cook Islands Party (CIP). This legislation was passed following efforts by political parties to mobilize external electors at general elections in 1974 and 1978, which the Cook Islands courts had subsequently found to be illegal. In those elections, the major political parties had chartered aircraft to fly in those who were registered as 'absentee voters'. In the 1974 elections the DP chartered an aircraft to transport approximately 75 voters to Rarotonga, and in the 1978 elections both the DP and the CIP chartered aircraft.

Both parties now realized that the increasing number of prospective absentee voters could swing the results of an election, and thus made elaborate efforts to register voters who were resident in New Zealand. Democratic Party voters paid for the charter air fares while the Cook Islands Party members were told that their flights would be free of charge. After the CIP victory in 1978, in which the 'fly-in' votes had been a decisive factor, the DP filed election petitions, challenging, among other things, the legality of the votes won by flying in voters at no cost or heavily subsidized by the CIP using government funds. On 24 July 1978 the Supreme Court determined that eight of the CIP's 15 seats had been gained by 'unlawful conduct' in that the CIP fly-in votes were tainted by bribery and corruption. These seats were awarded to the DP, and the CIP lost power. (High Court of the Cook Islands, Misc. nos 21, 22, 23, 24, 25, 26, 27, 28, 29, 30, 31 and 32.78, in the Matter of Elections of Members of the Legislative Assembly of the Cook Islands, unreported. See also Henry 2003.)

The use of 'flying voters' was made possible by the vagueness of the definition of 'ordinary residence' in the constitution, but there was no constitutional provision for external voting outside the Cook Islands, because when it was drafted in 1964 there were few Cook Islanders in New Zealand and no air service.

Following the establishment of the external seat in 1981, a debate ensued about whether Cook Islanders who had chosen to live elsewhere should have full representation in the Cook Islands legislature, and the high cost of the public sector in general (particularly in the context of the Cook Islands' small and struggling economy) brought into question the cost-effectiveness of the external seat. The cost of administering the external seat has never been made public. A 1998 Commission of Political Review was unable to determine exact costs but estimated that the costs of external voting—the salary costs, fares, living costs and so on of the team of officials sent from the Cook Islands to visit communities of Cook Islanders in New Zealand and Australia to advise them about the provisions—were too high, relative to the numbers of voters concerned, to make it worthwhile. Even the administrators of political parties agreed that there was too little interest among expatriate Cook Islanders to make the effort worthwhile. Moreover, under the terms of the free association arrangement between the Cook Islands and New Zealand, all Cook Islanders are New Zealand citizens and are therefore entitled to vote in New Zealand elections; New Zealand citizens can similarly move to Australia quite easily and take up citizenship rights in that country.

In a the general election of March 1994 voters were also asked at referendum whether the overseas constituency should be abolished. Approximately 55 per cent of the population voted in favour of keeping the seat, and the government thus took no action to remove it. However, although on this occasion the voters agreed to the continuance of the seat, public support for it declined within a few years.

In practice, while there are more Cook Islanders living outside their home country than in it, few have been motivated to register and vote in Cook Islands general elections. Out of approximately 60,000 Cook Islanders resident in New Zealand and 45,000 in Australia, only 737 registered as voters for the 1994 general election and some 569 Cook Islanders abroad actually voted (Cook Islands News and ABC News, 18 September 2002). (In 1994 there were four candidates for the overseas seat.) The reasons for the low registration numbers include a tendency for Cook Islanders to describe themselves on official forms as New Zealand citizens or as Maori, sometimes out of fear that they might be removed from these countries in the same manner as Samoans and Tongans are (although this is based on ignorance of the law, because Samoans and Tongans have less right of entry to New Zealand than Cook Islanders).

In 1998 the Commission of Political Review recommended a number of changes to the Cook Islands constitution, including reducing the number of parliamentary seats to 17—a formula that did not include an overseas seat (Commission of Political Review 1998). The future of the external seat gradually became the subject of intense speculation. At the general elections in 1999 three of the four political parties fielded candidates for the overseas seat, although an inquiry that suggested that the overseas seat cost some 100,000 NZD each year was a factor in a large proportion of the Cook Islands public favouring its abolition. In 1991 the High Court also ruled that candidates who are normally resident abroad are ineligible to represent Cook Islanders in Parliament.

In 2000 there were an estimated 55,000 Cook Islanders in New Zealand and another 30,000 in Australia. However, only 6,000 of these were eligible to vote because they had been abroad for less than three years.

In 2003 some 2,000 voters signed a petition calling not only for abolition of the overseas seat but also for a reduction in the parliamentary term from five years to three, a reduction in the number of MPs and a reduction in funding for ministerial support. When the legislature voted in 2003 on whether to abolish the overseas seat even its incumbent, Dr Joe Williams, agreed to its abolition.

CASE STUDY: Indonesia

# Indonesia: a long-established system for external voting at diplomatic missions

Alan Wall

In 2004 Indonesians participated in a historic series of elections, in April in what are widely regarded as the most democratic elections for legislatures held since the 1955 Sukarno-era elections, and in July and September for the first direct elections for the presidency. Between 200,000 and 250,000 voters (*c.* 0.2 per cent of total voter turnout) voted outside Indonesia at these elections. Voting outside Indonesia for national parliamentary bodies has been a constant feature of Indonesian elections since the first post-independence direct popular election—that for the national People's Representative Council in September 1955.

Concern to preserve the voting rights of a large external population of immigrant workers and students, mostly resident abroad for a relatively short period, had led to external voting provisions being included in the 1953 Election Law. External voting was managed by the Ministry of Foreign Affairs. Indonesians who met the qualifications to vote but were overseas and living in a city where Indonesia had diplomatic representation could register to vote for the national legislative body at the relevant embassy. They were registered to vote for the electoral district in which the Ministry of Foreign Affairs headquarters was located—the province of Jakarta. Overseas voting committees (PPLNs) were formed at each Indonesian diplomatic mission by the ambassador to manage electoral registration, voting and the counting of ballot papers.

Similar arrangements continued under the 1969 Election Law, which governed the six Suharto-era 'elections' for the national People's Representative Council (DPR) held between 1971 and 1997. The first post-Suharto era election, in 1999, also continued these arrangements, although PPLNs made up of party representatives now replaced the bureaucrats of the ministries of home affairs and foreign affairs of the Suharto era. External electors could still vote only for the DPR, and their votes continued to be added to votes for the province of Jakarta.

Constitutional changes between 1999 and 2002 significantly altered the structure of the organs of the Indonesian state. They resulted in a significant overhaul of electoral management—the setting up of an independent National Election Commission (KPU), and the adoption in 2002 and 2003 of new electoral laws. Elections for the DPR and regional representative councils (DPRDs) were now to be held using an open list proportional representation (PR) system. The system adopted requires that voters must vote for their preferred political party and may also vote for their preferred candidate from that party's candidate list for the relevant electoral district. (Previously, a closed List PR system, in which only party names/symbols appeared on the ballot papers, was used.) The KPU also now had to divide each council's area into electoral districts, each returning between three and 12 representatives. Previously, elections for the DPR had been based on the provinces as electoral districts, and elections for DPRDs were held 'at large' within each council's area. A new second chamber of the national parliament, the Regional Representatives Council (DPD), was to be elected by a Single Non-Transferable Vote (SNTV) system, using each province as an electoral district. All these elections were to be held on the same day. Subsequent presidential elections were to be held using a Two-Round election system.

The complexity of the new electoral arrangements made any significant changes to the external voting arrangements difficult. The vastly increased number of electoral districts provided even greater administrative difficulties in providing external voting facilities for elections to provincial and local representative councils. (For elections prior to 2004, electoral districts for the DPR and provincial DPRDs were equal to the number of provinces (27 in 1999), and for local DPRDs equal to the number of regencies/municipalities (c. 260 in 1999). For the 2004 elections there were 69 electoral districts for the DPR, 32 for the DPD, 211 for the provincial DPRDs and 1,745 for local DPRDs.) The relevant electoral laws (Law no. 12 of 2003 on Elections, and Law no. 23 of 2003 on the Election of the President and Vice-President) stated that external electors could vote only in elections for the DPR and the presidency.

The increase in the number of national electoral districts and the introduction of an open list voting system was also decisive in restricting change to the framework for external voting for DPR elections. It was argued, successfully, that it was not possible for external voting stations to cope with administrative materials for the 69 national electoral districts, and that neither the political parties nor the electoral administrators had the capacity to provide information at all external voting locations about the candidates standing on party lists in all these districts. To simplify the administration, the KPU determined that for the 2004 elections votes cast by external voters would continue to be amalgamated with votes cast in the Jakarta province. However, the Jakarta province was now split into two electoral districts for the DPR elections. Arguments were made for continuing the historical arrangement whereby all external votes were amalgamated into the votes for the electoral district where the headquarters of the Ministry of Foreign Affairs is located, but this was not accepted. Instead, external votes were divided into what the KPU believed would be relatively equal shares. Votes for the DPR from external voters in Malaysia and Singapore were amalgamated with votes for one Jakarta electoral district, and votes from external voters at all other locations were amalgamated with votes for the second Jakarta district.

The administrative arrangements for external voting for the 2004 elections were therefore similar to those for previous elections. The process was managed by the KPU, in coordination with the Ministry of Foreign Affairs. External voting facilities were located at Indonesian diplomatic missions and managed at each location by an independent PPLN, appointed by the KPU. Election supervisory committees (Panwas) were also established at each external voting location. Panwas are a uniquely Indonesian institution, formed at each election administration site. They are responsible to the KPU and charged with supervising the election processes, handling complaints, resolving disputes that do not involve a breach of the law, and reporting on alleged breaches of the law to the relevant authority.

Indonesians overseas who met the normal qualifications to vote were able to register at the Indonesian diplomatic mission in the city in which they were resident. PPLNs at each mission were responsible for registering them: registration could be done in person, by email or by post. Electors registering overseas were not included in the population counts used to determine the number of seats in the DPR allocated to the Jakarta province, or to the districts within the province. A single electoral register was constructed for each mission, later to be broken down into lists to be used at each polling station within the mission. (The electoral law sets a maximum of 300 electors per polling station.)

Voting in person at diplomatic missions was held simultaneously with voting in Indonesia. Observers, party agents and Panwas members had the same rights to observe the election processes at external voting locations as their counterparts in Indonesia. For the 2004 elections external voters could also apply to lodge postal votes, which had to be received by the relevant mission within ten days of election day. Votes lodged in person and by post at external voting locations were counted at that location and the results faxed or emailed to the KPU's headquarters in Jakarta.

For the three elections in 2004, between 405,000 and 460,000 persons registered as external electors, of an estimated 2 million Indonesians overseas. External voter turnout at these elections, at between 55 per cent and 60 per cent, was significantly lower than turnout within Indonesia.

Funding requirements for external voting are specifically recognized in the KPU's budget. For example, in its budget proposals for the 2004 elections, the KPU sought parliamentary approval for allocations of over 57.5 billion Indonesian rupiah (IDR—c. 6 million US dollars (USD), or 13 USD per registered external voter) for the costs of administering external voting for the April 2004 legislative elections. This did not include the costs of voter information, the printing of ballot papers, and central administration for external voting. Actual costs are not known.

During the period in which new election laws were being developed for the 2004 elections there was some discussion, initiated by civil society organizations, as to whether external electors could also be eligible to vote in elections other than those for the DPR and the presidency, but such proposals were not strongly argued or seriously considered. The administration of external voting for around 2,050 national, provincial and local government electoral districts was deemed too difficult. It was also argued that, while external voters may maintain a connection to Indonesia's national affairs, this could not be said to be true of the affairs of a particular province or local government area. Since the 2004 elections, there has been no further public discussion about altering the current external voting arrangements.

CASE STUDY: Zimbabwe

# Zimbabwe: highly restrictive provisions

Ozias Tungwarara

External voting by post was part of the electoral laws that were introduced in Zimbabwe after 1980 when the country attained political independence. It is limited to electors who are absent from Zimbabwe while in the service of the government, such as diplomats, civil servants, and members of the armed forces and police. An estimated 3.5 million Zimbabweans now live outside the country, mainly as a result of economic and political hardship, and about two-thirds of these are probably of voting age. This situation has given rise to increased demands by those living in the diaspora for external voting arrangements to be extended to them as well. Zimbabwean laws prohibit dual citizenship.

External voting is provided for in part XIV of the Electoral Act (Act no. 25/2005), which deals with postal voting. The act only makes reference to postal voting and does not provide for voting at a diplomatic mission. Eligibility to vote by post is limited to persons ordinarily resident in Zimbabwe who are resident in the constituency (electoral district) in which the election is to take place or were resident in that constituency 12 months preceding polling day and have good reason to believe that they will be absent from the constituency or unable to attend at the polling station by reason of being 'absent from Zimbabwe in the service of the Government of Zimbabwe' (section 71(1)(b)). The spouses of persons absent from Zimbabwe on government service are also eligible to vote by post.

Sections 71–81 of the Electoral Act describe in detail the procedure for applying for postal ballot papers, the issuing of the postal ballot papers, postal voting, the handling of the postal ballot boxes, and offences related to postal ballot votes. A person who is eligible to vote by post may apply to the chief elections officer for a postal ballot paper. The application, to be received by the chief elections officer ten days before polling day, is made on a prescribed form that the applicant signs in front of a competent witness. The chief elections officer shall number consecutively and keep every application received by him or her open for public inspection until the final result of the election is announced.

Once the chief elections officer is satisfied that the application satisfies the legal requirements, he or she will send the ballot paper to the applicant by registered post or by hand together with other documents stipulated in the act. The ballot paper shall be numbered and shall be indistinguishable from the ballot papers at other polling stations. Upon receiving the postal ballot, the voter shall produce the numbered ballot paper before a competent witness. Both the voter and the competent witness will sign a declaration of identity. The voter will then mark the ballot paper with the candidate of his preference in the presence of a competent witness but without disclosing how he or she has voted. The voter will place the marked ballot paper in an envelope marked 'ballot paper' and place it together with the identity declaration in a cover envelope for dispatch by registered post or hand it directly to the constituency election officer.

The constituency election officer shall, no later than three days after nomination day, notify each candidate of the time and place at which he or she will seal the postal ballot box. At the appointed time and place the constituency electoral officer will show the postal ballot box open and empty and then seal it with his seal and the seals of any candidates who wish to affix their seals. All postal votes received before the close of the poll will be placed unopened in that ballot box. The constituency elections officer will give each candidate 24 hours' notice of the place and time at which the postal ballot boxes and envelopes will be opened.

The electoral authorities have taken great care to ensure the transparency, credibility and security of the external voting process through the provisions described above. However, despite increasing demands, the government maintains that it has no obligation to introduce external voting arrangements to allow the growing number of Zimbabweans living outside the country to vote.

In a recent case a group of Zimbabwean citizens living in the United Kingdom, sought an order compelling the government to make arrangements to allow them to vote externally. The Zimbabwe Supreme Court (Case no. SC 22/05) ruled that the case had no merit. The ruling, made on 18 March 2005, indicated that full reasons for the judgement would be given later. At the time of writing the full judgement is still to be made available.

The applicants—who were not employed by the government but were legally resident in the UK—argued that they were entitled to exercise their right to vote in terms of the Zimbabwean Constitution and that their exclusion from voting was discriminatory and therefore unconstitutional. They further contended that the exclusion from voting of those living outside Zimbabwe curtailed their rights to freedom of expression to an extent that was not acceptable in a democratic society, and advanced the argument that the Zimbabwean Government was committed to full participation by its citizens in political and electoral processes by its citizens by virtue of being party to the Universal Declaration of Human Rights, the African Charter on Human and Peoples' Rights and the Southern African Development Community (SADC) Principles and Guidelines Governing Democratic Elections. They argued that there was a distinction between eligibility to register as a voter and eligibility to vote. The electoral law was therefore discriminatory to the extent that it permitted certain citizens to vote externally while excluding others.

In response, the Zimbabwean minister of justice, legal and parliamentary affairs, who was cited as first respondent in the case, denied that Zimbabweans living abroad were being discriminated against by the absence of external voting arrangements. He argued that the electoral law provided for the disqualification of voters who had been absent from Zimbabwe for 12 months or more. He contended that the SADC Principles and Guidelines are a political document pegging out a road map for the region that SADC countries must follow towards a a future democratic ideal, but that it is not a legal document that is binding on member states. He argued further that, while the Zimbabwean Government acknowledged that Zimbabwean citizens had the right to freedom of expression, assembly and association, the government was not discriminating against anyone but that, under the current political and economic situation, Zimbabwe was unable to allow electors from the diaspora to vote externally because of practical logistical problems. He pointed out that most of the countries in which Zimbabweans were living had adopted measures and sanctions that prohibited government officials from entering such countries. (Sanctions have been adopted by mainly the European Union countries and the United States.) This, he argued, would create an uneven political playing field where the ruling party would not have access to would-be voters while the opposition would have easy access.

It is clear that in Zimbabwe the provisions for external voting are elaborate but restrictive. There is no doubt that, given the growing number of citizens living outside the country, there is going to be increasing demand for similar arrangements to be extended to citizens who are not abroad on government service. The case referred above also raises the fundamental issue of a rights-based approach to electoral administration and how far governments should be held responsible for realizing citizens' right to vote.

CASE STUDY: Mozambique

# Mozambique: a system that is too subjective?

Simon-Pierre Nanitelamio

According to the constitution of the Republic of Mozambique (article 170, point 2), the parliament (the Assembly of the Republic) is composed of 250 seats. They are distributed as follows: 248 are allocated to the 11 internal electoral districts within Mozambique; and two are allocated to the two external electoral districts ('Africa' and the 'rest of the world'). The rationale behind the creation of electoral districts outside the national boundaries is to preserve the voting rights of migrants. The provisions of the 1990 constitution, revised in 2004, allow Mozambican citizens living abroad to vote, in their countries of residence, not only for their representatives to the Assembly of the Republic but also in presidential elections. However, the exercise of their voting rights hinges on the existence of some basic conditions.

Both the Voter Registration Law and the General Elections Law emphasize that Mozambican citizens living abroad have the right to register as electors and vote only if and when the National Electoral Commission (NEC) considers it possible. (Since 2002, the NEC has been made up of 20 members: 18 are appointed by political parties represented in the parliament, in proportion to the number of seats they won at the last election in 1999. Ten are appointed by the ruling party, the Mozambican Liberation Front (Frente de Libertação de Moçambique, Frelimo) and eight by the Mozambican National Resistance Resistência Nacional Moçambicana, Renamo)–Electoral Union coalition. One member is nominated by the government and the president, the 20th member, is designated by the civil society organizations. An electoral reform is currently under way and the composition of the NEC may change in the future.)

Article 9 of Law no. 18/2002 of 10 October 2002, on the institutionalization of systematic electoral registration for elections and referendums in Mozambique, states that: (a) electoral registration will be conducted both within the national territory and abroad; and (b) the geographical boundaries and locations for electoral registration are (i) in the national territory: the districts and Maputo city; and (ii) abroad: at diplomatic or consular missions. The electoral registration referred to in point (ii) will be carried out only if the NEC considers that the necessary 'material conditions and control, review and inspection mechanisms' are in place in all regions.

Article 10 of the General Elections Law, Law no. 7/2004 of 17 June 2004, states that 'Mozambican citizens registered abroad are eligible for the elections foreseen in the present law'. This is complemented by the provisions of article 11 (on Mozambican citizens living abroad) of the same law, as follows.

1. Registered citizens living abroad cast their vote at the respective diplomatic or consular mission of the Republic of Mozambique.

2. Electoral acts abroad shall take place only after the NEC has verified and confirmed that the necessary conditions with regard to the material conditions and control, review and inspection mechanisms are in place in the region(s) constituting the electoral districts of Mozambican communities abroad.

3. If the electoral acts referred to in the above point cannot take place, the NEC shall redistribute the parliamentary seats allocated to the external electoral districts to the internal electoral constituencies, according to the criteria determined in the present General Elections Law.

These provisions were also to be found in the previous electoral laws—the General Elections Law, no. 4/93 of 28 December 1993, the Voter Registration Law no. 5/97 of 28 May 1997, the General Elections Law no. 3/99 of 2 February 1999, and the Voter Registration Law no. 9/99 of 14 April 1999. One of the peculiarities of Mozambican electoral practice since the introduction of the multiparty system is that a new electoral legislation package (containing the law on electoral registration, the law on the electoral management bodies (EMBs), and a law on the type of election—municipal or general elections) has been passed each time the country has held elections—in 1993 for the 1994 general election, in 1997 for the 1998 municipal elections, in 1999 for the 1999 general election, in 2002 for the 2003 municipal elections, and in 2004 for the 2004 general election. The new electoral law usually amends and/or complements the provisions of some articles of the previous law. Once again, an ad hoc parliamentary electoral reform commission was established in March 2005, upon completion of the 2004 electoral process, to review and amend the current electoral legislation package in anticipation of the future electoral processes: the new electoral legislation package was expected to be passed at the first parliamentary session of 2006.

Thus, for electors to be registered and elections to be held abroad, the NEC must confirm that the material conditions and the control, follow-up and monitoring mechanisms are in place in the external electoral districts. However, the decision as to whether such conditions are in place could be very subjective and could become a real bone of contention among the electoral stakeholders. In fact, even though the external voting issue in Mozambique has been raised regularly since the preparations for the first democratic multiparty elections (held in October 1994), following a long period of a one-party system since independence, and even though it is provided for in the electoral law, external voting did not take place until the general elections held in December 2004.

The first attempt to carry out registration in the external electoral districts took place in 1997 in seven countries—in Malawi, South Africa, Swaziland, Tanzania, Zambia and Zimbabwe for the Africa electoral district; and in Portugal for the 'rest of the world' electoral district. The preparations failed, and the attempt was a setback: only 1,694 Mozambican citizens in total turned out to register out of an estimated population of approximately 200,000 expatriate citizens. Considering that the conditions were therefore not met, the NEC did not repeat the operation in 1999 in preparation for the country's second general election.

In 2004, in the course of preparations for the third general election, scheduled for 1 and 2 December, the external voting issue was raised again. A heated debate took place within the NEC as to whether the EMB should carry out electoral registration for Mozambican citizens living abroad. Frelimo, the ruling party, was very supportive of the idea, while almost all the opposition political parties, led by Renamo, were fiercely against it on the grounds that (a) the preconditions (material conditions, control and inspection mechanisms) had not been met and (b) the legal time frame had already elapsed (arguing that electoral registration should have been conducted simultaneously in Mozambique and abroad from 28 June to 15 July 2004). In the absence of a consensus, a vote was organized during the NEC plenary session of 21 July 2004. With eight votes against the idea and ten in favour, the decision to carry out electoral registration abroad was officially taken.

With a separate budget of 400,000 US dollars (USD) totally financed by the government of Mozambique, the electoral registration operation took place from 6 to 25 September 2004, as shown in table 1, in nine countries—seven in Africa and two in Europe.

Table 1. Mozambican citizens residing abroad and numbers of registered external electors, 2004

| Country of residence | Estimated population of Mozambican citizens | No. of registered external electors | No. of parliamentary seats allocated |
|---|---|---|---|
| Kenya | 2,571 | 699 | |
| Malawi | 1,724 | 676 | |
| Tanzania | 8,618 | 3,807 | |
| South Africa | 156,939 | 32,186 | |
| Swaziland | 30,000 | 2,921 | |
| Zambia | 1,000 | 764 | |
| Zimbabwe | 14,575 | 4,812 | |
| Germany | 2,811 | 190 | |
| Portugal | 7,860 | 911 | |
| Total | 226,098 | 46,966 | 2 |

The sole criterion for the selection of the countries where external registration would take place was demographic—the existence in each country of a minimum of 1,000 legally registered Mozambican citizens. The figures (taken from the population estimates) were provided to the NEC by the diplomatic missions in those countries through the Ministry of Foreign Affairs and Cooperation.

On 11 October 2004, notwithstanding another negative vote from its Renamo-appointed members, the NEC voted in favour of holding the general election in the two external electoral districts, thanks to the votes in favour of all its Frelimo-appointed members. In addition to Renamo, many other opposition political parties disagreed with the idea of holding the external voting operation on the grounds that the small number of registered electors (0.5 per cent of the total registered electorate of 9,142,151) did not justify the high costs involved and that the mechanisms for proper supervision and monitoring were not in place. However, it seems that the opposition political parties' resistance was most probably linked to the fact that the external electoral districts are considered to be strongholds of the ruling party, in addition to the fact that they did not consider the diplomatic and consular missions where the elections were to take place as politically neutral premises.

In South Africa external registration and voting were extended to the areas where migrant Mozambican citizens are concentrated, namely the mining areas. In the eight other countries those operations were limited to the premises of Mozambican diplomatic and consular missions.

No official budget for the voting operations abroad was disclosed, although part of it was included in the total budget for the 2004 elections: all the polling materials, for instance, for both internal and external voting, were produced at the same time by the same South African company.

The same voting requirements and procedures that applied in the national territory were applied for the external voting. The right to vote was exercised in person at the polling station where the elector was registered. No postal or remote voting was allowed. The NEC and the Technical Secretariat for Electoral Administration (STAE), its implementing body, sent supervision teams to the selected countries. Training programmes for the registration and polling station staff, as well as voter education campaigns, were designed by the EMBs at central and national level and run under their close supervision. The external voting took place over two successive days (1-2 December 2004), simultaneously with the voting in Mozambique.

For voters to cast their votes their names had to be included on the electoral register and the polling station staff had to verify their identity. When the polling station closed, the presiding officer proceeded immediately with the partial counting and the results were displayed at the polling station. The presiding officer immediately informed the diplomatic or consular representation of all elements of the partial count contained in the results tally sheet. The NEC supervisory teams present at each diplomatic or consular mission in turn informed the NEC headquarters in Mozambique. (In the case of in-country voting, the presiding officer of each polling station immediately informs the district or city electoral commission of all elements of the partial count contained in the results tally sheet, and the city or district electoral commission, in turn, must inform the provincial electoral commission, which must directly inform the NEC.) The NEC collated and published the results obtained by each candidate or political party in each electoral district, as well as the distribution of parliamentary seats won by each party. The official external voting results were also subject to validation by the Constitutional

Council before being publicly announced together with the in-country results.

Tables 2 and 3 show the results of external voting in the 2004 presidential and legislative elections, as validated and announced by the Constitutional Council on 21 January 2005.

Table 2: Numbers of external votes in the Mozambican presidential election, 2004

| Description | Africa | Rest of the world |
| --- | --- | --- |
| No. of polling stations | 62 | 3 |
| No. of registered electors | 45,865 | 1,101 |
| No. of votes cast | 27,237 | 732 |
| No. of valid votes | 26,748 | 699 |
| No. of void votes | 171 | 24 |
| No. of null votes | 318 | 9 |

Table 3: Numbers of external votes in the Mozambican legislative election, 2004

| Description | Africa | Rest of the world |
| --- | --- | --- |
| No. of polling stations | 62 | 3 |
| No. of registered electors | 45,865 | 1,101 |
| No. of votes cast | 26,128 | 732 |
| No. of valid votes | 25,638 | 704 |
| No. of void votes | 253 | 23 |
| No. of null votes | 237 | 5 |

The insignificant number of registered electors abroad may have been one of the arguments used by the stakeholders who opposed external voting in 2004, but their higher turnout (57 per cent in Africa and 64 per cent in the rest of the world, as compared to 36 per cent in-country) demonstrated migrants' willingness to participate in the political debate by electing their representatives, thus reinforcing the conviction of the stakeholders who had defended the idea that Mozambican citizens living outside their country should not be denied the right to vote in national elections.

# CHAPTER 3

# 3. The legal framework and an overview of electoral legislation

Dieter Nohlen and Florian Grotz*

## 1. External voting: a challenge for democracies in the 21st century?

Historically, external voting is quite a recent phenomenon. Even in some long-established democracies citizens who were resident in other countries were not granted the right to vote until the 1980s (in the Federal Republic of Germany (FRG) and the United Kingdom (UK)) or the 1990s (Japan). Currently, 115 countries have legal provisions allowing their citizens to vote while abroad (see chapter 1 and annex A) but, in spite of this relatively high number, there has been almost no international debate about external voting until recently.

External voting is nonetheless now on the political agenda in many countries. Its sudden relevance in different regions of the world clearly derives from the worldwide political changes of the 1990s. First, as a result of the rapid increase in the number of democracies after the break-up of the communist bloc, the design of democratic electoral rules has received more attention. Second, external voting becomes more significant in the face of increasing migration.

Against this background, a considerable problem emerges: how can people living outside their country of origin have their political rights assured? The answer to this question that is most often heard is that in our 'globalized' world the principle of universal suffrage can only be fully achieved if citizens living abroad are entitled to vote in the national elections of their home country. This argument is mainly based on different international declarations in which universal, equal, free and secret suffrage is recognized as an inalienable part of human rights (for example, the 1948 Universal Declaration of Human Rights, article 21; the 1948 American Declaration of Human Rights and Duties, article 20; and the 1969 American Convention on Human Rights,

---

*The authors would like to thank Matthias Catón, Emilia Conejo, Julia Leininger and Steffanie Richter for their valuable research assistance.

article 23). These documents do not mention external voting as an integral part of universal suffrage. The 1990 International Convention on the Protection of the Rights of All Migrant Workers, however, explicitly states that:

> Migrant workers and members of their families shall have the right to participate in public affairs of their State of origin and to vote and to be elected at elections of that State, in accordance with its legislation.
>
> The States concerned shall, as appropriate and in accordance with their legislation, facilitate the exercise of these rights (International Convention on the Protection of the Rights of All Migrant Workers and Members of Their Families, UN document A/RES/45/158, 18 December 1990, article 41).

The notion of external voting as part of universal suffrage is neither self-evident nor unproblematic. The concept goes against one of the classic requirements for voting rights—residency inside the state territory. Furthermore, the implementation of external voting involves major technical and administrative problems that might interfere with other crucial features of the franchise, in particular the principle of free elections.

Nevertheless, the idea of external voting is currently highly attractive. Even in new democracies with little experience of free elections and problems with electoral administration, external voting has either already been introduced or is on the way to being implemented. One notable case is that of Mexico, where free elections were established only recently.

Although this is such a topical issue, the related debates remain at an intuitive level. Political elites are not generally familiar with the normative arguments in favour of or against external voting. Nor do they consider the potential problems arising out of such an extension of voting rights. As a result, there is great demand for expertise on external voting and on the options for its institutionalization, but there is not yet agreement on the basic concepts. Terms such as 'political community' and 'citizenship' are used differently in different contexts; their interrelationship remains unspecified.

Little comparative research has been carried out on the subject of external voting. Some articles on the topic can be found in the legal literature for certain countries, but there are almost none in the social sciences field (see annex C). There is a general absence of systematic information on the relevant legal provisions of individual countries. Furthermore, a set of criteria is needed by which the functioning of some of the institutional arrangements associated with external voting can be evaluated. This is all the more important because a number of countries have already scheduled external voting for future elections but have still no regulations in place for implementing it.

The aim of this chapter is to introduce the issue of external voting in a systematic–comparative manner. This is done in three steps. Section 2 examines the exact meaning of external voting and provides a systematic overview of the legal framework of external voting. It discusses three different dimensions of the legal provisions for external voting and outlines the basic institutional alternatives with regard to these dimensions. (Chapters 4 and 5 provide more detail.) Section 3 presents three main structural problems which are typical for external voting and should therefore be considered in political debates about its introduction. These are: (a) the problem of the political representation of citizens living abroad; (b) the problems of organizing free and fair elections, the transparency of external voting procedures, and the freedom and fairness of party competition, and (c) the problem of judicial review of elections held abroad. Finally, section 4 provides a summary and concludes that: external voting can only reasonably be introduced if the specific context of each country is taken into account. Similarly, the legal and administrative provisions that are decided upon should depend on the most important contextual factors. This chapter presents some recommendations which deserve special attention when the introduction of or reforms to external voting are being considered.

## 2. The concept and provisions of external voting: basic features and institutional choices

### *2.1. The concept of external voting*

According to the definition used in this Handbook, external voting is understood as 'provisions and procedures which enable some or all electors of a country who are temporarily or permanently outside the country to exercise their voting rights from outside the territory of the country'.

External voting must be distinguished from two other types of voting which are easily confused with it. The first is the *franchise for foreigners* in a host country, which is applied for instance within the European Union at municipal level, allowing people who are not citizens of the host country to vote in certain elections in that country. This is in effect the opposite of external voting, and is not covered by this Handbook. The second is where some countries' electoral laws allow citizens who are resident abroad to vote at home after entering their homeland. This provision—long applied in Italy—is applied nowadays in some new democracies in Eastern Europe, such as Albania or Slovakia. However, the right of overseas citizens to vote back home is not the same thing as external voting. The main point is *where* the overseas elector is when his or her vote is cast. Since these elections are held exclusively *inside* the state territory, this cannot be regarded as an instance of external voting.

### *2.2. Legal sources for external voting*

There are three major types of source that contain the legal provisions for external voting:

- constitutions;
- electoral laws; and
- administrative regulations.

67

In reality, external voting is seldom provided for explicitly in constitutions. Notable exceptions include Portugal (article 172 of the constitution) and Spain (article 68/5 of the constitution). Most countries enable external voting through general provisions in their electoral laws. Additional regulations on its implementation are also often set out by legislatures or electoral commissions.

## 2.3. Entitlement to an external vote and requirements for registration as an external elector

The right to vote externally may be limited to certain types of election.

The institutional arrangements for external voting will depend first of all on who can be registered as an external elector. Various options are possible:

- all citizens living outside the state territory may be allowed to vote in national elections;
- certain legal limitations may determine which citizens can be registered as external electors;
- citizens living abroad may have the right to vote if a specified minimum number of them register with diplomatic missions in the foreign country; and
- the right to an external vote may be limited in time.

The entitlement to an external vote is discussed in chapter 4.

## 2.4. The procedures for external voting

There are three basic options for the procedure for external voting:

- postal voting;
- voting in diplomatic missions or military bases, or other designated places; and
- voting by proxy.

Chapter 5 looks at these in more detail. In future, electronic voting will increasingly be another option; this is discussed in chapter 10.

It may be disputed whether voting by proxy can strictly speaking be treated as a case of external voting, since the act of voting actually takes place *in* the state territory. Similarly, consulates or military bases are usually the sovereign territory of the state in question. However, voting by proxy and voting in diplomatic missions or military bases are included here as types of external voting because the electors concerned need not enter their home country in order to vote, but may do so from their place of residence.

These alternatives should be examined in the context of the fundamental principle of the free, equal, secret and secure ballot. Proxy voting may be rather problematic from the perspective of democratic theory because there is no guarantee that the vote cast by the proxy—and thus possibly even the result of the election—reflects the will of the original voter. A proxy could use this procedure to obtain an additional vote and thus infringe the principle of equal suffrage. Voting in diplomatic missions may deny some external electors the right to vote if they cannot travel to the polling stations. Voting by mail may not be as transparent as voting in a diplomatic mission in the presence of state officials—and voting in a diplomatic mission depends on the perceived impartiality and integrity of those state officials. There is thus no 'best procedure' for external voting. Much will depend on the context, such as the infrastructure of those foreign countries where external voting is to be held. The decision on suitability will depend on the costs and practical aspects of the different procedures for external voting, which are discussed in chapter 5.

### 2.5. The assignment of external votes to electoral districts

The last institutional aspect of external voting is the assignment of external electors to electoral districts. The institutional provisions for the assignment of external votes are politically important because they define how external votes are translated into parliamentary seats. In other words, these regulations will largely decide the extent to which external voters can influence domestic politics.

The main point of reference in the systematic classification of assignment provisions is the structure of electoral districts. Two basic options may be distinguished:

- There are extraterritorial electoral districts for external electors.
- External votes are assigned to existing electoral districts inside the country, for example, in the electoral district in which the external elector was last registered.

Each alternative has its own logic. Whereas the first stresses the special extraterritorial character of external votes, the second stresses the relation of overseas citizens to the state territory, and thus reflects the classic legal requirement of residency. The impact the external vote can have on domestic politics is different for each alternative. The political influence of external voters depends not only on the choice between the fundamental alternatives, but also on the 'institutional fine-tuning' within these models. Where there is an extraterritorial electoral district or districts, the political significance of external voters is basically determined by the representation attached to those districts in the institutional framework. This is especially true where electoral laws establish a fixed number of extraterritorial seats, often assigned to the world regions where citizens of the country live. The classic example is Portugal, where two parliamentary seats are reserved for citizens living abroad, one for European countries and one for the rest (see the case study). This institutional arrangement was adopted by several former Portuguese colonies in Africa (Angola, Cape Verde (see the case study) and Guinea-

Bissau). Croatia introduced a different extraterritorial model in 1999. The new electoral law also established separate electoral districts for Croats living abroad. The number of external seats, however, is not settled a priori but is calculated by dividing the total number of external votes by the number of votes cast nationwide to arrive at the Hare quota.[1] In other words, in Croatia the number of external seats depends on the relation between the actual number of external voters and the number of in-country valid votes. In comparison with the 'Portuguese model', this institutional framework is more sensitive to the actual levels of electoral participation and political competition.

In fact few countries have extraterritorial electoral districts for their overseas citizens. In most cases, external votes are assigned to domestic electoral districts and are included in the seat allocation of the respective electoral district. It is clearly more difficult to appraise the political significance of external voters in these cases than in arrangements with a fixed number of extraterritorial seats. Furthermore, institutional variations are also important in this model. There is a difference between those electoral systems with one nationwide electoral district and those with sub-national electoral districts. All else being equal, the political influence of external electors tends to be greater where sub-national districts are used, because external votes can be concentrated in some electoral districts and can even make up a plurality within those districts, although nationwide their share in the total number of voters may be insignificant. The actual effect will once more depend on the concrete institutional provisions. If overseas electors are assigned to electoral districts according to their former place of residence, as happens in the majority of cases (e.g. in Canada, Estonia and the UK), a regional concentration of external votes is unlikely. The political weight of external votes becomes more significant if they are assigned to the electoral district or districts of the capital, as in Indonesia (see the case study), Kazakhstan, Latvia and Poland. This solution is administratively simpler: the votes can be collected in the Ministry of Foreign Affairs and directly transferred into the domestic electoral district(s). Politically, however, this option may attract criticism because external votes could produce an election result in the capital electoral district which differs from the result that would have happened without the external votes, even in countries with a relatively small number of citizens living abroad. In such cases the legitimacy of external voting—and perhaps of democratic elections as such—may be questioned by domestic public opinion.

Against this background, the regulation of the 1999 Russian electoral law is a useful example. First, it assigns external electors to domestic single-member electoral districts according to their former place of residence; second, it provides for a maximum quota of citizens abroad (10 per cent of the registered electors residing in the respective electoral districts). Thus it reduces the risk of election results being externally determined. Belarus, on the other hand, offers an unusual and highly dubious arrangement. It assigns external votes to those electoral districts where the number of registered electors is lower than the average. In reality, this provision allows the ruling elite to allocate the external votes arbitrarily according to their own political advantage. Such a practice, in the absence of strict normative criteria, will clearly not enhance the transparency and legitimacy of the electoral process.

## 3. Three structural problems of external voting

Specific provisions for voter registration, voting procedures, and ways of assigning external votes to electoral districts can be combined in many ways. Two points have to be made in relation to this potentially vast array of institutional arrangements: first, some individual countries have developed highly specific provisions; and, second, political decision makers must choose the 'right design' of external voting from an almost endless variety of institutional possibilities. At this point one question becomes most significant. Which *criteria* should be considered before deciding in favour of or against external voting or a certain form of external voting?

To answer this question we now look at three challenges of external voting which are essential elements when shaping the legal framework, and the normative criteria which may relate to them. The challenges are:

- political representation of citizens who are not resident or not present in their country of citizenship;
- organization of elections outside the national borders, which introduces organizational problems, questions of the transparency of voting procedures, the issue of equality of party competition and transparency in electoral fraud; and
- the resolution of disputes if the results of elections held on foreign ground, outside the judicial territory, are contested.

### 3.1. External voting: the problem of representation

The arguments in favour of external voting are related to the democratic principle of universal suffrage. The basic idea is that every citizen has the right to participate in every direct election to representative state organs because the formal–judicial equality of all citizens is guaranteed by the law or the constitution.

One normative criterion underlies this argument—political rights are human rights, the right to vote being one of them. This perspective regards universal suffrage exclusively as an individual right. There are also, however, two functional dimensions: (a) the contribution the popular vote makes to the creation of state institutions; and (b) the importance of electoral participation to the legitimacy of the elected institutions.

It follows that it is desirable to guarantee the right to vote even where special circumstances, such as illness, disability, and so on, make it difficult for the citizen to vote. Temporary and perhaps involuntary residence abroad is considered another special circumstance.

Residency in the country or even in the electoral district has been one of the classic conditions of universal suffrage written into national constitutions and electoral laws, as well as into some international declarations of human rights. According to the 1969 American Convention on Human Rights (article 23, 2), for example, residency is one of the conditions which may limit the exercise of political rights. Yet in the current debate about external voting the requirement of residency has seemingly become irrelevant. (On the concepts of residency and citizenship as requirements for the entitlement to vote, see also chapter 4.)

A difficult problem arises in cases of long-standing residency abroad. Should these citizens living outside a country keep their right to influence the composition of the representative organs whose decisions are only binding on citizens residing *inside* the state territory? From the point of view of the theory of political representation, it may be argued that only those individuals who bear the consequences of their electoral decisions should be entitled to vote.

This problem of representation is particularly important in countries which have a considerable number of citizens living abroad (e.g. El Salvador, Mexico or Russia). In these contexts external votes are likely to become significant or even crucial for the overall election result (on the case of Mexico, see also chapter 8 and the case study). Since the political consequences of national elections concern mainly the citizens living in the country, the participation of external voters might be considered illegitimate by the domestic public. A classic example of such a case is provided by the Cook Islands, where more citizens live outside than inside the country. Before 1981 all Cook Islanders, regardless of residency, had the right to participate in national elections *inside* the state territory. Under this legal framework, citizens living abroad actually determined the overall result of the 1978 election to the legislature, as Albert Henry's Cook Island Party had flown in a decisive number of voters from New Zealand. Following an appeal to the courts on the ground that this was unconstitutional, these votes were disqualified by the court. Furthermore, the parliament changed the electoral law so that from then on only one single-member electoral district was reserved for citizens abroad. The influence of overseas citizens has been limited ever since, and the single overseas electoral district was abolished in 2004 (see the case study).

Similar problems of representation can arise in states that are territorially larger, especially if the pattern of political support among external voters differs significantly from that among domestic voters. In these cases overseas citizens would become a powerful factor in domestic politics if they were granted the right to vote. Political forces which would benefit would then be likely to deem external voting to be legitimate, while those who would suffer would be likely to take the opposite view. Under these circumstances, the legitimacy of the political system may be brought into question by the introduction of external voting. This was the case in Croatia during the Yugoslavian wars of the 1990s. In this period, the government of President Franjo Tudjman took advantage of the nationalistic leanings of the Croats residing abroad. The government parties passed an electoral law providing for 12 'external seats' out of 127 in the parliament. As expected, in the 1995 election all those 12 seats went to Tudjman's Hrvatska Demokratska Zajednica (Croat Democratic Union, HDZ). The institutional structure of external voting helped the incumbent government to win a majority, and there were vehement complaints from both lawyers and public opinion. In the new electoral law of 1999, worked out jointly by the government and the opposition, the fixed number of extraterritorial seats disappeared. Instead, a new allocation procedure made the number of external seats dependent on the ratio of the number of external valid votes to the total number of domestic valid votes. This institutional reform of external seats has contributed to increase the legitimacy of elections in Croatia.

In markedly turbulent contexts, a thorough and profound analysis of the political effects of external voting is especially necessary. The question has to be answered whether the introduction of external voting will increase the legitimacy of a democratic system or undermine it by being perceived as an instrument of specific political interests. In any event, the institutional form of external voting—if it is appropriate at all—needs to be developed with the involvement of major stakeholders in the electoral process, and thus to reflect the specific context. There is no 'one size fits all' approach.

### *3.2. External voting: the challenge of electoral organization*

Apart from the formal and legal difficulties described above, the acceptance of external voting poses a serious problem of electoral organization. Elections held beyond a country's borders usually imply organizational problems, greater personal and financial cost, and greater logistical effort per voter than in-country elections (see in particular chapter 5). In the light of these practical difficulties, a crucial problem is how to guarantee the maintenance of the principles of universal, equal and secret suffrage, maintain the equality of electoral competition, and prevent offences against the electoral law.

Countries which have external voting must come to terms with the fact that the freedom and security of the votes of their citizens cast abroad may not be guaranteed to the same extent as those cast inside the country. Electoral management bodies cannot fulfil their functions autonomously in foreign host countries. They have to collaborate with the institutions of the host country (see chapter 6) and possibly also with branches of the executive of the home country (typically the foreign ministry and ministry of the interior). How is registration abroad to be organized? How are double registration and double voting based on different documents to be prevented? What about the political rights of persons living illegally in the host country?

Ensuring that electoral procedures are free of influence by party interests may be a problem for countries which face challenges in organizing legitimate elections at home, especially if they have a great number of citizens not only living abroad but also concentrated in one single country. The electoral campaign may take place among external electors with no effective control by the administrative bodies of the home country. The possibility of interference by political actors which are not subject to the legislation of the home country aggravates the danger of the equality of electoral party competition being violated.

The introduction of external voting where a high percentage of the population resides abroad poses particular challenges in new democracies. In Mexico, a country in which electoral fraud had been the order of the day over decades, the electoral management body—the Federal Electoral Institute (Instituto Federal Electoral, IFE)—has made huge and effective efforts since the early 1990s to achieve a high degree of transparency in the organization of elections. Deficiencies in the organization of external voting could pose dangers to the reputation that the IFE has built up as an effective and independent body.

### 3.3. External voting and electoral dispute resolution

The practicalities of electoral dispute resolution may involve organizational problems similar to those that can be seen in the practical aspects of organizing external voting. When irregularities are alleged, documents may not be readily available. There may be physical problems in holding hearings and summoning witnesses. As a result, the quality of judicial decisions may be more contentious and their implementation more difficult.

### 3.4. A preliminary summary of the structural problems

The degree of fairness, transparency and electoral justice of external voting bears on the whole electoral process, especially if the results abroad deviate greatly from the in-country results. In debating proposals to introduce or maintain external voting, issues of electoral justice—the transparency of electoral registration, the equality of electoral competition, the legal conduct of the act of voting, and the control mechanisms to ensure all of these—are essential in informing the process of decision. When citizens living abroad are claiming the right to vote, denying it may result in some loss of legitimacy. But it is equally important to bear in mind that an external voting process which is perceived as biased in favour of particular political interests or as chaotic may cause electoral events to lose legitimacy in the eyes of the domestic public.

## 4. Conclusions

Institutional reforms never involve one single objective, but rather several objectives simultaneously. For external voting, these objectives are:

- the realization of the principle of universal suffrage, associated with the other principles of democratic voting rights;
- the maintenance of the rule of law;
- a real increase in political participation (which justifies the political effort involved in and the financial costs of external voting);
- the enhancement of the legitimacy of the democratic system; and
- an effective contribution to democratic consolidation.

At this stage other questions also arise: should external voting be extended to both representative organs and referendums or should it be restricted to one single type of electoral event, such as a direct election to the presidency? In the case of external voting for legislatures, is it convenient to establish a fixed threshold of representation for citizens living abroad or should such a threshold be arranged according to the actual electoral participation by external voters (perhaps by specifying minimum and maximum numbers of 'external seats')?

Table 3.1: Overview of the arguments for and against the introduction of external voting

|  | For | Against |
|---|---|---|
| **Theoretical arguments** | Full implementation of the *universal suffrage* as a part of human rights | *Residency* as a central criterion of suffrage and of political representation |
|  | Increased *political participation* | Problematic *transparency* of external election process |
|  |  | Problematic *dispute resolution* of external voting |
| **Historical and empirical circumstances** | Small number of permanent external electors in relation to domestic electors | Large number of permanent external electors in relation to domestic electors |
|  | Equal distribution of political preferences of external electors | Uniform ideological orientation of external electors |
|  | Democracies with long experience of elections and a well-established electoral organization | New democracies with problems of electoral administration and/or a history of electoral fraud |

Three major conclusions may be drawn when considering reforms relating to external voting.

1. *The introduction of external voting is likely to give rise to political controversy.* There are solid theoretical arguments both in favour of and against external voting. On the one hand, the recognition of the principle of universal suffrage is regarded as a civil right, which can be realized by the widening of political participation. On the other hand, external voting implies the electoral participation of individuals who may not be directly affected by whatever effects the result brings about.

The historical trend clearly points towards the understanding of the right to vote as an individual right of every citizen, regardless of his or her place of residence. But a move to adopt or extend external voting by a particular country needs to ensure that all stakeholders are involved in the decision-making process, and that consequent trade-offs or drawbacks—for example, restrictions on electoral freedom such as inequalities in the political rights enjoyed by different people—are considered and are thus less likely to give rise to subsequent questioning of the constitutionality or legitimacy of the electoral process.

It is also good practice for the decision-making process to take into account not merely the substance of reform proposals, but also the perception of the proposals by the electorate and by the media. As with other areas of reform of electoral process, law and regulation, the success of change may depend not only on the substance of what is agreed but on the extent and effectiveness of civic and voter education activities to explain changes to the electorate both inside and outside the country.

As with any electoral reform proposal, external voting will be particularly controversial if the votes cast externally affect the result decisively and determine the winner. Such election results will be highly controversial among the relevant political actors.

2. The debate on external voting should not be allowed to overshadow consideration of *the political inclusion of foreign citizens in their country of residence*. A move has been made towards this principle through the introduction in many European Union member states of voting rights for citizens of other member states. A more widespread introduction of the right to vote in the country of residence would enable individuals with foreign nationality to take part in decisions that affect their personal interest and thus create a context of responsibility—although such a move could also generate political controversy, especially if foreign citizens were thought likely to give support disproportionately to one political group and if their votes were decisive in determining the result.

3. *There is no ideal institutional design for external voting*. Once a decision is made in favour of introducing external voting, the resulting legal provisions must be designed to suit the particular context of the country. Above all, attention must be paid to minimizing the possible trade-offs and unintended negative side effects.

### Notes

1 The Hare Quota, used in proportional representation (PR) systems, is the total valid vote divided by the number of seats to be filled in the electoral district.

CASE STUDY: Colombia

# Colombia: representation of emigrants in the Congress

Nydia Restrepo de Acosta

The first Colombian electoral legislation (Law no. 39) was issued in 1961. It established that Colombians with permanent residence abroad could vote in presidential elections. Agreement on this provision was promoted by the exodus caused by political instability and the dictatorial regime (1953–7). The provision was first applied in the 1962 election, when there were 3,227 registered electors outside Colombia. In 1986, when the existing Electoral Code was decreed, article 116 confirmed the possibility of voting abroad in presidential elections.

Although this was not expressly contemplated in the electoral legislation, in November 1990 Colombian residents abroad were called on to participate in the election of members of a Constituent National Assembly, which prepared a new text of the constitution. Article 171 of the new constitution (1991) established that not only Colombian permanent residents abroad, but also those who were temporarily out of the country could vote. It also allowed residents abroad to vote in elections to the Senate, which took place for the first time in 1994.

Article 176 of the constitution also created a special electoral district in the Chamber of Representatives in order to ensure the participation of ethnic groups, political minorities and Colombians resident abroad. However, this did not come into effect until 2001, when Law no. 649 established that the special electoral district would have a total of five seats, one of which would be for a representative of Colombians residing abroad, two for black communities, one for indigenous communities and one for political minorities. This provision was first applied in 2002. It is important to note that this election was controversial as a result of a ruling by the Constitutional Court which gave electors in-country the option of voting in the election for the external voters' seat. The result of this ruling was that only 3,000 of the 9,000 votes in favour of the winning candidate were actually cast by Colombians living abroad. Subsequently, in December 2005, the international electoral district was specifically regulated by a decree which established that only votes cast by Colombian citizens abroad would be counted to determine who would be the special representative of Colombians abroad in the lower chamber. It was applied in March 2006, in the most recent legislative election.

Although the electoral legislation does not refer specifically to the participation of Colombians abroad in the mechanisms of direct democracy, this has happened twice: (a) in the election of members for the Constituent National Assembly of 1991; and (b) in the referendum on corruption and bad political practices, promoted by the president and held in 2003, in which a wide-ranging constitutional reform was submitted to the people of Colombia, and 41,398 citizens abroad voted.

On 28 August 2006 the National Electoral Council handed the Senate a draft a proposal for reform of the Electoral Code. It suggests adding one paragraph that lists all types of election for which external voting is allowed. Although external voting arrangements for presidential elections are contained in the Electoral Code. The paragraph in the constitution, dispositions for legislative elections are only contained in the constitution; and it would also include all direct democracy practices at national level.

## Electoral registration and the conduct of elections

Regarding the procedure and requirements for the registration of electors abroad, the national government issues a decree before every election enabling the premises of Colombian embassies and consulates to be used as polling stations for external voters. Later, the National Registry of the Civil State (NRCS, Registraduria Nacional del Estado Civil), which is the authority that organizes and runs elections both in-country and out-of-country, sends a resolution by which it fixes the period when identity documents can be issued abroad, at least 15 days ahead of election day. (There are two electoral management bodies, the National Electoral Council (NEC), which is responsible for guaranteeing the impartiality and transparency of the electoral processes and general scrutiny, and for resolving challenges presented by the candidates, their proxies or electoral witnesses, according to the relevant articles of the Electoral Code; and the NRCS, whose president is designated by the NEC, and which is in charge of the electoral registers and the organization of elections.) The NRCS also determines at what places this is to be done and appoints polling station staff. It is possible to register as an elector simply by presenting a certificate of citizenship or a valid passport, but to actually vote it is compulsory to have the latter, which is issued by the NRCS.

The Directorate of the Electoral Census of the NRCS compares the certificates of the citizens who are registered as electors abroad with those who are registered in-country. If an elector is found to be registered twice, the first registration is annulled. On election day, the electoral register is posted in a public place next to the election precinct, a copy is given to the polling site managing committee, and a third copy is given to the embassy or consulate.

The senior diplomat at the embassy or consulate designates as polling station staff four Colombian citizens who are resident locally—two incumbents and two substitutes—who must belong to different political parties which have representation in the Congress, in such a way that no one political grouping is dominant. The list of polling station staff is established 15 days before election day and is posted in a visible place at the embassy or consulate ten days before the election.

Candidates for the external voters' seat in the special electoral district must present a registration form at the appropriate Colombian embassy or consulate at their place of residence and have to comply with the following requirements: they must be over 25 years of age on the date of the election; they must demonstrate to the electoral authorities that they have resided abroad for a minimum of five continuous years; and they must be endorsed by a political party or a political movement which is properly recognized by the NEC, or a social movement or a significant group of citizens.

The representative in the Chamber of Representatives who is chosen for this special electoral district is subject to the general rules on congressmen's incapacities and conflicts of interest, and must reside on the national territory while he or she holds the position.

The voting abroad, like the voting in-country, is by means of universal, direct, equal and secret suffrage. Article 258 of the constitution obliges the electoral authorities to offer the tools that guarantee electors the exercise of their right to vote by means of a printed paper ballot or electronic device. (In 2004 a bill was approved assigning to the electoral authorities the responsibility of implementing electronic registration and voting, both in Colombia and abroad, within five years, that is, not later than 2009. This provision is being considered as part of a bill to reform the Electoral Code which is currently before the Congress at the initiative of the NEC.)

Currently, to organize elections abroad, the National Registry of the Civil State provides the necessary elements in the 'election package', which consists of ballot papers and electoral certificates (voting proof or written evidence showing that the voter has actually voted), the electoral register, special envelopes, the forms for registering the results and the ballot boxes. This package is sent ten days ahead of election day, thus guaranteeing that it will be received at its destination two days before election day.

The scrutiny of the votes cast abroad is the responsibility of the National Electoral Council, which is the authority in charge of the scrutiny of all national voting, declaring the results of the election and issuing the relevant credentials (certificates given to the candidates chosen).

In matters of access to the mass media, election propaganda and the financing of political parties abroad, there are no specific stipulations: the electoral campaigns and election propaganda are governed by the provisions of the constitution in the terms of the political reform of 2003, and by the Basic Statute on the Parties and Political Movements (Law no. 130 of 1994). The norms established by this law and the constitution are interpreted and applied to the activities of candidates abroad. The campaign can only start six months before election day, and there is a time limit on election propaganda of three months before election day.

The electoral campaigns of the political parties and movements, as well as the significant groups of citizens that candidates represent, are financed out of state resources in proportion to the number of valid votes obtained by each list, according to a formula previously determined by the National Electoral Council. The NEC also establishes the limits on campaign expenditure, and verifies that the resources the parties and political movements receive are legal, and that they observe the established ceiling on campaign expenditure; to ensure this, the political parties and movements must publish this information within one month of election day. There are quite severe sanctions for violations of the ceiling on campaign expenditure, including the loss of rights to reimbursement of expenses, and loss of the seat won by the candidate. In the latter case, when the parties register lists for multi-member electoral districts, if a single member of a list exceeds the ceiling on expenditure, the party loses all the seats it has obtained in that electoral district.

The implementation of voting abroad does present difficulties of a technical, administrative and operational nature. Because of distance, lack of technology and the short time that passes between the closing of the electoral registers and the actual election, the main difficulty lies in carrying out the electoral census abroad in order to confirm the list of people who are entitled to vote; however, in the elections of 2002 it was possible, for the first time, to set up a daily exchange of information with the diplomatic missions by email. This helped to integrate the Electoral Roll of Resident Colombian Citizens Abroad rapidly and smoothly, as well as assisting comparison with the National File of Identification, and the subsequent deletion of duplicate names to avoid the issuing of duplicate ballot papers.

On polling day itself, technical problems related to data transmission do appear, preventing electoral material from being sent and distributed in one delivery. Thanks to technological advances, however, these problems are on the verge of being overcome.

## Cost

In the Senate elections of 2002, 365 polling stations abroad were set up. The production of election packages cost 22,600 US dollars (USD); their shipment and set up costs in the 66 countries where voting took place came to 161,930 USD, making an approximate total of 184,530 USD, or approximately 2 USD per registered elector. This funding originates from the election budget of the National Registry of the Civil State.

## Turnout

In 1998, in elections to the Senate, external voters cast 17,049 votes. In 2002, that number increased to 40,688. In the March 2006 legislative elections, participation by external voters was expected to increase considerably, since as of 2005 the electoral census included many more external electors, but participation remained almost the same as in 2002, with turnout at roughly 15 per cent of external electors (see the tables).

Turnout is usually higher in presidential elections than in legislative elections. In the presidential elections of May 2002, participation by external voters represented over 64 per cent of the 165,631 registered external electors. In the May 2006 presidential election, 38 per cent of registered external electors voted. Usually a higher number of potential external voters register for presidential elections than for other elections. The main reasons for this are that external electors, as opposed to in-country electors, have to register for each and every election, and interest in presidential elections is normally higher than interest in legislative elections.

## Table 1: Participation of Colombians abroad in the 2002 elections

| Election | No. of registered external electors | No. of polling stations installed | Total no. of votes | No. of valid votes | Turnout (%) |
|---|---|---|---|---|---|
| Presidential (1 round, May) | 165,631 | 534 | 106,931 | 106,375 | *64.56* |
| Senate (10 March) | 94,296 | 365 | 40,688 | 38,918 | *43.149* |
| Special representative in the Chamber of Representatives (10 March) | 94,296 | 365 | 39,983 | 37,672 | *42.402* |

Source: Calculated from data of the National Registry of the Civil State (Registraduria Nacional del Estado Civil de Colombia), <http://www.registraduria.gov.co/elecciones2002/e/vsenadoi.htm?1>.

## Table 2: Participation of Colombians abroad in the 2006 elections

| Election | No. of registered external electors | Total no. of votes | No. of valid votes | Turnout (%) |
|---|---|---|---|---|
| Presidential (28 May) | 319,045 | 121,155 | 120,540 | *37.97* |
| Senate (March) | 273,385 | 42,588 | 38,767 | *15.57* |
| Special representative in the Chamber of Representatives (March) | 273,385 | 41,165 | 37,176 | *15.05* |

Source: Calculated from data of the National Registry of the Civil State (Registraduria Nacional del Estado Civil de Colombia), <http://www.registraduria.gov.co/elecciones2002/e/vsenadoi.htm?1>.

CASE STUDY: Portugal

# Portugal: extended voting rights and decreasing participation

Marina Costa Lobo

Portugal has held free elections since the fall of the dictatorship in 1974, and since that time the voting rights of Portuguese citizens living abroad have been substantially expanded. External voting rights were granted from the outset, but only for elections to the national parliament. Following Portugal's entry into the European Community in 1986, external voting rights were granted for Portuguese citizens abroad to vote for the national lists for the European Parliament elections.

More recently, 1997 marked a major change in the process of external voting in Portugal. The constitution was revised for the fourth time, and one of the specific topics for reform was the rules governing elections. Only minor changes were introduced, but in this constitutional package, agreed by the two major parties, the centre–left Socialist Party (Partido Socialista, PS) and the centre–right Social Democratic Party (Partido Social Democrata, PSD), Portuguese citizens resident abroad became eligible to vote in both presidential elections and national referendums as well as legislative elections. This had been promoted in particular by the PSD in the constitutional negotiations. (The experience of legislative elections since 1976 had shown that the PSD has consistently had a majority of votes among external voters, which helps to explain why that party lobbied for an extension of emigrants' voting rights.)

These changes equalized the electoral rights of Portuguese citizens inside and outside Portugal for all national-level elections, although external voting was not extended to local elections. Portuguese citizens with external voting rights were first able to exercise their right to vote for the president of the republic in 2001. Ironically, the extension of voting rights has coincided with a marked decrease in external voting participation as measured by turnout in legislative elections.

In legislative elections, the electoral system that has been adopted is the proportional representation (PR) d'Hondt system, with closed lists presented in multi-member districts. Portuguese citizens living abroad are grouped into two electoral districts, each electing two members of parliament (MPs). One electoral district covers all European countries, the other the rest of the world ('outside Europe'). The principle of proportionality is therefore not fully observed in the external voting for legislative elections. This is because in 1976 there were fears that the large Portuguese emigrant community would elect a high proportion of MPs, which was considered unfair given that they do not live in Portugal.

## Eligibility for an external vote

External voting can only be exercised if citizens register, although (unlike for citizens residing in Portuguese territory) registration is not mandatory (article 3, no. 3, Law no. 13/99, 22 March 1999). Registration can be done at any time up to 60 days before an election. Those whose 18th birthday falls between registration and election day can, however, register up to 55 days before the election.

For external voting, registration occurs mostly at consulates. If there is no consulate in a particular country, then registration normally occurs at the embassy or another designated registration centre. There are around 200 registration centres abroad, some of which cover more than one country. There are also a few countries where there is more than one registration centre because of the large number of Portuguese citizens in those countries.

Eligibility criteria vary according to the type of election. For legislative elections, the criteria are the same as those for internal electors (voters have to be 18 years or older). For European Parliament elections, until recently only Portuguese citizens resident abroad who were living in another European Union (EU) country could vote, thus excluding all those Portuguese citizens who lived outside the EU. However, this has recently been changed: Organic Law no. 1/2005 of January 2005 allows all electors resident abroad to vote in elections to the European Parliament. The eligibility criteria for external voting in presidential elections have changed since voting rights were extended. All those who were registered to vote in legislative elections by 31 December 1996 can also vote in presidential elections. The criteria for voting eligibility of all other Portuguese nationals residing abroad were to be defined by ordinary law, which should 'take into account the existence of effective ties to the national community' (Constitution of the Republic, article 121, no. 2). However, because these criteria had not been defined when the next presidential election occurred, in 2001, all those registered to vote for legislative elections both before and after 1996 were eligible to vote in those elections. Recently, the criteria for establishing 'effective ties' have been adopted: citizens must (a) have lived in an EU country or in a Portuguese-speaking country for not more than 15 years; (b) have lived in any other country for not more than ten years; or (c) have been to Portugal and stayed there at least 30 days in the previous five years, and be able to prove that they can speak Portuguese (Law no. 5/2005 of 8 September 2005).

Finally, Law no. 5/2005 also states that the eligibility criteria for Portuguese citizens residing abroad for voting in referendums are identical to the criteria applied for such citizens in presidential elections. However, this should be interpreted with caution: Portuguese citizens resident abroad have never actually been called to vote on any referendum, and it is not quite clear whether these rules would indeed apply in any future national referendum (see also below).

## External voting procedure

Here as well there are differences between types of election. Decree-Law no. 95-C/76 of 30 January 1976 sets out the procedural aspects of external voting in legislative elections. In these elections, as well as in European Parliament elections, the external voting right is exercised by post. However, Organic Law no. 1/2005 changed voting procedures for European Parliament elections: voting is now done in person at the designated polling sites.

For elections to the national parliament and the European Parliament (from 1987 to 2004), the Ministry of Internal Administration in Portugal sends a ballot paper with two envelopes to all citizens registered in electoral registers abroad around two to three weeks before polling day. The voter fills in his or her ballot paper, folds it and inserts it in one of the envelopes which he or she then seals and places in the other envelope together with a photocopy of his or her elector's card. All must be sent back to the designated reception point in Portugal and can be posted up until (and including) the day of the election. Ten days following the election, the external ballot papers are opened and counted. In legislative elections, the four parliamentary seats reserved for external voters are then allocated. In European Parliament elections, the external votes are added to the internal national totals (Decree-Law no. 95C/76).

In presidential elections and referendums, Portuguese residents abroad have to vote in person. In these cases, external voting takes place over a period of three days up to and including election day. Registered electors can go to the voting centre closest to their place of residence to cast their vote, which is then opened and counted.

## Registration and turnout patterns in different types of election

Table 1 shows the number of registered external electors and the turnout in each legislative election since 1976. The number of electors grew until 1999, since when it has fallen a little. This may be due to an effort to 'clean' the electoral registers of those who had died or moved—a process that also occurred for the national register in the late 1990s. The drop in turnout is remarkable—from 86.7 per cent in 1976 to 25.2 per cent in 2005. While electoral participation in Portugal has declined substantially, participation by external electors has dropped even more. (It should be noted that there are different patterns of turnout in Europe and outside Europe, with turnout being higher in Europe.)

Table 1: External voting in Portuguese legislative elections

| Election year | No. of registered electors | No. of votes cast | Turnout (%) |
|---|---|---|---|
| 1976 | 105,709 | 91,740 | 86.7 |
| 1979 | 132,273 | 88,379 | 66.8 |
| 1980 | 175,577 | 108,096 | 61.6 |
| 1983 | 159,188 | 83,984 | 45.3 |
| 1985 | 190,818 | 57,531 | 30.1 |

| Election year | No. of registered electors | No. of votes cast | Turnout (%) |
|---|---|---|---|
| 1987 | 187,581 | 49,849 | 26.5 |
| 1991 | 187,598 | 61,128 | 32.6 |
| 1995 | 183,351 | 43,040 | 23.5 |
| 1999 | 192,329 | 45,852 | 23.8 |
| 2002 | 162,412 | 39,711 | 24.4 |
| 2005 | 146,354 | 36,938 | 25.2 |

Source: National Electoral Commission (Comissão Nacional de Eleições, CNE), <http://www.cne.pt>.

In European Parliament elections, the electoral system is identical to that for legislative elections, with the important exception that there is only one electoral district. The external vote is simply added to the national vote. Table 2 shows external voting in these elections. Turnout has been very low from the outset.

Table 2: External voting in European Parliament elections in Portugal

| Election year | No. of registered electors | No. of votes cast | Turnout (%) |
|---|---|---|---|
| 1987 | 71,880 | 14,572 | 20.3 |
| 1989 | 54,526 | 19,360 | 35.5 |
| 1994 | 84,643 | 20,722 | 24.5 |
| 1999 | 84,073 | 16,079 | 19.1 |
| 2004 | 70,504 | 13,269 | 18.8 |

Source: National Electoral Commission (Comissão Nacional de Eleições, CNE), <http://www.cne.pt>.

The same procedure is also used for presidential elections, which are held using the Two-Round System. Again, there is one electoral district that comprises all electors, both internal and external. External votes are added to internal votes. In the first presidential election where external voting was allowed, participation was extremely low, even by Portugal's external voting standards. In the most recent presidential election, in January 2005, the size of the electoral register and turnout increased slightly but the participation of Portuguese citizens living abroad was still low.

Table 3: External voting in presidential elections in Portugal

| Election year | No. of registered electors | No. of votes cast | Turnout (%) |
|---|---|---|---|
| 2001 | 185,223 | 15,431 | 8.33 |
| 2005 | 187,109 | 18,840 | 10.07 |

Source: Technical Secretariat for Electoral Processes Matters (Secretariado Técnico dos Assuntos para o Processo Eleitoral, STAPE), <http://www.stape.pt>.

## Referendums

There were no provisions for referendums in the 1976 constitution. Only with the third revision of the constitution in 1989 was a national referendum allowed under specific circumstances, but the possibility of external voting was not foreseen. The constitutional revision of 1997 introduced a number of modifications to the referendum law. It allows Portuguese nationals resident abroad to vote in referendums, provided they are correctly registered, whenever the referendum deals with issues that concern them specifically. This last provision is ambiguous and lends itself to significant political argument about whether in any given referendum Portuguese citizens resident abroad may or may not vote. In practice, there have been two referendums in Portugal: one in 1998 on abortion and another in 1999 on the issue of regionalization. In both instances, following Constitutional Court rulings (Ruling 288/98 and Ruling 532/98), external voting was not allowed.

# CHAPTER 4

# 4. Entitlement to vote

Phil Green

## 1. Introduction

Many countries allow their citizens the right to vote in elections when they are not present in their home country. This chapter examines the ways in which countries may determine who is entitled to vote while outside the country.

Entitlement to cast an external vote is usually linked to the general entitlement to vote that applies to all eligible electors in a country. However, there are sometimes extra requirements imposed on external electors, such as a minimum period of previous residence or an intention to return to the country. In some cases only limited groups of external electors may be eligible to vote, such as diplomats, other public officials and members of the armed forces, and their families. Some countries extend the right to vote to all their citizens living abroad, regardless of the length of time they have spent out of their home country, while others impose time restrictions or require evidence of an intention to return.

Eligibility to vote is usually linked to citizenship. The definitions of citizenship that are applied can also affect which classes of people are eligible to cast external votes. This chapter discusses citizenship in this context.

Some countries, such as New Zealand and Sweden, also extend the right to an external vote to residents who are not citizens: this is sometimes referred to as the 'franchise for foreigners'. In this case different rules from those that apply to citizens are usually needed to determine whether these non-citizen residents are eligible to cast external votes.

In some countries the numbers of people eligible for an external vote are relatively small. Other countries do not allow anyone to vote if they are outside their home country. In some cases, for example, following major civil or political unrest or where national borders have changed, or where there are large numbers of migrant workers abroad, large numbers of people may be resident outside the country and have a legitimate claim to vote. In these cases the question of who is eligible to cast an external vote may be a major issue, and determining eligibility may be crucial to the election outcome.

Once a person's eligibility to cast an external vote is established, there is usually a second requirement to be met—the need to be registered on the electoral register in order to show that that person is entitled to vote. Special registration requirements may be necessary for external electors, or external electors may be required to register in the same way as all others. Registration requirements thus introduce a second stage into the entitlement process and may serve to limit the numbers of persons who are eligible to cast an external vote.

Another aspect of entitlement, where countries are divided into electoral districts, is the electoral district in which an elector is entitled to vote. This could be determined by reference to the address at which the elector most recently resided before leaving the country, or by reference to the person's place of birth, or, where a person has never resided in the country, by reference to the address of a parent or grandparent. Another option is to provide for special districts composed entirely of external electors, particularly where large numbers of electors are concerned. In some cases, countries will also limit the types of ballot in which external electors may participate. For example, external electors may be permitted to vote in national elections for head of state or national parliament but not in local government elections. (In Switzerland, different rules apply in different cantons: see the case study.)

The chapter concludes by considering whether it is possible to identify 'best practice' principles to guide those considering adopting or amending external voting eligibility criteria.

## 2. Types of election

Entitlement to vote is sometimes limited to particular types of election. For example, external electors may be permitted to vote in national elections for head of state or national parliament but not in local government elections. In some presidential systems in Africa and Asia, citizens living abroad have the right to vote for a president but not in elections to the legislature. Because of their distance from their mother country, citizens living abroad are allowed to influence domestic politics only to a limited extent and consequently are granted only selective rights in national elections and referendums.

## 3. Conditions for entitlement to vote

To be entitled to cast an external vote, a person must first satisfy the general qualifications for electoral registration and voting that apply in their home country.

The entitlement to vote is generally linked to citizenship, age and residency. For example, a country may only permit a person to vote if he or she is a citizen of that country, is

18 years of age or older and has been resident in that country for at least 12 months. Determining whether a person meets these qualifications is generally straightforward while resident in the home country. However, where a person is not resident in the home country—either temporarily or permanently—determining their entitlement to an external vote generally requires the application of more complex tests of eligibility.

Determining the citizenship of a person who is absent from the home country, particularly where the person has adopted the citizenship of another country, involves interpretation of the applicable laws of citizenship. This issue is discussed below in section 3.1.

Determining a person's age may raise difficulties if the registration process requires the person to provide proof of age. In some cases, particularly that of refugees, a person may not possess documentary proof of age. Even where a person does possess proof of age, if they are applying to register to vote while outside the home country, providing that proof of age to the registration authority may be difficult. This is an issue that will need to be addressed when determining exactly how a person may register for external voting (this is discussed further below in section 5).

Applying a residency test to a person who is not resident in their home country is perhaps the most difficult aspect of determining entitlement to vote externally. Some countries deal with this issue by providing that all their citizens are entitled to vote for its elections, regardless of whether they have ever having resided in the home country. Others apply rules related to the length of time spent by the citizen in the home country and/or time spent away from the home country. This issue is discussed in section 3.2.

Some countries also impose further limitations on entitlement that restrict the classes of people who can vote while absent from the home country. For example, some countries limit the right to vote externally to citizens employed in particular occupations, such as diplomats and members of the armed forces (see table 1.4). Others restrict voting to those who are resident in particular locations, such as places where there is a specified minimum number of electors or the locations of diplomatic missions of the home country. Section 3.2 looks at this in more detail.

### 3.1. Citizenship

Citizenship can be defined as the status of a citizen. A citizen can be defined as a member of a state or a nation. Citizenship carries with it a range of rights and duties. One of the key rights of a citizen who is of voting age is the right to vote.

Citizenship can be conferred on a person in a number of ways. A person can become a citizen by descent, by place of birth, or by naturalization.

Citizenship by descent (*jus sanguinis*, or 'law of the blood') is one of the two internationally recognized legal principles used to determine an individual's country of citizenship at birth. Generally, where this principle is applied, if one or both parents are citizens of a country their offspring are automatically given this citizenship at birth. Under this principle, it is possible of a person to attain citizenship for a country they have never been in, or to attain citizenship for more than one country if the parents have two different nationalities.

Citizenship by place of birth (*jus soli*, or 'law of the soil') is the other internationally recognized legal principle used to determine an individual's country of citizenship at birth. Where this principle applies, a person has citizenship of the country in which he or she was born. In some cases, both *jus sanguinis* and *jus soli* may apply, and this is another way in which a person may attain citizenship of more than one country.

Finally, a person may acquire a different citizenship by naturalization. While there are several ways in which this can be done, naturalization is usually granted to an immigrant after a specified period of residence.

Citizenship can also be lost. In some cases, naturalization can involve renouncing any previous citizenship held. In other cases, a person can lose his or her citizenship automatically upon becoming a naturalized citizen of another country.

In other cases, a naturalized citizen is permitted to retain other citizenships. Some countries do not permit their citizens to renounce their citizenship (for example, Greece and the United Kingdom (UK)). In these ways, many people can hold dual (or multiple) citizenship.

In determining whether a person is eligible to cast an external vote, an understanding of the relevant citizenship laws is therefore essential. Different countries' citizenship laws vary. While a person who is currently abroad from a country might have had the status of citizen there before leaving that country, he or she may have lost the entitlement to be a citizen of that country by taking on a different citizenship.

As there are several ways in which a person may obtain dual or multiple citizenship, dual or multiple citizenship is quite common. This is not usually a cause for denying a person the right to vote in any of the countries in which they hold citizenship. However, policy makers may wish to consider whether holders of dual citizenship might have a conflict of interest in some circumstances.

Where a person who is living abroad changes citizenship by naturalization, and in the course of doing so renounces his or her previous citizenship, that person would not retain the right to vote in the country for which citizenship has been renounced.

Where the right to vote while abroad is based on citizenship, it is important that any forms used for electoral registration and for external voting ask the voter whether he or she holds citizenship of the country concerned. In the unlikely event of dual or multiple citizenship being relevant to the franchise, the relevant forms should also ask the elector whether they hold any other citizenship.

In almost all cases, the right to cast an external vote is granted only to citizens of the home country. Citizenship is therefore a minimum requirement for determining eligibility to vote externally. However, some countries, for example New Zealand and Sweden (for elections to the European Parliament) also extend the right to vote externally to residents who are not citizens. In this case different rules from those that apply to citizens are needed to determine whether these non-citizen residents are eligible to cast external votes.

### 3.2. Place of residence

Applying a residency test to a person who is not resident in their home country is perhaps the most difficult aspect of determining entitlement to an external vote.

External electors can be categorized according to a range of typical residential circumstances. The more common categories include:

- citizens resident outside their home country who do not have a fixed intention to return to that country;
- citizens temporarily resident outside their home country who intend to return to live in that country;
- citizens in defined occupations, such as military personnel, public officials or diplomatic staff (and their families);
- citizens resident outside their home country who live in specified countries and who may be subject to special circumstances, such as refugees or migrant workers; and
- non-citizens who have been granted the right to vote in a country through residency but are temporarily outside that country.

These categories can be further qualified by limiting the right to vote externally by imposing time limits on the length of absence from the home country.

The broadest category of residential entitlement to an external vote is the first—that extended to citizens who are resident outside their home country without regard to their intention to return. Several countries extend this right to their citizens. Some allow any citizens living abroad the right to register and vote regardless of the amount of time they have spent away from the country, while others place a time limit on that right.

For example, Belarus, Bosnia and Herzegovina, Estonia, Norway, Poland, South Africa, Sweden and the United States of America all give their citizens living abroad the right to register to vote regardless of the amount of time they have spent away from the country. Countries that impose time limits on this right include Germany (25 years for persons resident in countries that are not members of the Council of Europe), New Zealand (three years for citizens, 12 months for permanent residents) and the UK (15 years).

One rationale for imposing time limits on the right to vote is that the longer citizens stay away from the home country the more they lose their ties to it. Those who have been away from the home country for a long time cannot arguably aspire to make decisions with regard to domestic politics. It is of course difficult to measure the degree of an absent citizen's attachment to his or her home country. It can depend on more than the length of absence, as the German legislation illustrates. The rationale behind the German provision is that, because of the cultural context, German citizens living in Council of Europe countries are more closely linked to their country of origin. Moreover, because about their geographical proximity they have easier access to the current political information of their home country than they would in other regions of the world (Schreiber 1985).

In some of these cases, citizens may only be registered as external electors after satisfying a minimum residency requirement in their country of citizenship (as in Germany, New Zealand and the UK). In other cases, it is possible that a person who is granted citizenship through descent may be eligible to vote in elections for their country of citizenship even though they may have never been resident in that country.

However, granting citizens living abroad the right to vote regardless of intention to return could result in citizens who have no close links with the country beyond holding citizenship exercising significant influence over the results of elections. The greater the number of citizens living abroad, the greater the influence they could have. Whether this is desirable will depend on the particular circumstances of the country. It may be desirable to extend voting rights to citizens living abroad where large numbers of citizens have left the country as refugees or as a result of civil or political unrest. The 1994 general election in South Africa is an example of such a case. In other cases such an approach has been adopted as part of a post-conflict transition to democracy, as in Cambodia in 1993, and Bosnia and Herzegovina in 1996.

The second category of entitlement to an external vote—the right extended to citizens and other permanent residents who are temporarily abroad and intend to return to their home country—is the next-broadest category. Countries that provide for this kind of voting include Australia (for registered electors who are abroad for six years or less, although extensions may be granted) and Canada (for citizens who are abroad for five years or less).

Granting the right to an external vote to persons temporarily absent from their home country caters for those people who are absent on holiday or who are out of their home country for work, study or personal reasons for relatively short periods of time. This model has the advantage of retaining the right to vote for people who have clear ties to their home country, while ensuring that people who may not have such close ties do not have the opportunity to influence elections in which they do not have a personal stake.

Third, several countries have special entitlement provisions for citizens in defined occupations, such as military personnel, public officials or diplomatic staff, and their families. Usually this involves waiving time limits and/or providing for automatic registration. Some countries that do not have a general entitlement allowing citizens abroad to vote have special provisions that apply only to citizens in defined occupations. For example, Lesotho only provides for external voting for public officials employed at diplomatic missions and their dependents or employees, and the Republic of Ireland only provides for external voting for officials employed at diplomatic missions and for members of the armed forces. Non-resident Indian citizens who are employed by the Government of India in a post outside India (this includes the military) are eligible to register as electors. In most cases, where special entitlement provisions are made for citizens of defined occupations, those entitlements are extended to members of their families resident with them who are otherwise entitled to vote.

Fourth, the right to vote externally can be linked to residence in specified countries and/or may be limited to electors who may be subject to special circumstances, such as refugees or migrant workers.

Such restrictions on the right to vote externally may be pragmatic solutions for limiting the number of persons who are eligible for an external vote. Allowing all citizens to vote while they are abroad can add considerably to the cost of running elections, depending on the numbers involved (see chapter 5, and annex D). It is a matter of judgement whether this additional expense is justified. An interesting example is that of Senegal, where the electoral law states that citizens living abroad have the right to vote if at least 500 of them register with diplomatic missions in the foreign country. The underlying reason for this limitation is a pragmatic one—the financial and administrative costs of implementing external voting in extremely small overseas communities are out of proportion to the increase in electoral participation which its introduction might bring about (see the case study). However, such restrictions might violate the principle of electoral equality. The scope of this potential danger depends on the number of external electors involved and the geographical distribution of overseas citizens.

Similarly, another pragmatic approach that has been adopted that has limited the categories of citizens entitled to vote externally has been to restrict voting rights to those who are able to attend a particular location to vote. For example, for the Ukraine elections of December 2004, the election law provided that polling stations could be created in 'diplomatic and other official representations and consular offices of Ukraine abroad, and in military units located outside the borders of Ukraine'. Consequently, 113 polling stations were established abroad, all located in diplomatic and consular offices. For the Iraqi elections of 2005, the Iraq Out-Of-Country Voting Program facilitated polling in 36 cities in 14 countries. Only those Iraqi voters who could attend at one of the specified polling places were able to vote outside Iraq (see the case study).

Chapter 8 discusses the special circumstances that might apply to migrant workers.

Finally, some countries extend the right to vote externally to non-citizen permanent residents. This is sometimes referred to as the 'franchise for foreigners'. Where such non-citizen permanent residents are normally entitled to vote while resident in the country, they may be permitted to vote if they are temporarily (but not permanently) abroad. For example, in Sweden citizens of any member state of the European Union and citizens of Iceland and Norway are entitled to vote in municipal and regional elections if they have been registered residents of Sweden for three consecutive years on election day. In some cases the rules applying to citizens and non-citizen permanent residents are different. For example, New Zealand citizens overseas are qualified to register and vote if they have been in New Zealand within the last three years; whereas permanent non-citizen residents are only qualified to register and vote if they have been in New Zealand within the last 12 months.

### 3.3. Compulsory voting and external voting

Those countries that have compulsory voting add another layer of complexity to the issue of determining entitlement to vote externally. In general, countries which have compulsory voting allow registered electors to escape a fine for not voting if they have a valid reason for failure to vote. Being absent from the home country would be expected to be an acceptable reason for failing to vote. In Australia, the electoral law specifically states that absence from Australia on polling day is sufficient reason for not voting. However, under a compulsory voting system, failure to vote while absent from the home country may impact on a person's ongoing right to remain registered to vote externally. For example, Australia removes a person's name from its register of external electors if the person fails to vote or fails to apply for a postal vote for a national general election.

## 4. Qualification to stand as a candidate in elections

In determining the eligibility rules for external electors, it is important to consider whether the same eligibility rules should apply to candidates for election. Particularly where the right to vote is extended to all citizens who are resident abroad, regardless of intention to return, it may be desirable to have stricter eligibility rules for candidates. This would usually take the form of a residence requirement.

In some cases where political players may be in exile from their home country it might be desirable to allow persons resident outside the country to be candidates. This could be appropriate where a country is undergoing a transition to a new, democratic form of government, as in South Africa in 1994.

Considerations of dual or multiple citizenship may be more important for candidates than for voters. It may be desirable to prevent holders of dual citizenship from standing as candidates. For example, Australia's constitution does not allow 'a citizen of a foreign power' to sit in its national parliament. Such a provision is intended to ensure that elected members do not have divided loyalties that could lead to conflicts of interest. In practice, dual citizenship is so common that this type of provision can lead to candidates and elected members being ruled ineligible for what is arguably a technicality.

## 5. Registration of external electors

Once a person's eligibility to cast an external vote is established, there is usually a second requirement to be met—the need to be registered on the electoral register in order to show that he or she is entitled to vote. Special registration requirements may be necessary for external electors, or they may be required to register in the same way as all other electors. Registration requirements thus introduce a second stage into the entitlement process and may serve to limit the numbers of persons who are eligible to cast an external vote.

In most countries ordinary electors are registered in respect of particular locations—usually their home residence—so that they can establish their right to vote in particular electoral districts and for regional levels of government. As it may be difficult or impossible to allocate an external elector to a particular locality in the home country, it is sometimes desirable to use a special registration process for external electors.

Where the eligibility requirements and/or voting rights for external electors are different from those for in-country electors, it is essential that external electors use a separate registration process. For example, where they are entitled to vote for national elections but not local elections, the electoral register must clearly distinguish external electors.

Whether external electors are listed on a special external electoral register or are listed on the normal electoral register will depend on local circumstances. One relevant factor would be whether a country has one national electoral register or different registers for different levels of government. Another would be the level of technical sophistication of the electoral register. Australia, for example, essentially maintains one computerized national electoral register that is used for elections for all levels of government. While it has a separate registration form for external electors, their names are stored on the national electoral register with all other registered electors, with an annotation indicating that they have registered as external electors. Other countries, particularly those that have different electoral registers for different regions and/or levels of government, might be more likely to maintain separate electoral registers for external electors. Where electoral registers are kept by different authorities for different levels of government or for different regions, such as the different states in the USA, the process for registration as an external elector may vary from jurisdiction to jurisdiction and/or from place to place.

In some cases, simple registration on the normal electoral register is sufficient for an external elector to retain the right to vote, without the need for special registration as an external elector. For example, Swedish residents living abroad remain on the electoral register for an absence of up to ten years. Only those who are absent for longer than ten years need to register in order to remain on the electoral register.

People who are absent for short periods, such as those who are on holiday, generally do not need to apply for special external elector status if they are listed on the normal electoral register.

Where a person is absent for a longer period, many countries require special registration as an external elector. This is particularly important where the electoral register is regularly reviewed, and people are removed from it if they do not appear to be resident at their registered address.

Registration as an external elector usually requires the elector to complete a form, which is then processed by the authority responsible for keeping the electoral register. In some cases, the person may be required to provide documentary proof of eligibility, such as proof of citizenship, age or residence. When considering whether such evidence should be required, attention should be given to the feasibility of this requirement. If a person is applying for registration from outside the home country, the requirement that identity documents (IDs) be provided may be impractical or unreasonable. Where a country is in transition or is otherwise subject to civil instability, many citizens, particularly refugees, may not have valid IDs (see chapter 7 and the case studies on Afghanistan, Bosnia and Herzegovina, and Iraq). In these cases, the registration process may need to rely on a declaration signed by the applicant and/or a declaration signed by a witness.

In most cases it would be appropriate to apply the same level of authentication requirements to registration as an external elector as apply to the normal electoal registration process.

Where a specific external elector registration form is required, care should be taken to ensure that the form seeks sufficient information to demonstrate that the applicant is entitled to be registered. A registration form could for example require the applicant to state how they acquired citizenship, when they last lived in the home country, whether and when they intend to return to the home country (if relevant) and when they were born.

Keeping a register of external electors up to date is a difficult task. Electoral registration authorities are unlikely be able to review the status of registered external electors who are resident abroad. In practice, the most feasible approach is to rely on external electors to update their details when applying to register or when actually voting. One way to keep the electoral register free of out-of-date entries is to remove the names of those who do not vote, for example, for one or two national elections in a row.

## 6. Examples of qualifications for external voting

While most countries' qualifications for external voting fit within the broad categories outlined above, the details usually vary from case to case. Box 4.1 lists some examples of different external voting qualifications. In most cases, the qualifications listed relate to national elections. Different rules may apply for provincial and local government elections. The list of examples is not, of course, complete. Other countries also allow their citizens to vote while abroad.

**Box 4.1: Examples of qualifications for external voting**

**Australia:** External electors must satisfy the normal requirement for electoral registration in Australia, which means that they must be Australian citizens (or British subjects who were on the electoral register in Australia on 25 January 1984). Registered electors who leave Australia and intend to return within six years can apply to be registered as 'eligible overseas electors' and retain the right to remain on the electoral register and vote while overseas; eligible overseas electors who are overseas for longer than six years can apply for 12-month extensions indefinitely. Spouses or children of eligible overseas electors who become entitled to register to vote while overseas by turning 18 or becoming Australian citizens may also apply for registration as eligible overseas electors. Eligible overseas electors can lose their right to be registered and to vote if they do not attempt to vote at a national general election held while they are overseas. Registered electors who go abroad but have an intention to return to live at the same address can remain on the electoral register and entitled to vote without having to register as eligible overseas electors. In this case there is no time limit.

**Belarus:** Citizens living outside Belarus can participate in elections by applying to specified diplomatic missions.

**Bosnia and Herzegovina:** Citizens living outside Bosnia and Herzegovina can register to vote.

**Canada:** Citizens who have lived abroad for less than five consecutive years since their last stay in Canada and who intend to resume their residence in Canada may apply for registration on the register of non-resident Canadians, and thereby become entitled to vote while abroad. Canadian members of the armed forces, public servants or employees of other specified organizations, and their families, are eligible to apply for registration on the register of non-resident Canadians regardless of their length of absence from Canada.

**Estonia:** Citizens residing temporarily or permanently outside Estonia may apply for registration to vote at their nearest Estonian diplomatic mission.

**Germany:** Germany has three categories of external electors qualified to apply for entry on the register of electors—German citizens who are civil servants or armed forces personnel and other salaried public employees, and their family members; German citizens resident in another Council of Europe member state, provided that after 23 May 1949 and prior to their departure they were permanently resident in Germany for an uninterrupted period of at least three months; and German citizens resident outside the Council of Europe member countries who were, prior to their departure, permanently resident in Germany for an uninterrupted period of at least three months, and not more than 25 years have elapsed since their departure.

**India:** Non-resident Indian citizens who are employed by the government of India in a post outside India, including military personnel, are eligible to be registered as electors.

**Iraq:** For the Iraqi elections of 2005, the Iraq Out-Of-Country Voting Program facilitated polling in 36 cities in 14 countries. Only those Iraqi electors who could attend one of the specified polling places were able to vote outside Iraq.

**Ireland:** Public officials employed at diplomatic missions and members of the armed forces are the only categories of elector permitted to vote while abroad.

**Namibia:** Any holders of a valid voter registration card are eligible to vote, including citizens resident abroad.

**New Zealand:** Citizens overseas are qualified to register and vote if they have been in New Zealand within the past three years; permanent residents are qualified to register and vote if they have been in New Zealand within the past 12 months; New Zealand public servants and defence personnel and their spouses and children over 18 years of age are qualified to register and vote regardless of length of time overseas.

**Norway:** Norwegian citizens resident abroad retain the right to be registered to vote if at any time previously they have been registered at the population registry as resident in Norway. All Norwegian public servants employed as diplomatic or consular staff and their families are entitled to vote even if they have never been registered in the population register.

**Poland:** Citizens living abroad and holding a valid Polish passport may apply to be entered on the register of electors.

**Sweden:** Citizens resident abroad are included on the electoral register and remain entitled to vote if they left Sweden within the previous ten years; after an absence of longer than ten years they must notify the relevant authority if they wish to remain on the electoral register.

**United Kingdom:** British citizens living abroad are eligible to register and vote as overseas electors if their name was previously on the electoral register for an address in the UK and no more than 15 years have passed between the qualification date of that register and the date on their application to register as an overseas elector; or if they have reached the age of 18 while living abroad and they were too young to be on an electoral register before they left the UK and a parent or guardian was on the electoral register for the address at which they were living on that date.

**United States of America:** The Uniformed and Overseas Citizens Absentee Voting Act (UOCAVA) guarantees US citizens overseas the right to vote in federal elections in the United States. (Federal elections include primaries, general and special elections for the president, vice-president, senators and representatives to Congress.) The UOCAVA applies only to federal elections. However, many states in the United States have enacted legislation whereby certain categories of citizens residing overseas can vote by absentee ballot for state or local officials. The same procedures for obtaining local election ballots are used for obtaining federal election ballots.

In order to vote in either federal or state elections in the United States, most states require citizens residing abroad to register in the state of their 'voting residence'. A voting residence is the legal residence or domicile in which the elector could vote if present in that state. Military and Merchant Marine members, and their spouses and dependents, may register to vote in the domicile (state) that the member claims as his or her residence. Civilian US Government employees overseas, their spouses and dependents will generally register in the state they claim as their legal residence. In accordance with the UOCAVA, overseas citizens (not affiliated to the US Government) must vote in their last state of residence immediately prior to departure from the United States. This applies even if many years have elapsed and the person maintains no abode and has no intention of returning to that state.

Note: More comprehensive data are available on the website of the ACE Electoral Knowledge Network, http://www.aceproject.org (select Comparative Data).

## 7. Conclusions

The extension of the right to vote to citizens outside their home country varies enormously from country to country. Some countries allow no one to vote who is not physically present in their home country. Others allow any of their citizens to vote from anywhere in the world, regardless of whether their citizens have ever resided in the country of their citizenship. In between these two extremes, there are many variations that allow certain classes of citizens to vote.

As with so many other aspects of the electoral process, there is no single 'correct' way of deciding who should be entitled to vote externally. A model that will suit one country may be totally inappropriate in another. For example, it may be feasible to allow any citizen of a country to vote externally, regardless of their intention to return, where the population of the home country is large and the voting influence of expatriates would not be expected to outweigh that of the home population. On the other hand, a country with a small population and a relatively large number of expatriates might be wary of handing electoral influence to a body of persons who may no longer have a direct interest in their home country.

In attempting to specify 'best practice' principles to guide those who are considering adopting or amending external voting eligibility criteria, it may be worthwhile to consider the purpose of the franchise. Chapter 3 discusses external voting in relation to the right to representation. The franchise is the right to vote for elected representatives. Its purpose is to allow persons to elect representatives to sit in parliament and/or the executive and to determine and administer laws on their behalf. It would therefore appear reasonable to limit the right to vote to those who have a direct interest in the determination and administration of those laws. However, if it is accepted that the franchise should *only* be granted to those with a direct interest in the process, it follows that extending the right to vote to absent citizens who have no intention to return to the home country—or to persons who hold dual citizenship and are permanent residents in another country where they are also citizens—may be seen as too generous. Indeed, it could be argued that a country's sovereignty could be at risk if its representatives are elected in part by voters who reside abroad. It would also follow that the right to vote should be extended to absent citizens who intend to return in the foreseeable future, as they too would have a direct interest in the government of their home country. This argument would particularly apply to those who are temporarily absent in the service of their country, such as diplomats and members of the armed forces.

However, while it is easier to justify, using the principle of 'intent to return' as a determining factor to grant voting rights to citizens abroad may be more difficult to administer than allowing all citizens to vote while abroad. It requires, at a minimum, some form of notification from citizens who are abroad (or are going abroad) that their absence is temporary and that they intend to return to their home country. The question then arises whether notice of intent to return ought to be accepted at face value, or whether an objective test should be applied. It may be difficult to devise an objective test that is not discriminatory and contrary to the principles of universal suffrage. For example, requiring evidence of ownership of a house or property would clearly discriminate against those who do not own property and could be seen as a return to a property-based voting right. Whether this is necessary will depend on the circumstances of each country, and particularly on whether large numbers of electors are likely to register to vote while they are abroad.

Finally, what voting rights should permanent residents who are not citizens have? It is arguable that, in today's global economy with an increasingly mobile population, the concept of citizenship may be losing its value as a determinant for the franchise. In future, countries may have to look at other criteria to determine whether a person residing abroad is eligible to vote in their elections. For the present, most countries continue to use citizenship as the main determinant of the franchise, and many grant the franchise to their citizens abroad regardless of intention to return. No doubt the issue of the extension of the eligibility to vote externally will continue to evolve in different ways in different places.

CASE STUDY: Senegal

# Senegal: a significant external electorate

Richard Vengroff

In the period leading up to the 1993 presidential elections in Senegal, under pressure from the international community and domestic opponents, the Senegalese Government convened a conference to reform and democratize the electoral processes. With the involvement of all political parties, the conference produced an important set of political reforms. These included a new electoral code; an opportunity for all political parties to be represented at polling stations; a guaranteed secret ballot; a lower voting age (18 instead of 21); an easier and expanded system of electoral registration; guaranteed access to the state media for all parties; the acceptance of foreign election monitors; a change in the balance in the allocation of seats, increasing the number of proportional representation (PR) seats decided by a national list from 60 to 70 and reducing the number of plurality seats by 10 to 50; and the putting in place for the first time of a system of external voting for both presidential and legislative elections. This new system was approved and strongly supported by all political parties. Although several opposition leaders retained some doubts about implementation, the policy itself was considered to be a sound base for free and fair elections. An independent election commission (the Observatoire National des Elections, ONEL) was established to see that the new rules were in fact implemented and to monitor the results both within Senegal and in the external constituencies. (It was replaced in 2005 by the Autonomous National Election Commission (Commission Nationale Electorale Autonome, CENA), which is responsible for control and supervision of the registration and electoral processes.)

Three important interrelated factors underlay the desire to include a mechanism for external voting beginning in 1993 and included in all subsequent electoral codes. They are (a) demographic, (b) economic and (c) social. The demographic factor is associated with the rapidly growing number of overseas Senegalese and their improving status. Many of these individuals, previously mostly involved in the informal sector, gained economic 'clout' and became more and more involved in the formal sector. They and the generation which followed were better educated, better informed politically and better placed to influence public affairs back home. They rapidly became a significant target for political parties which were looking to expand their support base not just in terms of votes but also to increase their lists of reliable donors of funds.

From an economic perspective, the financial power that Senegalese in the diaspora have vis-à-vis relatives who stayed behind in Senegal is of great importance. Overseas Senegalese, as is the case in many developing countries, remit significant sums to the home economy. Many Senegalese have learned to depend on them for financial assistance, the construction and improvement of homes, health-care costs, special events such as baptisms, marriages and funerals, and other needs. Many rural community projects which the Senegalese Government is unable to fund come to fruition thanks to remittances from abroad. As they became more aware of their potential power, overseas Senegalese became difficult for the authorities to ignore.

From a social perspective, the Conseil des Sénégalais de l'Extérieur, a government-sponsored organization designed to provide assistance to Senegalese in the diaspora, began to take on new roles. Increasingly, its members expressed the desire to make their voices heard and to get involved in making choices that affect the handling of public affairs in the mother country. Most overseas Senegalese use modern technology such as the Internet to maintain close contact with their extended families and thereby potentially exert a disproportionate influence on their networks of relations in Senegal. The government felt that providing them with an outlet in the electoral politics arena would act as a safety valve and would entail only limited costs and risks for the regime. Opposition parties saw the inclusion of external votes as an opportunity to expand their influence and revenue sources. Hence it was in the interests of all parties to concede the vote to overseas Senegalese.

## Legal provisions

The formal legal provision for external voting, as part of the electoral code, is established by and can be modified by the legislature (the Chambre des Députés) rather than being constitutionally mandated. All Senegalese nationals resident overseas who are 18 years of age or older (as of the date of the vote) and who are not active members of the armed forces, the police or the public service (designated positions only) are technically eligible to be included on the list of registered electors. However, for practical purposes three additional constraints are imposed. First, there must be official diplomatic representation in the country of residence. Second, voting will only take place in countries in which the official electoral register reaches at least 500 when registration officially closes. Fifteen different countries qualified during the 2000 presidential election in Senegal: nine in Africa (Burkina Faso, Côte d'Ivoire, Gabon, Gambia, Guinea, Mali, Mauritania, Morocco and Nigeria); four in Europe (Belgium, France, Germany and Italy), and the USA plus Canada in North America. Third, the formal permission of the host country for such elections to be conducted on its territory is required. There has been some limited demand for voting opportunities to be offered in additional countries, but usually only after the registered Senegalese community has grown and surpassed the 500 level, as is the case now in Canada. There is a separate register of electors in each overseas country rather than an overall list of registered overseas electors.

The elections themselves are technically overseen by Senegal's independent election commission, ONEL, with the full participation of representatives of the various political parties and candidates with a presence in the host country. Provided that a minimum of 500 electors have registered, the head of the diplomatic mission, in collaboration with the Ministry of Foreign Affairs, will establish polling locations around the host country. Polling places are headed by a president who is a designated representative of the head of the diplomatic mission. The conditions for the actual balloting are rigorously laid out, including the use of the French-style ballot paper, private voting booths, election observers, and careful procedures for counting, verifying and controlling a voting process. Election locations are distributed in key areas of the host countries in which there are significant concentrations of Senegalese. In France, for example, there were 32 polling places set up for the over 16,000 registered electors in 2000.

The system for presidential elections is a majority Two-Round System (TRS), with the second round taking place between the two leading candidates, unless one candidate secures an absolute majority of votes in the first round. Overseas Senegalese are eligible to vote in both rounds and their votes contribute directly to the national presidential total. For legislative elections Senegal uses a mixed-member majoritarian (MMM) system, with some of the seats allocated on the basis of a plurality block vote at the department level (in 31 departments) with the district magnitude ranging from one to five seats. The remaining seats are distributed by PR using a Hare Quota system with largest remainders in a single national constituency (for the 2002 elections the distribution was 65 department seats and 55 national list seats). Voters use a single ballot paper (voting for the party only) with the party vote cumulating to both the district (department) and the national list. External votes, however, contribute only to the allocation of the national list seats. They have no separate plurality constituency and their votes are not allocated at that level. Because of the highly proportional nature of the distribution of list seats, the influence of overseas Senegalese votes could potentially be quite significant at the margins in deciding the final distribution of seats among parties.

## Electoral impact

To assess the importance of external voting we need only look at several recent elections. Because of the difficulty of getting to the limited number of polling stations, work demands, a shortage of information, and limited campaigning and interest, voter turnout tends to be considerably lower than it is in-country. In the critical presidential election of 2000, which produced a dramatic democratic transition, the turnout nationally was about 60 per cent in both rounds, while only 41 and 37 per cent of the registered overseas Senegalese participated in the two rounds, respectively. There is considerable variation in turnout between host countries, varying from highs of 80 per cent in Mali, and 59 per cent in Morocco, Burkina Faso and Guinea, to lows of 16 per cent in Italy, 25 per cent in Nigeria and 30 per cent per cent in Gambia. The largest numbers of external votes are cast in Côte d'Ivoire and Gambia (with over 8,300 votes each counted in 2000), Mali (7,417) and France (5,522). As few as 189 external votes were counted in Belgium, followed by Nigeria (327). The same trend holds for elections to the legislature as well.

Always of concern is the potential differential voting preferences of external and domestic voters. In the case of Senegal the larger parties, and particularly the party in power, have a clear advantage in mobilizing their supporters overseas. Some of the smaller parties lack the financial resources and local personnel to mount campaigns in so many countries and concentrate instead on those closer to home, such as Mali and Gambia. In the presidential election of 2000 the total national vote gave the incumbent president,

Abdou Diouf, 41.3 per cent of the vote while external voters offered 48 per cent support for Diouf in the first round. In the second round of the election, the advantage of the incumbent overseas was again demonstrated. Whereas Diouf received only 41.5 per cent of the second-round votes nationally, his overseas share rose to 55.5 per cent as the PS used its influence, political, regulatory and financial, to good advantage in a vain effort to mobilize enough external supporters to save the day. Since external voters account for between 4 and 5 per cent of the total vote, they can clearly have a significant influence on a close presidential election in either or both rounds.

At the legislative level those numbers can be translated directly into about three seats in the National Assembly. This can also have an important influence in a close race for control of the legislature, especially if external votes do not mirror the domestic vote. (This external vote power would of course be considerably more important if these votes counted at the department level, where a simple plurality win translates into a block of up to five seats.)

In sum, external voting enhances the legitimacy of the regime and its democratic image, and symbolically integrates a key economic group into the public affairs of the nation. While it tends to reinforce support for the largest parties, its overall political impact so far has been limited. The cost to the nation is not insignificant but the overall gains in terms of image are clearly viewed as worth the cost.

CASE STUDY: The Marshall Islands

# The Marshall Islands: a high proportion of external voters

Jon Fraenkel

In the Republic of the Marshall Islands, the majority of the population vote from somewhere other than their place of residence. Not only those who are resident or working temporarily overseas, but also inter-island migrants and displaced people from the atolls that are affected by US nuclear tests are entitled to vote in their electoral district on their home island. Absentees can therefore determine the outcome of elections, and party agents travel widely overseas to attract voter support, campaigning in Hawaii, in California, and among Marshallese employed at the Tyson Foods chicken factory in Arkansas.

The Marshall Islands comprise two parallel chains of islands, the Ratak ('sunrise') and Ralik ('sunset') groups, spread across 2 million square kilometres (km) of the Pacific Ocean. Towards the north, the peoples of the Bikini, Rongelap, Enewetak and Utrik atolls were displaced by 67 US nuclear tests conducted between 1946 and 1958. Further south, Kwajalein Atoll is the site of a sizeable US military base and missile testing facility. It has the world's largest lagoon, which is used as a target for missiles fired from California under the Star Wars II programme. Nearly half of the domestic population of 50,850 (46.6 per cent) lives on Majuro, where the capital is located, and another 21.4 per cent live on Kwajalein, most of them on the islet of Ebeye near the US base (Office of Planning and Statistics 1999: 16, table 3.2).

Over 20 per cent of the population is resident outside the country. Owing to the country's Compact of Free Association with the USA, Marshallese are able to enter the USA without visas to reside or work, but they are not automatically eligible for US citizenship. Around 14,000 currently live on the US mainland, in Hawaii or in the nearby US territories of Guam and the Commonwealth of the Northern Marianas.

The 1979 constitution provides for a unicameral parliament (the Nitijela) with 33 members, including at least one member for each of the 24 inhabited atolls and coral islands, with members elected on a First Past The Post (or plurality) basis (article IV, section 2(1) of the constitution). The more populous islands have multi-member electoral districts with members elected by means of the Block Vote system. Five members are elected from Majuro, three from Kwajalein and two each from Arno, Ailinglaplap and

Jaluit. All other inhabited atolls and coral islands have a single representative. Although the population of the country increased by 65 per cent between 1980 and 1999, there were no changes in the distribution of Nitijela seats. Substantial inter-island migration to Majuro and Kwajalein has left the outer islands sparsely populated. Had electoral registration had been based on residence, the result would have been significant inequities: the 1979 constitution (article 4, section 2[4]) specifies that 'every member of the Nitijela should represent approximately the same number of voters; but account shall also be taken of geographical features, community interests, the boundaries of existing administrative and recognized traditional areas, means of communication and density and mobility of population'. However, potential under-representation of the more urbanized atolls which receive migrants was avoided (a) by allowing electors to continue to register on their ancestral islands in the outer islands and (b) by a curious spontaneous redistricting process.

The 1979 constitution entitles electors to register either where they reside or where they hold land rights. Every person otherwise qualified to vote shall have the right to vote in one and only one electoral district, being an electoral district in which he either resides or has land rights, but a person who has a choice of electoral districts pursuant to this paragraph shall exercise that choice in any manner prescribed by law (1979 constitution, article 4, section 3[3]). Most Marshall Islanders have land rights on several atolls or islands, and hence multiple potential constituencies where they can register as electors. Marshallese society is based on a system of exogamous matrilineal clans. Clans are usually spread across several atolls, and intermarriage between peoples from different atolls is frequent. However, matrilineal inheritance does not exhaust the range of lineages and associated lands in which an individual has rights. Particularly towards the south of the group of islands, bilateral inheritance is common, and even in the more firmly matrilineal systems children may claim patrilineal land-use rights back at least five generations. Many of those who move to the urbanized centres of Majuro and Kwajalein remain on the electoral register on their island of origin. Many also shift regularly between electoral districts, either to accompany favoured candidates or to avoid 'wasting' votes on unlikely victors or to vote in smaller constituencies where votes count more. Strategic re-registration of urban electors to outer island electorates evens out the inequities arising from the maldistribution of seats across the country.

One study of the 1999 electoral data found that 57.1 per cent of electors registered on the outer islands (the outer islands are all the islands in the group other than Majuro and Kwajalein) were in fact resident on Mauro and Kwajalein. Absentee voters living on Majuro and Kwajalein accounted for 43.6 and 13.5 per cent of the outer island vote, respectively, with an additional 4.4 per cent coming from overseas and 6.7 per cent casting absentee ballots from one outer island to another. In the outer islands electoral districts the proportion of votes cast by people actually living there (the on-island vote) was on average less than one-third of the total, although with considerable variation between the different atolls. For nuclear-affected Rongelap, the 14.9 per cent of the voters shown as 'on-island' were in fact people resettled on Mejatto Island, in the northern part of Kwajalein atoll. Similarly, on-island voters shown in the Bikini constituency were people now living on the island of Kili, where the population relocated after Operation Bravo and other nuclear tests.

For most of the outer islands, the offshore vote is larger than the on-island vote and therefore sufficient to determine electoral outcomes. When the reformist Kessai Note administration came into office in 1999, many of its crucial victories in remote constituencies occurred thanks to the addition of the votes of people living on Majuro.

According to the 1979 constitution, all Marshall Islands citizens over 18 years of age, except those who are imprisoned or certified insane, are eligible to vote. Provisions for absentee voting are contained in the 1993 Electoral Act. To qualify for registration by land rights, citizens require a supporting affidavit from customary chiefs or, in the case of qualification by residence, from local government officials. In practice, most requests for registration are granted without affidavits being submitted. In theory, registration rights can be challenged before the High Court, but this seldom occurs. The procedure for registration of overseas electors is exactly the same as the that for registration in the home electoral district. Applications for postal ballots require 'an affidavit sworn before a notary public in the country of residence' (Elections and Referenda Regulations, 1993, section 118(6)).

There are no geographical restrictions on the countries from which the voters can cast an external vote.

External voting is done exclusively by post. There is no provision for voting stations outside the republic. Those who are temporarily or permanently outside the republic vote by means of a postal ballot paper (Elections and Referenda Regulations, 1993, section 118 (1)(b)). Historically, ballot papers have been mailed in to the electoral office and, provided they meet the various requirements, are accepted no matter where they are from.

In the 2003 election, the government sent election teams to distribute ballot papers to registered voters living in the USA, which resulted in a much higher turnout on the postal absentee front.

In the wake of the 1999 election, the Marshallese Government restricted the scope for re-registration of voters between constituencies. Citizens were required to lodge applications at least a year before the 2003 polls. Yet, owing to intensification of political competition accompanying the advent of a political party-based system, a large number of voters continued to shift registration to their preferred electoral district.

# CHAPTER 5

# 5. The implementation of external voting

Judy Thompson

## 1. Introduction

The practical implementation of external voting is complicated by factors such as the number of electors, their locations, the distances involved and the complexity of the voting system in place. Election planning becomes a two-tiered process as the tasks involved in organizing an election in-country are duplicated, under very different circumstances, for the external voting.

At each stage of the external electoral process, emphasis must be placed on implementing procedures and processes that are not only faithful to the legislation but also as close as possible to those in place for in-country voters. All electors must have access to a similar registration and polling process, no matter where they are located. Administrative creativity and flexibility are needed, but the process must always be in accordance with the law.

The problems of implementation will vary depending on the methods of registration and voting, the geographical distribution of expatriates and the political situation (e.g. during a transition after violent conflict). In all cases, *security* and *privacy* are central to the process, whether voting is done in person, by post, by proxy (essentially an internal process) or by electronic means. Many groups of external electors (such as refugee populations) may be vulnerable to intimidation and will need assurances that they are protected by the secrecy built in to the process. Other groups (e.g. military serving outside the home country and members of the diplomatic community) will have more confidence in the system but will expect the same protection.

In first or transitional elections, the political players will watch the external voting with suspicion. If any political force is seeking a reason to challenge the results of an election, anomalies in the external voting can often be pointed out to justify any complaints. For this reason, the planning for external voting requires a carefully integrated approach to ensure that it is as transparent and administratively correct as the internal voting.

Administrative problems or delays in the external voting are often viewed as deliberate acts of fraud by an incumbent government or even by the election management body (EMB). 'Transition elections should be viewed as accidents waiting to happen at the intersection between political suspicion and administrative incapacity. Every administrative problem is interpreted by one side as designed by its opponent to do it harm' (Pastor 1999). This is particularly true for external voting. It is important to eliminate any potential cause for suspicion when planning the implementation of external voting.

Finally, disputes and complaints will need to be resolved quickly and fairly. All participants in the electoral process must have the right to appeal to an independent, impartial body. Procedures need to be established for the appeal process to ensure it is accessible for the external electors and within the election timeline. All complaints will need to be dealt with in an equitable and timely manner.

## 2. The procedures for external voting

There are four basic options for the procedure for external voting:

- voting by proxy;
- personal voting—voting in person in diplomatic missions or military bases;
- postal voting; and
- electronic voting.

The advantages of proxy voting are that it is technically simple and does not involve the huge financial and administrative costs that are customary in elections held outside the state territory. It does, however, have one problematic feature: the proxy could use this procedure to obtain an additional vote and thus infringe the principle of equal suffrage, with the electoral authorities being unable to intervene.

The main advantage of voting in diplomatic missions is that there is a highly transparent electoral process, supervised by diplomatic staff. However, they must be, and be perceived to be, independent and unbiased. Moreover, in some countries getting to the nearest embassy or consulate may be a problem, especially for citizens of those states that have few diplomatic missions in those foreign countries or in countries where the infrastructure is poor. Oversight issues also need to be considered with voting at military bases abroad.

It is clearly easier to organize postal voting than to establish polling stations in all diplomatic missions worldwide, but the transparency of voting by post is not so high as when the vote is cast in person in a consulate under the observation of state officials (problems of 'family voting', for instance, have been known to arise); moreover, postal services may be slow and unreliable. Whether postal voting is more or less suitable than voting in diplomatic missions will depend to a great extent on the context, such as the infrastructure of those foreign countries where external voting is to be held. The costs associated with postal voting are generally lower than those for personal voting because the management structure can be centralized for postal voting. However, due to timelines, it may be necessary to use courier services to move the ballot papers to a central point in each country for mailing, and also to return them for counting. Costs for these services are high but they ensure timely delivery. The local mailing costs are also high because the package contains ballot papers, a series of envelopes, instructions, candidate lists and so on.

Voting by electronic means is considered in chapter 10.

Thus there is no 'best procedure' for external voting. The EMB will have to consider the procedure that best meets the needs of its electorate.

Table 5.1: Advantages and disadvantages of external voting procedures

|  | **Tentative advantages** | **Tentative disadvantages** |
|---|---|---|
| Postal voting | Lower financial and organizational costs  Able to reach most eligible electors | Problematic transparency of voting procedure  Dependent on a speedy and reliable postal service |
| Voting in diplomatic missions | High transparency of voting procedure | Higher financial and organizational costs  Many eligible electors do not live near the location of the mission |
| Proxy voting | Almost no additional expenses | Principle of electoral equality not sufficiently guaranteed |
| Electronic voting | No delays  Available worldwide  Facilitates counting | Security concerns  Financial costs of implementation |

## 3. Timelines

The planning process is made difficult by the particular features of external voting. However, if there is early planning and careful preparation, the process will naturally parallel that of the election in-country. For external voting, however, extra time is required at the registration and voting stages, especially if the external electors are widely distributed geographically, as table 5.2 shows. A short election period can effectively exclude external voting, and is indeed sometimes used for that purpose (e.g., in Sierra Leone 2002, the timeline was one of the reasons for excluding external voting).

One of the pre-election tasks that can be time-consuming is the negotiation and signing of a memorandum of understanding (MOU) with each country that will have external registration and voting (see chapter 6). The MOU is the basis for all the arrangements, assistance and needs of the EMB in that country. When several countries are involved, a delayed MOU with one or more can jeopardize the process. This happened in the 2005 Iraqi election, with the last MOU being signed just four weeks before the election.

The managers of the external voting must be an integral part of the EMB's management and planning team so that all the players are aware of the special problems to be faced and the timelines. This is particularly important if the external voting is being administered by an agency outside the EMB of the country for which the election is being held. The fact that there is external voting impacts on every step of the process—from procurement and printing to distribution of the ballot papers, and from training of election workers and voter education to procedures. Only by working closely together can the internal and external voting be consistent and function well and efficiently.

The campaign period will need special attention because candidates and political parties may not have the resources to reach external electors. The EMB may have to print and distribute information about the candidates and political parties to these electors, particularly if it is a postal vote. Although the campaign period would be the same as that for the in-country campaign, the time needed for preparation of materials has to be considered. Timelines will be affected differently depending on the locations of external electors, on the method of registration and on the process for voting. Technology is offering new options and electronic methods of voting (discussed in chapter 10).

Table 5.2: Examples of election timelines for external and in-country voting

| External voting | Countdown | In-country voting |
| --- | --- | --- |
| Sign MOU with each government Make arrangements with non-governmental organizations (NGOs) for cooperation | - 8 months | Order registration materials |
| Hire registration staff | | |
| Establish number/location of external electors | - 6 months | Establish registration sites |
| Start information campaign | | |
| Select registration/voting sites and/or mailing points | | |
| Receive registration materials | - 5 months | Distribute materials to registration sites |
| Train registration staff | | Start information campaign Hire and train registration staff |

| External voting | Countdown | In-country voting |
|---|---|---|
| Register electors (in person or by post) | - 4 months | Registration of electors |
| Transport registration information to the election commission Exhibition/corrections to list (if separate from internal list) | - 3 months | Order election equipment/materials Nomination Order ballot papers Prepare electoral register |
| Arrange for voting equipment | - 2 months | Preliminary register of electors |
| Campaign period: print and distribute information on parties/candidates for external electors | | Challenges to registration and appeals Corrections to electoral register |
| Hire and train voting staff | | Campaign period |
| Receive ballot papers and other secure materials Election observers arrive | - 1 month | Print final electoral register Recruit and train voting staff |
| Voting (if by post) | - 3 weeks | Deliver non-secure materials to voting sites |
| Transport ballot papers to election commission (postal voting) | - 2 weeks | Deliver ballot papers and other secure materials to voting sites |
| | - 1 week | Election observers arrive |
| Voting (if personal) and counting (or transport ballot papers to election commission for the count) | Election day | Voting and counting |
| | +1–7 days | Challenges to voting and count |
| | + 1 week | Investigate complaints/recounts |
| | + 3 weeks | Official announcement of results |

This timeline assumes full registration of all eligible electors specifically for the election in question prior to election day. It will be considerably shorter if other registration methods are used. For example, a permanent register that includes those who are outside the country would only need an updating period, which will usually be shorter than the time full registration would take. The use of established lists, such as registers of refugees, military registers and diplomatic staff lists may also be used to cut down the registration period if there is a way of checking the eligibility to vote of the persons concerned. Bosnia and Herzegovina in 1996 used the pre-war census as the basis for the voting, and Iraq in 2005 used the Food Distribution List. Earlier electoral registers can be used in the same way if necessary.

## 4. Costing and budgeting*

External voting can add considerably to the costs of an election. The costs of external voting will vary with the prevailing conditions. Once a decision has been made to have external voting, it is necessary to be aware of where extra funds will be needed and what the actual costs will be. In transitional elections, if international donors are involved, they will want oversight of detailed costing and budgets. All the costing factors must be known early in the process so that a realistic budget can be presented to governments and donors. When programmes are established well in advance within a recognized structure, they are likely to be less costly.

The extra costs may be a reason to limit the extent the external voting. For instance, the option of external voting may be offered only where the number of registered external electors exceeds a certain threshold (e.g. Ukraine in 2004) or only in countries where the country holding the election has an embassy or consulate. In some cases, decision makers may determine that the challenges of external voting are too costly and insurmountable against tight timetables. This has been the case in a number of post-conflict elections. Indeed, in the 2005 Iraqi elections, the United Nations initially advised against external voting due to the complexity of such an operation. However, the Iraqi political parties advocated strongly for external voting and the Independent Electoral Commission of Iraq (IECI) ultimately (in November 2004) decided to incorporate external voting.

External voting programme costs might include:

- security—of persons, locations, materials, events. Special security arrangements may be needed if there is a perceived risk for the voters and/or ballot papers during the process;
- staffing—including recruitment, salaries, training;
- office space (it may also be necessary to administer the external voting from an office outside the country if there are communications or other infrastructure problems internally);
- travel—for oversight and administrative staff;
- training. Special training materials and programmes will be needed for both external registration and the external voting itself;
- the electoral registration programme;
- election materials—the printing of ballot papers, the installation of voting booths and so on;
- the transport of materials. This can be a major expense, depending on the number of countries involved. It will often be necessary to use couriers in order to meet timelines (e.g. for returning the ballot papers from external voting if they are to be counted in-country);
- the cost of registration, polling and office locations;
- information materials and distribution/media. Special communication programmes will be needed to reach external electors with information and to raise awareness

---

* Parts of this section were kindly contributed by Brett Lacy.

about the procedures for registration and voting, and this may involve media costs in several countries;
- communications—constant communication is needed between the EMB and its external operation;
- observation—The EMB may want to provide its own observers for the external registration and voting or it may want to help political party representatives attend these events; and
- implementing partner organizations' costs.

Many of the basic election costs for items such as procurement and printing will be included in the general election budget (e.g. the number of ballot papers to be printed will include internal and external electors).

If a large number of countries and a large number of electors are involved, negotiations can be started early to involve the diplomatic community, national EMBs and where relevant international agencies in those countries. It may be possible to borrow much of the polling station equipment locally and local election officials may assist in the preparations in each country, but an agreement will need to be reached with the local or national EMB (see chapter 6). This assistance will vary greatly from country to country and will need to be negotiated separately. In Bosnia and Herzegovina, international support was crucial. 'Most of the countries hosting Bosnian refugees were sufficiently affluent and politically stable to permit, and even fund, election activities on their soil. The same cannot be expected of host countries in other regions' (Organization for Security and Co-operation in Europe, Refugee Election Steering Group 1997: 61). Where the number of external electors is small (e.g. diplomats, workers and travellers), the embassy of the country concerned can usually handle the arrangements without input by the local EMBs.

Table 5.3 gives some examples of the costs of external voting programmes. However, it is not always possible to ascertain what is included in the different figures, and the figures here cannot be treated as directly comparable.

### Table 5.3: Examples of the cost of external voting programmes

|  | Estimated costs of external voting programme (million US dollars (USD)) | Cost per registered elector (USD) |
|---|---|---|
| Iraq (January 2005) | 92 | 300–400 |
| Iran (December 2005) | 17 | 45 |
| Afghanistan (2004) | 24 | 20 Iran/32 Pakistan |
| Indonesia (2004) | 6 | 13* |
| East Timor (1999) | 1 | 161** |

\* These figures are the allocation for which approval was sought. Actual expenditure is not known. Ultimately only about 0.2 per cent of total voter turnout was accounted for by external voters. See the Indonesia case study.
\*\* International Organization for Migration, 'Out of Country Voting Case Studies: East Timor'.

The Iraq external voting programme was the most expensive in history. Much of the costs in both Iraq and Afghanistan—particularly in Iraq—can be attributed to security requirements, although another factor in the case of Iraq was directly related to the institutional arrangements that were put in place to organize and conduct the external voting programme within a very short period of time: the entire external voting programme was contracted out to the International Organization for Migration (IOM), resulting in an organizational overhead being charged for the whole programme. The cost of external voting for Iraq in the December 2005 election, organised mainly by the IECI and Iraqi servants, was considerably lower than in the January election, organised with the assistance of international partners. East Timor's external voting programme for its 1999 referendum on independence cost a fraction of what the programmes in Iraq and Afghanistan have cost. It registered about 6,220 electors in six countries and external voter turnout was 96.5 per cent.

Breaking external voting programmes down into parts, with the EMB of the home country itself contracting out directly for smaller pieces, such as the printing of ballot papers, can significantly reduce overall costs. Costs will be higher when external voting programmes have to establish an electoral register for the first time or to reconstruct a significantly flawed one. Other methods of reducing costs include eliminating the production of new identity documents.

Most costs are borne by a combination of the country of origin, the international community, and in a more limited way the host countries, but other costs can be borne by the voters themselves. Voters often pay their own travel fees associated with registration and voting. Depending on the election timetable, voters may need to make two trips, one to register and a second to cast their vote. These travel costs can be a significant obstacle to participation, particularly where eligible electors have to travel over large distances, and can result in low external voter turnout. For the January 2005 Iraqi elections, the costs for electors to travel to register and then again to vote were prohibitively high, particularly in countries such as Sweden and the United States (where an estimated 10 per cent of external votes were cast) where there were only a limited number of polling and registration sites. The Danish Government subsidized the travel of voters to participate in the Iraqi external voting programme, but most host countries did not provide such support.

Budget issues can produce creative and innovative solutions to some of the problems of external voting. In areas where large numbers of refugees live in close proximity, volunteers from refugee groups and other community or civic groups who have the necessary language skills could handle much of the education and training activities. In some cases it may be possible to draw on these groups to provide election officials. The expatriate community often suggests other cost-saving measures (although there could be a risk of these suggestions being biased).

Naturally, any financial costs should be considered alongside the non-financial costs of not conducting external voting, such as the implications for the consolidation of democracy, peace and stability, or national reconciliation, particularly in post-conflict societies. In some cases, the costs of not conducting out-of-country voting can in the long run far exceed the costs of any single external voting programme.

## 5. Logistics

The procurement and distribution of election materials and equipment take on added dimensions when external voting takes place. If external electors are living in several different countries, the problems of delivering items to coincide with the delivery of the same items inside the country grow in proportion.

Special arrangements may have to be made with providers such as printers and manufacturers to deliver to several locations, both inside and outside the country. This raises questions of security and timing, which have to be carefully controlled. Infrastructure problems of transport and communications must always be considered in planning these deliveries. The transport of ballot papers can be complicated by the electoral system used. In an election where proportional representation (PR) is used nationally, the same ballot paper is used everywhere. However, in an electoral system where each electoral district or province or region has a unique ballot paper, distribution becomes more complex. Voters have to be identified by constituency, adding another step to the process, unless a postal ballot is used. This, of course, has its own complexities because each voter then needs a list of candidates or parties for the particular electoral district.

A breakdown in the delivery of materials can create a tense situation, as was experienced in the Central African Republic National Assembly election in 1998:

> There was bitterness in neighbouring Gabon and in France, where angry migrant voters surrounded their diplomatic missions insisting on voting. A protestor in Libreville, Gabon, told newsmen that 'we've not been able to vote here in Libreville because the consulate did not receive the necessary materials to enable it to organise the elections. This is why we're protesting against the flagrant violation of the constitution by blocking Central Africans in Gabon from freely exercising their civic duties. We're contesting with all our energy' (Tumanjong 1999: 41–42).

Even countries with excellent infrastructure and communications can experience difficulties. Some Canadian electors working in Kosovo at the time of the Canadian election in 2000 were unable to vote when many ballot papers did not arrive at the Canadian Co-ordination Office in Kosovo on time.

An important aspect of the logistical plans is the appointment and training of staff for the external voting. Whether they are hired directly or appointed by a national or international agency in each country, the election officials will need specific and detailed training. Although registration and voting manuals prepared for in-country training will be useful, there will also be specific matters that need to be addressed for the staff managing the external voting. These may include the context (e.g. peace agreements, country background), the particular challenges (e.g. reaching electors in refugee camps and finding out how to reach those who are scattered), and special instructions for returning registration materials and ballot papers to the EMB.

Voter education and communication with prospective voters are also a part of the logistical preparations. Materials designed for internal voting may need to be modified for use outside the country (including language). Close cooperation with international and national organizations will be needed to reach prospective voters and to conduct education programmes. The use of the mass media needs to be kept to a minimum in order to keep down costs unless there is a large population of external electors in a particular country. The host country's regulations on the media may also need to be checked. Announcements and information must be targeted carefully to reach eligible electors in different locations. The election officials may also be involved in distributing campaign information if the political parties do not have the means to do this outside the country. Toll-free telephone lines may be needed to answer queries if large numbers of external electors are resident in a particular country.

As with the planning process, the logistical preparations have to be carefully monitored and worked out to ensure that all contingencies are provided for where the timelines for registration and voting are concerned.

## 6. The security of election materials

The security and control of registration and voting materials require special attention for external voting. Security is as essential externally as it is internally but there is the added challenge of securing sensitive materials during transport to and from several countries. Once the ballot papers are returned to the EMB, they may also need to be transported further to the provincial or municipal level, depending on the counting and reconciliation arrangements. Each step requires a security plan to prevent fraud.

Observers and political party representatives often want to follow the trail of the ballot papers and other election materials from origin to destination. Secure transport, such as a courier or diplomatic pouch, is required to reassure observers, candidates and voters that the ballot papers cannot be tampered with in any way.

Security will also be an issue during the registration process. In some circumstances, providing the data necessary to register to vote may be dangerous for the individual. Refugees may be concerned about losing their refugee status or being forced to return prematurely to their country of origin. For this reason they may want assurance that the registration data will remain confidential to the EMB. This, however, may conflict with the ideal of an open list to which the political parties have access. Measures can be devised to protect the information on the elector's location or status by carefully selecting the information that will be printed on the electoral registers. This type of problem requires careful consideration if the needs of the displaced citizen are to be balanced with the needs of the electoral system.

## 7. Voter registration

Legislation defines who is eligible to vote and an EMB establishes the procedures for registering eligible electors and preventing fraud. The electoral registers are generally a matter of public record, which means that the data to be published in the lists must be agreed upon and other data collected must remain confidential.

External electors may be registered on the electoral register of the electoral district of their previous place of residence, or on another national list (for example, if the country concerned has a single consolidated electoral register), or there may be a special electoral register of external electors. In the latter case, the list can be by country, by type of residence (permanent or temporary), by category (refugee, guest worker etc.) or by any combination of these. There may be a permanent register of electors that has to be updated regularly, or registration may be regular and automatic, or electors may need to register in advance of each election.

External electors who are working or travelling in another country will need to confirm that their names are on the electoral register. The onus is on the elector to check this by post or by the Internet. For large displaced populations, it is usually necessary to hold a new registration because any electoral registers that exist are generally out of date. This process can be very costly to organize and manage. In these cases, the onus is on the EMB to ensure the process occurs. The registration process must be designed so that the register of external electors will meet the requirements set out in the law as well as meeting any specific problems in host countries. Registration can be carried out by trained local officials, by embassy staff or by post. Whatever process is used, controls are needed to prevent fraud. Registration cards and the data need to be secure in order to avoid duplication or loss. Controls over the distribution of cards and other materials and their return must be in place so that those handling them account for every item.

Prior to registration, the locations of potential electors have to be targeted as closely as possible. The communication plan devised to reach the eligible electors with information about the process will need to be reasonably specific. The information can be channelled through international organizations, local non-governmental organizations (NGOs) and community groups, as well as Internet websites.

External electors, especially refugees, often do not have official identification documents. Procedures need to be adopted to allow eligible electors to register using some other means of identification (e.g. United Nations High Commissioner for Refugees (UNHCR) records) or on oath. At the same time, the procedures have to ensure that non-eligible persons are not registering fraudulently. The procedures also have to give equal access to all eligible external electors, regardless of ethnicity or religion. Members of minority groups often find it more difficult among other things to establish their identification and citizenship, and may need more attention in the registration process.

Any special procedures must remain within the spirit of the existing legislation and may require amendments to the law. If the election officials in each host country make their own decisions about who is eligible or about what forms of identification will be accepted, this can have great ramifications for the acceptance of the results of an election.

The accurate registration of external electors can become a political issue, as happened in Guyana after the franchise was extended to non-resident electors after 1968:

> There were persistent allegations that the lists of overseas voters were often inaccurate and made without the prior knowledge or participation of the Elections Commission. The lists were said to be heavily padded with fictitious and ineligible voters, having an inaccuracy rate of about 75 percent of the entries. Voters were found to be living at non-existent addresses, in vacant lots, in open pastures and in abandoned premises. Another criticism levelled at overseas voting was that up to 95 percent of those votes went to the ruling party . . . [An amendment in 1985 attempted] to change the regime of overseas voting, but the basic scheme was left intact and remained flawed since it was susceptible to serious election manipulation (Dundas 1993: 145–6).

Legal methods for objecting to the registration of a name or correcting an entry on the register of external electors also need to be in place if the list is not integrated into the internal electoral register. Minimum standards must be met, similar to those that apply for internal registration, to ensure the integrity of the electoral registers.

## 8. External voting and the secret ballot

All the measures that are used to protect the secrecy of the vote internally must be duplicated in the external setting. The training of election workers, including any diplomats or members of the military who are involved in establishing polling stations, is an essential step in ensuring the integrity of the vote. In most cases it will be possible to duplicate the polling station procedures and voting procedures in the external polls. In other cases it may not be practical—for instance, if there are only a few electors. When a postal return system is used, extra steps are needed to ensure secrecy. This can prove difficult when a voter receives the ballot paper by post and marks it at home. It may be necessary to require voters to go to an embassy or a public institution to mark the ballot paper in secrecy. An instruction must be included with the ballot paper to inform the voter that he or she must mark the ballot paper in private and that any interference is a breach of the law.

The choice of polling station locations for personal voting is based on the registration information. However, contingency plans must be in place for changes in the status of electors. A large-scale return of refugees prior to polling day can affect the number and location of polling stations. There may also be numbers of externally registered electors who choose to return for voting day, wanting to vote in-country.

The ballot papers marked by external voters generally require the use of a series of envelopes to keep the ballot and the voter's identity secret at each step—at the poll, during return to the EMB, and finally at the count (see figure 5.1). The voter's identification is indicated on an outer envelope so it can be double-checked against the electoral register for eligibility and to prevent voting more than once. If it is a postal ballot, this envelope will also be pre-printed with the address of the EMB (or the organization that is administering the vote). An inner envelope, marked with the address of the body to which the ballot paper will be sent for the count, allows the ballot papers to be distributed to the proper national, provincial or municipal level. Finally, an unmarked inner envelope containing the actual ballot paper is placed in the appropriate ballot box for the count. Some combination of two or three envelopes will allow the voter's eligibility to be confirmed, the ballot paper to be delivered correctly and the ballot paper to be counted without it being traced back to the voter. This process in the vote is important and careful instructions will be needed so that the voters and the election officials understand the system and are fully confident in it.

Figure 5.1: Envelopes used for external voting

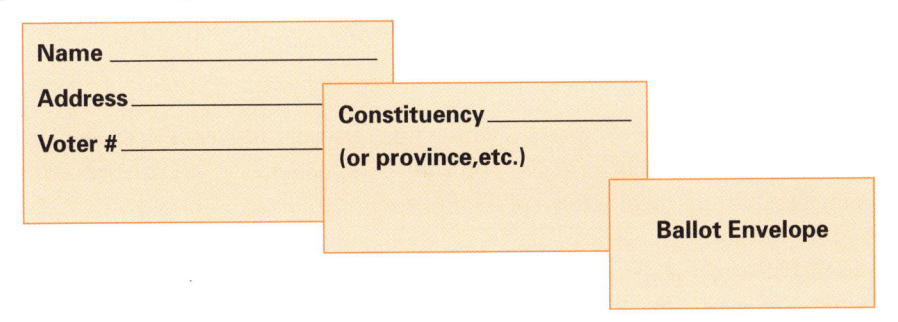

Decisions about how the ballot papers are counted are also an important part of the secrecy of the vote. If there are only a few external ballot papers, they may need to be mixed with internal ballot papers to prevent disclosure. For instance, in Lesotho in 1998 some provinces had only one external ballot paper, which was mixed with other ballot papers at a specified poll. If there are very large numbers of external ballots, the decision is often made to count them centrally either at the polling stations (as in Croatia in 1997) or after return to the EMB (as in South Africa in 1994 and Kosovo in 2000). The numbers are then added to the totals. Unfortunately, in post-conflict situations, the reconciliation process can break down, and sometimes political party representatives object to all external ballot papers at the count. This happened in Lesotho in 1998.

Security at the external registration and polling stations is often subsumed by the embassy or consulate where the station is located. Local police, if necessary, can enhance the security. If there is a specific threat or a perceived security risk such as during the 2005 Iraqi election, special arrangements are made for extra security procedures. This needs to be factored into the budget process. Observers and political party representatives are another integral part of the secrecy of the vote. These participants ensure that procedures are followed and that the secrecy of the vote is maintained at each step of the electoral process. It is often difficult for political parties to send representatives, so international observers have to be relied upon to carry out the duties of oversight of external voting.

International observers have been deployed to observe the external vote in some elections. However, the costs for international organizations to send observers to several countries for an external vote has led to other solutions. Diplomatic staff and other international staff (e.g. NGOs) in each country are often recruited to do the observation on behalf of an international organization. These observers are trained and report back to the organization, which prepares an overall report. The EMB also sends its own staff to each location to ensure procedures are followed.

## 9. Contracting out external voting

The electoral management body can run the election itself or contract it out. The latter option is unusual where an established EMB is in control of the electoral process, but is used more frequently in transitional elections with substantial direct input from the international community. The EMB in conjunction with the subcontractor will also need to interact with various government departments (e.g. the department for foreign affairs).

Prior to 1996, where it existed, external voting was a part of the overall election planning process. For instance, the refugee registration and voting operation in Cambodia in 1993 was an integral part of the functions of the Electoral Component of the United Nations Transitional Authority in Cambodia (UNTAC). However, for the 1996 election in Bosnia and Herzegovina, because of the scale of external voting, other approaches were considered. Refugees from Bosnia and Herzegovina were living in over 50 countries, but the largest numbers were in the neighbouring countries. The Organization for Security and Co-operation in Europe (OSCE) established a Steering Group to coordinate this task. The group worked with the International Centre for Migration Policy Development (ICMPD) and the IOM. Processes were established for registration and voting both by post (in most countries) and in person (in neighbouring countries). Subsequently, the IOM was contracted to manage the participation of refugees in the municipal elections in Bosnia and Herzegovina and later for the external voting in Kosovo (in 2000) and several other countries (see also chapter 7 and the case studies on Afghanistan, Bosnia and Herzegovina, and Iraq).

The contractor coordinates and liaises with the EMB and is responsible for infrastructure arrangements, information, registration, database preparation (in some cases), polling, and challenges to the inclusion of names on the electoral registers. The contractor can also be responsible for archiving and documentation.

## 10. Conclusions

As with the internal electoral process, the system to be used for external voting needs careful planning and implementation. It also needs to be methodically coordinated to ensure that all electors are treated equally under the relevant election law. The cost per voter for external voting will be higher than the cost for in-country voting but the budget will have to be integrated so that there is no discrimination against the external elector.

External voting adds complexity to the process but is a necessary part of extending the franchise to all eligible electors. 'Today we have come to assume that democracy must guarantee virtually every adult citizen the right to vote' (Dahl 1998: 3).

Although flexibility is important in order to meet the challenges, all decisions must be in compliance with the law. External voting, properly administered and implemented, will facilitate the democratic process and, in the case of refugee populations, encourage unity and reconciliation.

## CASE STUDY: Brazil

# Brazil: compulsory voting and renewed interest among external voters

Leticia Calderón-Chelius*

Paradoxically, it was in 1965, at the beginning of a military regime that was to last into the 1980s, that an arrangement was introduced in Brazil's electoral legislation to allow citizens living abroad to vote in presidential and vice-presidential elections for the first time. However, it was not until the return to democracy, starting in 1985—and more specifically within the framework of the new constitution, adopted in 1988— that the law was ratified and regulated and the conditions for the implementation of external voting were actually put in place. Since the external voting law was part of the democratization process in the Brazilian political system, the right to the external vote was not questioned. Politicians who discussed the topic assumed that Brazilians who had left the country had done so because of the political conditions under the dictatorship, and therefore democracy needed to recognize and guarantee their political rights.

External voting was implemented for the first presidential election after the return to democracy, in 1989, and from that time on Brazilian migrants have been able to exercise their right to vote in the subsequent presidential elections—in 1994, 1998, 2002 and 2006—including during the second electoral rounds under the Two-Round System.

The law states that the right to an external vote shall be limited to presidential and vice-presidential elections. In addition, for a plebiscite held on 21 April 1993, when the citizens were invited to define the system of government the nation would adopt (presidential or parliamentary) and to choose between a republican system and a monarchy, exceptional arrangements were approved so that Brazilians living abroad could participate in this type of plebiscite. Although there has not been any other experience of this kind, a precedent had been set so that external voting could be allowed in other kinds of electoral event.

## Entitlement to an external vote

The right to vote externally extends to every elector abroad who has Brazilian nationality, including those who have acquired another nationality, but only when they have

---

* Isabel Morales assisted with updating this case study.

done so as a condition of remaining in the foreign country or of exercising their civil rights, because this is the only situation in which Brazilian legislation acknowledges dual nationality. Thus, every Brazilian citizen by birth or by naturalization, and those with dual nationality, retain the right and the obligation to participate in presidential elections.

According to the electoral legislation, the right to an external vote does not extend to those who are outside the country temporarily or provisionally or to those who are not formally resident abroad, such as students, temporary workers or tourists. However, it has to be said that the legislation does not establish precise criteria for the application of this rule; indeed, the dynamics of international migration make it impossible to determine clearly who is formally and definitively a migrant. Thus all those Brazilian citizens who register in time as external electors at an embassy or consulate are qualified to vote.

## Compulsory voting and the external vote

Voting is compulsory in Brazil, and this extends to external electors. Those external electors who do not vote have to justify their abstention; if they do not they will be forced to pay a fine as soon as they return to the country. If they do not pay the fine, they become subject to a series of sanctions which come into effect two months after their return to the country. Among those sanctions are the following.

- They cannot apply for any public position or function.
- They cannot receive any remuneration or salary from a public post.
- There are restrictions on the types of loan they can obtain from federal or local government sources, or from any credit institution administered totally or partially by the government.
- There are restrictions on their obtaining a passport or identity card.
- There are restrictions on their renewing their teaching licences in public educational institutions or those that are controlled by the government.

## The mechanism for external voting

The current legislation provides that external voting will be done in person at Brazilian embassies and consulates worldwide, where electors are registered according to their address in the foreign country. All the procedures for registering and voting are the responsibility of the diplomatic mission, and it is the diplomatic missions which compile and send the lists of electors registered for each electoral event to the Ministry of Foreign Affairs in Brasilia. An electoral judge from the First Zone of the Federal District approves the new electoral registers, cancels the previous registers and produces the ballot papers. This material is then sent to the diplomatic mission concerned, which is responsible for notifying electors of the date of the election and place where they are to vote.

While responsibility for the legislative issues related to external voting lies essentially in the Superior Electoral Tribunal (Tribunal Electoral Superior, TSE), implementation is shared by the Ministry of Foreign Affairs and the Regional Electoral Tribunal of the Federal District.

For an electoral centre overseas to be accredited, it must have at least 30 external electors registered. If there are more than 400, a new electoral centre has to be installed at some official building that is the property of the Brazilian Government. The Regional Electoral Tribunal of the Federal District appoints the staff at the voting centres in the first round as well as in the second electoral round, taking into account the suggestions of those in charge of the respective diplomatic missions.

All the material used during the entire electoral process—ballot papers and so on—is supplied by the TSE, which must dispatch it at least 72 hours prior to the election. The voting centres should be open at the same times as they are open in-country, allowing for different time zones. After the counting, the results are sent to the Regional Electoral Tribunal of the Federal District by diplomatic telex. This procedure allows the results of the external vote to be included in the general results immediately. The ballot papers are then placed in a special envelope which is sent by diplomatic bag to the TSE in Brasilia.

The procedure for external voting has remained essentially the same since the first experience in 1989. Through the different elections, some adjustments have been made to the electoral law (defined by the TSE as resolutions) renewing and adapting procedures when considered appropriate. For instance, during the 1998 presidential election computers were installed in Brazil itself to allow electronic voting, but it was not possible to use this method abroad because of the high costs. Electronic devices are now used for voting throughout the country, but for external voting the traditional ballot paper was still in use until the presidential election of 2006; then the TSE authorized 240 electronic 'urns' to be sent to 30 countries where Brazilians are concentrated abroad (out of 91 in all). The biggest group is in the United States, where 32,000 potential voters out of 86,360 in all on the electoral register of citizens abroad were registered. There are also considerable groups of Brazilian migrants in Canada, Germany, Italy, Portugal and the United Kingdom.

## Turnout

Although the figures for registration and turnout abroad are not high, they illustrate some interesting trends. For the 1994 presidential election there were 39,367 electors registered abroad, of whom 27,831 voted—a 70 per cent turnout. In 1998, the number of electors registered abroad increased by almost 20 per cent, to 47,961, but only 21,844 (45.5 per cent) voted. For the 2002 presidential election, registration increased to 69,937 electors—almost 45 per cent more than four years before. The presidential election had to be decided in a second round of voting; in the first round, 38,618 external electors voted (55.5 per cent) and in the second round 36,043 (51.7 per cent). These figures indicate a sustained increase in voter registration abroad and fairly stable turnout. Then, in the presidential election of October 2006, when President Lula da Silva was re-elected, almost 50 per cent of the registered Brazilians abroad voted in the first and second rounds.

## Challenges

There are two major challenges in the implementation of external voting for Brazilian citizens.

The first is that the period allowed for voter registration has not been established with precision. It is usually modified from one election to another and, in general, it has been considered short (between a month and two months and a half prior to the election). This has caused confusion and has left some potential voters excluded from the electoral process. To mitigate this problem, the period of electoral registration abroad needs to be clearly defined, and the tendency to extend the period of registration should continue.

The second challenge lies in the fact that the electoral authorities have no programme to promote registration among Brazilian citizens abroad, with the result that the call to register as external electors has succeeded only among those abroad who are politically involved, and has not even always been successful among those who are not consistently involved in associations or groups linked to political life in Brazil. This is one of the Achilles heels of the Brazilian system of external voting. However, this same situation has given rise to increasing interest on the part of the activists from the political parties in participating in the political life of their country of origin—mainly the supporters of the party currently in power, the Labour Party (Partido Trabalhista, PT). In this context Brazil is currently witnessing a novel process whereby candidates are promoting themselves abroad. During the presidential election campaign of 2002, in the two cities that have the largest concentrations of Brazilian citizens abroad—Boston in the United States and Lisbon in Portugal—expatriate groups demanded that the candidates, and specifically the candidate of the PT, Luiz Inacio Lula da Silva, include in their political agenda a section about Brazilian migrants. This had a direct impact on Brazilian people's perceptions about the migration of their fellow nationals, as well as in the redefinition of Brazil's migration policy, during the first term of President Lula da Silva's regime. This fact alone shows the importance of the external vote in Brazil.

Even though only a relatively small proportion of eligible electors abroad vote, the strength of the external voting provision lies in the facts (a) that it guarantees the political rights of the citizens and (b) that it includes those who, whatever their geographical location, decide to maintain a close bond with their country.

Finally, it should be stressed that the costs associated with the implementation of external voting are part, and only represent a small share, of the operating expenses of the electoral management body, and are not the subject of any controversy.

CASE STUDY: Honduras

# Honduras: a decision based on political calculations

Jacobo Hernández Cruz

As a fundamental part of the process of democratic change in Honduras which took place when power was transferred from a military to a civilian government, the Electoral and Political Organizations Law was approved in November 1979. This law was to govern the election of members of the Constituent National Assembly, who were trusted with writing a new constitutional text.

Article 10 of that law recognized specifically that Honduran citizens residing abroad would have the opportunity to vote in the election for deputies to the Constituent National Assembly as long as they were in the country on election day and were registered in the National Electoral Census—which cannot be considered as external voting in the strict sense of the term.

However, external voting in the true sense was provided for two years later. The Constituent National Assembly, installed in June 1980, not only wrote the new constitutional text, which was promulgated in January 1982, but also issued a new Electoral and Political Organizations Law with the purpose of calling the Honduran people to general elections to the presidency, to be held in November 1981. In the new electoral legislation, the vote for Honduran citizens who were resident outside the national territory was considered again, and this time specifically voting from abroad. However, its implementation was put on hold until the appropriate conditions in the organization of electoral affairs were in place (article 11) and until the electoral management body (the National Electoral Tribunal) was able to decide on the detailed regulation of external voting by a unanimous vote of its members.

The provision in fact was not implemented for almost 20 years because the right conditions never occurred for the electoral authority (the National Electoral Tribunal became the Supreme Electoral Tribunal in 2004) to proceed with its effective assessment and regulation. By initiative of the then ruling party, the Liberal Party of Honduras, the Congress, at the end of 2000, approved a decree that gave the National Electoral Tribunal three months in which to regulate the voting by Hondurans abroad within the terms of article 11 of the electoral law. The decree stipulated that if the electoral body did not fulfil this mandate within that time frame it would be up to the National Congress to develop and decide on the regulation.

The members of the National Electoral Tribunal did not reach unanimous agreement within the time stipulated, and the responsibility of preparing the regulation was indeed transferred to the Congress. Accordingly, it was the president of the Congress (who at the time was virtually a candidate for the presidency of the republic, expected to stand as the candidate of the National Party) to take the initiative on the regulation of voting for abroad, which, if approved, would be applied for the presidential election to be held in late 2001.

In spite of objections by the opposition and counter-arguments related to the high financial cost of external voting and to the lack of consultation with other interested sectors, by the end of May 2001 a majority in the Congress had approved the Special Law for the Exercise of Suffrage of Hondurans Abroad, thereby restoring this potential benefit for nearly 600,000 Honduran citizens who were permanently resident abroad.

This was clearly the result of a political calculation by the ruling party. There is also no doubt that the amount of money remitted to Honduras by residents abroad (known as the 'economic mattress', and estimated at the time at 1 billion US dollars (USD) per year), was also influential in the decision to approve this law.

The special law established that external voting for Hondurans living abroad will only apply for presidential elections; that the consular offices will be considered as auxiliary electoral bodies, which implies that voting will be in-person in these precincts (postal voting from abroad is not possible), and that it is up to the electoral authority to select the cities where electors will be able to vote. In spite of all of the above, it was decided that in the presidential election of 2001 external voting would be carried out but only in six cities in the United States—New Orleans, Miami, Washington, New York, Los Angeles and Houston. These cities were selected because it was estimated that they were home to the great majority of Hondurans living abroad. The same cities were chosen to organize external voting in the presidential election of 2005, although it was not possible to offer it in all of them.

## Voter registration and electoral logistics abroad

For the implementation of external voting by Hondurans abroad in the 2001 and 2005 presidential elections, a Local Electoral Board was established in each of the consular offices of the six US cities selected. These boards were formed by a representative of the consular office plus a representative of each legally recognized political party (there were only five at the time) and were to administer and supervise the entire electoral process, including the establishment of the electoral register.

The law establishes that to vote from outside the national territory Honduran citizens residing abroad must be registered in the National Electoral Census. To achieve this, they must present themselves at the corresponding consulate, register on a preliminary list, and provide their general information, current address and identity card number. It is important to note that potential voters must possess an identity card in order to register and vote abroad.

For the 2001 presidential election, Honduran residents abroad in those jurisdictions had a period of over a month, from 1 July to 5 August, in which to request registration on the preliminary electoral register. For the 2005 election the registration period also finished in early August, since the Special Law for the Exercise of Suffrage of Hondurans

Abroad states that all consulates must issue the preliminary list of electors abroad before 25 August of the year of the election. In both the 2001 and the 2005 elections there were complaints about the short time allowed to register. Many Honduran citizens abroad do not have a Honduran identity card, so, in accordance with the Special Law, the office of the electoral authority which was in charge of issuing the unique identity cards sent specialist technical personnel in to the six selected cities where voting was to take place to deal with all requests for the granting, renewal or replacement of identity cards. All requests are sent to the national registry which issues the ID cards and then sent them back to the consulates in September and October to be delivered to the citizens concerned.

Citizens of Honduran origin who are naturalized in the USA or in another country and have not recovered their Honduran citizenship, according to the provisions of the constitution, cannot participate in this process.

The National Electoral Tribunal is responsible for integrating the definitive list of electors abroad and sending it, together with all the materials and electoral documentation, via the Foreign Ministry, to those consular offices that are qualified to act as auxiliary election bodies one month before polling day. The law establishes that if the name of an elector does not appear in the definitive list prepared by the electoral authority, that person cannot cast a vote.

According to the special law, the polling abroad is carried out the same day as the general elections in Honduras.

The law does not include specific provisions concerning election campaign activities abroad, but these take place by means of personal contacts, printed campaign literature, and messages in some Spanish-language broadcasts.

## Turnout

The definitive register of electors abroad for the 2001 election included 10,826 Hondurans, of whom only 4,541, or 42 per cent, voted. The table shows how they were distributed.

Table 1: Voting by Hondurans abroad in the 2001 presidential election

| City | No. of registered electors | No. of votes cast |
|---|---|---|
| Miami | 3,590 | 1,770 |
| Houston | 1,599 | 519 |
| Washington | 982 | 399 |
| New York | 2,196 | 676 |
| Los Angeles | 1,665 | 678 |
| New Orleans | 794 | 499 |
| Total | **10,826** | **3,931** |

At the time of the most recent presidential election, in 2005, it was estimated that a total of 1 million Hondurans were living in the United States, most of whom held ID cards. At 11,590, the total number of external electors registered was not much larger than the total in 2001. Moreover, even when the electoral authority knew about the apathy or lack of interest on the part of Hondurans living abroad in voting, they did not expect the very low turnout obtained in this second experience.

On this occasion, only 336 valid external votes were cast. This situation was caused by more than one factor. First, the external voting in New Orleans was cancelled because of Hurricane Katrina in August 2005. In New York the electoral officer of the two polling stations experienced problems and decided to suspend the election. Then the Miami and Washington ballot papers were not certificated, so they could not be taken to the data processing centre. The number of votes cast in these cities was estimated at 400. Of the two ballot boxes installed in Houston, only one was considered valid. So, in the end, only one urn from Houston and the ballot papers from Los Angeles were counted.

Table 2: Voting by Hondurans abroad in the 2005 presidential election

| Political party | Houston | Los Angeles | |
|---|---|---|---|
| Pinu | 5 | 2 | |
| National Party | 50 | 115 | |
| Liberal Party | 58 | 92 | |
| Democratic Unification (UD) | 1 | 4 | |
| Christian Democracy (DC) | 2 | 7 | |
| Total | 116 | 220 | 336 |

## The costs of external voting

The costs of the first implementation of voting abroad—in 2001—amounted to 10 million lempiras (HNL—c. 600,000 USD). The high costs, the low rates of registration and participation, and the presumed discord or political polarization in the Honduran communities abroad as a result of the electoral competition, have given rise to different criticisms and demands for this regulation to be reviewed, and even repealed. The Supreme Electoral Tribunal recognizes that the second experience of external voting was a failure. Improving this mechanism is a major challenge for the electoral authority. However, even though there has been talk of abolishing the Special Law for the Exercise of Suffrage of Hondurans Abroad, the introduction of external voting by post for the next election is still being considered.

# CHAPTER 6

# 6. Host country issues

Brett Lacy

This chapter explores the political aspects of organizing elections in another country. It addresses issues that pertain to the roles and responsibilities of the countries which host foreign nationals voting in elections of their country of origin, including security, the prevention of fraud, electoral registration, election campaigning, voter information and education, and the costs to the host country of external voting programmes. Finally, it offers some guidelines for institutional arrangements that address these and other issues. However, as the context of each and every external voting programme is different and may require different procedures and processes to be in place, they should be considered as broad guidelines only.

External voting has two main purposes: it is a means of ensuring the realization of political rights for people living outside their country, and it is a means of increasing political participation and thereby building trust and confidence in electoral processes and the democratic governments they produce. Growing cross-border migration has produced populations that are excluded from politics in both their home countries and their countries of residence. If a part of the population is excluded from the electoral process, the resulting system of governance suffers from a lack of legitimacy, accountability and sustainability, particularly in fragile democracies or post-conflict environments.

Despite making a critical contribution to democratization, external voting has not been used extensively—partly because it is perceived as straining financial, security and human resources, but also because of the complexities of negotiating with governments which may be potentially eligible electors, particularly when those electors are refugees or undocumented migrant workers. Conducting external voting presents a number of organizational and political issues, many of which can be addressed by the establishment of certain institutional arrangements in coordination with host countries.

## 1. Negotiating with host countries

Negotiating with host governments is one of the main challenges in developing external voting systems. Decisions regarding external voting, including the roles and responsibilities of host countries, are often made hastily against tight timetables. Moreover there is little clarity within the international community regarding who has the mandate to advocate, facilitate and evaluate external voting. There are no consistent policies, practices or standards to guide host governments on the question of foreign electoral activities being conducted on their soil, much less the responsibilities of host governments. Processes chosen build on a mix of precedents, relations, and ad hoc opportunities.

Host countries can be selected for external voting on the basis of a number of criteria, including histories of bilateral, regional or international relations. Other criteria can include the availability of resources, the existence of support infrastructures, and anticipated costs. Perhaps the most important would be the estimated numbers of potential voters they host. Countries which have hosted external electors range from those hosting refugees from a neighbouring country or regional conflict, to those hosting members of a diaspora and those hosting foreign workers. They vary in size, culture, language and infrastructure, as well as their level of development, type of government, foreign relations, human rights standards, and degree of democratization.

Despite these differences, host governments often share the same concerns about security, stability and sovereignty. Each of these concerns contributes to resistance to the idea of the political activity of a foreign country occurring on the host country's soil. States generally exhibit greater willingness when there is motivation, such as international advocacy and pressure, support for an identified political cause of the eligible electors they host, or sympathy for a particular religious or ethnic group (Newland 2001). Although these sympathies can sometimes be positive motivators, more often such political 'baggage' hinders the universal realization of the human right to political participation, threatening the consolidation of democracy and ultimately threatening international peace and security.

When external electors are refugee populations, their status, under international protection, mandates the participation of host governments in advocacy, facilitation and decision-making roles. However, the national interests of these governments, particularly in complex regional contexts, often influence their participation and the degree of international support for external voting.

Foreign relations and negotiations are generally outside the responsibilities of electoral commissions, and exceed their capacities. To negotiate external voting agreements with host countries, therefore, countries generally employ their diplomatic missions. In Estonia and Indonesia, for example, the respective ministries of foreign affairs not only negotiate host country agreements but are responsible for the coordination of external voting programmes.

Some governments have refused to allow foreign electoral activity within their borders. Switzerland, for example, did not allow foreigners to vote in foreign elections on its soil until 1989 (see the case study). Governments hosting Liberian (1997, 2005) and Cambodian (1993) refugees did not allow electoral activities, forcing refugees to repatriate in order to exercise their right to political participation and threatening the credibility of the electoral process and the sustainability of peace. In the case of Bosnia and Herzegovina (1996), some European countries refused to allow out-of-country voting on their soil, and in these countries registration and voting were carried out exclusively by post. Of the countries that have not allowed foreign electoral activity on their soil, some have a law that prevents such activity, while others have refused such requests for reasons ranging from sovereignty to security to politics. When a host country does resist foreign electoral activity taking place on its soil, fear of its sovereignty being violated is often the primary concern. Many scholars today are reframing the concept of sovereignty as one that is not territorial but rather based on a moral foundation of rights and obligations to a population that may transcend fixed geographical boundaries (see chapter 3). Such a morally based non-territorial conception of sovereignty suggests that external voting is not a violation of a host country's sovereignty but rather a means of the country of origin fulfilling its obligations as a sovereign to its people through the extension of the rights of political participation to all its citizens, wherever they may reside.

Canada is one of the countries that allow external voting within their borders only by post or inside foreign consulates and embassies. However, in the case of Iraq, given the lack of diplomatic missions, the tight time frame, Canada's overall support for democratization in Iraq and (presumably) considerable international pressure, Canada made a unique exception for the January 2005 Iraq National Assembly election to allow external voting in other locations within the country. However, other Canadian policies, such as a ban on campaigning, remained in full effect.

## 2. The roles and responsibilities of host countries

The roles and responsibilities of host countries in external voting programmes have ranged widely depending on context, available resources, and the degree of international interest and support. In most cases the duties and responsibilities of countries hosting foreign electoral activity on their soil are minimal, being confined to the role of facilitator rather than that of organizer or implementer. While host countries can assist in the external voting process, their role should not threaten the secrecy of the ballot or the neutrality or transparency of the programme. It is critical that external voting programmes be conducted without political or government influence or interference.

The following are some of the areas where host countries can play a role in external voting programmes:

- providing and protecting data, including demographic information;

- locating suitable office space;
- ensuring freedom of movement (of election staff, monitors and observers, party officials and voters);
- providing customs clearances for election materials, including ballot papers;
- providing permits;
- providing travel documents, including visas;
- waiving any taxes or other fees;
- assisting in the recruitment of staff;
- providing adequate security; and
- facilitating the deployment of election observers, monitors, and political party agents.

*Providing data.* A primary role of host countries in external voting programmes has been to provide a range of data and information to facilitate the process. Demographic data can help with estimating the numbers of eligible electors and identifying where they are resident within the host country, and can contribute to determining where registration and voting will take place. Data on infrastructure within host countries can also assist an external voting programme.

*Data protection.* It is essential that any data collected as part of an external voting programme be protected. Ensuring data protection can be a critical component of the overall programme, as the lack of adequate data protection can directly influence turnout. Any information on individuals eligible to participate in the vote that may come into the hands of the host country as a result of the external voting programme should be used exclusively for the external voting programme. These obligations should extend permanently beyond the expiry of any memoranda of understanding (MOUs) or agreements signed by the host country.

*Identifying locations.* In addition to providing data, host countries can help by making public facilities and similar premises available as registration and polling sites, or with identifying suitable premises for election activities or for temporary office space as needed. However, while host countries can help by providing information, it is important that the country conducting the election make the decisions regarding registration and polling sites. (In the Iraq case (January 2005), the United States emphasized that its role was simply that of a facilitator and that it did not have any authority in deciding on registration and voting sites.) The number and location of registration and polling sites can influence turnout and possibly affect election results, particularly where travel costs are high and are borne by voters themselves.

*Freedom of movement.* Host countries can help by facilitating and supporting the freedom of movement of election staff, monitors and observers, political party officials and potential voters. Such assistance can include the provision of multiple entry visas or travel permits in a timely fashion. Additionally, host countries can ensure any air, land or sea clearances or permissions necessary for the transport of persons or materials related to the external voting programme. Host countries may also subsidize travel costs or otherwise facilitate voters' travel to register and to vote.

*Customs.* Host countries can ensure that all necessary customs clearances and permits will be provided for any equipment and materials that may need to be brought into the country in order to conduct the external voting programme. This can include waiving taxes or other fees. However, in the case of the Iraqi external voting programme in Canada, Canada did not recognize the facilitating organization, the International Organization for Migration (IOM), as having any special legal status in Canada, and therefore did not consider the IOM to be eligible for any visa waivers, immunity or duty-free treatment. In fact, Canada specifically held that any imported election material would have to go through the normal customs clearance procedures.

*Legality of residency and documentation.* In some cases there may be eligible electors who are undocumented or residing illegally in the host country. The legality of one's residency does not affect one's right to political participation: undocumented or illegal residents in host countries have legal citizenship in their countries of origin and the rights and responsibilities that come with that citizenship, including the right to vote. However, the government of the country conducting the election may wish to negotiate with the host country to ensure that participation does not result in deportation or other potentially harmful ramifications for individuals. Such risks could significantly affect levels of participation, and could affect turnout unequally across sectors of a population, thus threatening the legitimacy of the election in the eyes of some citizens.

*Points of contact.* Host country responsibilities can include the appointment of points of contact in relevant government offices to assist in the processes of issuing visas or permits, customs clearance, providing security, and other matters.

*Staff.* Recruiting and training staff to run election-related activities in host countries, including electoral registration and polling, can be logistically and financially challenging. While host countries can provide invaluable help by providing data to assist with identifying and locating potential staff, the recruitment, hiring and training of staff should generally be conducted under the direct supervision of the country of origin or its designees.

In the case of the 2004 Afghanistan elections, when external voting was conducted in neighbouring Pakistan and Iran, the IOM, with a mandate from the Afghan Joint Electoral Management Body (JEMB), recruited and trained international and national core staff, community mobilizers, and registration and polling station staff. Overall, thousands of staff were recruited, the majority of them (95 per cent) Afghan nationals, and hiring policies maintained a gender and ethnic balance at all staffing levels. Training was conducted in less than one week. In the case of the 2005 Iraq elections, a number of host countries paid particular attention to staffing issues. Turkey, for example, specified that any locally recruited staff must have clean judicial records. Germany specified that any staff must be subject to local labour laws.

*Security.* Ensuring security, in terms of both the physical safety and security of participants, staff and materials, and the integrity of the electoral process itself, is of critical importance. External voting poses unique challenges in both these respects. Cooperation between host countries and the country of origin is essential to ensuring that the external voting programme is conducted in an atmosphere that is free of violence, intimidation or coercion.

While there are no clear standards or best practices in this highly sensitive area, it is generally most convenient and cost-effective for the host country to provide security during the electoral event. Other alternatives could be the use of international peacekeepers (in appropriate situations) or the use of private security companies. One of the most important questions when considering security provisions is whether freedom and security can be guaranteed in external voting programmes to the same degree as within the country of origin.

Agreements with host countries generally include specific security stipulations, particularly regarding registration and voting sites and the transport of election materials. Agreements can specify support from local and national police and security forces and can establish communications structures between the host state and election administrators. Where additional training may be required for the forces providing security, election officials and administrators can make recommendations regarding training and observe the process.

During the external voting programmes in the 2004 Afghanistan and January 2005 Iraq elections, the host countries provided security for registration and polling sites in most cases. They also assisted with providing security for the movement of election materials. For Iraqis voting in the United States, the responsibility (and costs) fell on local law enforcement agencies. The US Government facilitated the provision of adequate security by informing state and local authorities and encouraging them to work with the IOM, which ran the external voting programme. In Germany, the IOM was ultimately responsible for maintaining order at registration and voting sites, while German security and order agencies were responsible for maintaining security outside the locations where registration and voting took place.

*Preventing fraud.* One of the most serious obstacles to external voting has been the view that it opens additional avenues to fraud which can undermine the entire electoral process. Some observers have argued that the introduction of external voting in countries with a history of electoral fraud can undermine the public's confidence in the process and threaten the consolidation of democracy.

While ensuring the integrity of the electoral process itself and preventing fraud are generally the responsibility of the country holding the election, host countries can help by guaranteeing certain safeguards to protect against fraud. The host country may be able to provide invaluable assistance in this regard, particularly in terms of sharing data.

*Electoral registration.* The conduct of the electoral registration is a critical component of external voting programmes. The role of host countries in the registration process is extremely sensitive and highly political, particularly where host countries may have an interest in the outcome of the election or may have ethnic, religious or other ties to the country conducting the election. While host countries may have a role in the registration process, usually through providing demographic data, it is important that protection is put in place to prevent foreign governments from influencing the outcome of an election by screening the registration process and thus 'engineering' turnout.

Even where polling does not take place on foreign soil, timetables may make it necessary to conduct electoral registration or other activities out-of-country, particularly where time does not allow full repatriation of refugee communities before registration takes place. In the case of the 1993 Cambodian elections, Cambodian laws prohibited any electoral activity on foreign soil. As a consequence, refugees were forced to return in order to participate in the election. However, the repatriation of Cambodians from Thailand progressed more slowly than had been expected, thus affecting electoral registration timetables and jeopardizing the integrity of the electoral process. In order to register returnees in time, the United Nations and the Thai Government reached an agreement to allow most of the registration process to be conducted in Thailand. However, because Cambodia's electoral law did not allow for electors to register on foreign soil, electors did not receive registration cards until they reached Cambodia. (For additional discussion, see Gallagher and Schowengerdt October 1997 and 1998: 205.) In this case a combination of in- and out-of-country electoral activity was devised to ensure enfranchisement.

*Information dissemination: campaigning, voter information and civic education.* Host government cooperation, support and facilitation of the dissemination of information, including campaign materials as well as voter and civic education, is critical to the success of any external voting programme. In the Eritrean referendum of 1991, for example, Sudan's cooperation and initiative were essential to the education of voters in refugee camps.

Host governments can help in information campaigns of all types by making available local and national forms of electronic and print media, including television and radio, for the purposes of the electoral process. When external voting is being conducted in refugee camps, voter information and education should be tied to existing communication systems, particularly those linked to refugee priorities such as food and shelter.

External voting also poses questions about whether external electors will have less, equal or greater access to information than their counterparts in the country of origin. For example, Bosnian refugees in 1996 had access to the international press and other sources of information, while electors within Bosnia and Herzegovina had access to more limited media. Administrators of external voting programmes must consider whether differences in access to information might influence the overall integrity of the process or the outcome of the election. These differences become particularly important where one group of electors is limited by its access to government-controlled or otherwise unbalanced media.

The campaign period can be critical to an electoral process, providing potential voters with essential information about the choices before them. Where campaigning is allowed, host governments can help by authorizing candidates to campaign within the guidelines of any codes of conduct that may exist. While most countries do permit voter and civic education activities, it is not uncommon for a country to prohibit foreign nationals from campaigning on its soil. In the January 2005 Iraq elections, neither Turkey nor Canada allowed foreign political parties to conduct election campaigns on their soil.

Campaigning aside, the distribution of general political information is highly sensitive. In the case of the 1997 Liberian elections, not only did host governments resist external voting on their soil, but they also banned the dissemination of election-related information within their borders. For Bosnian electors in Croatia, the 1997 MOU between Croatia and the Refugee Elections Steering Group (RESG), an ad hoc organization tasked with coordinating Bosnia's out-of-country voting, prevented Bosnian political parties from campaigning on Croatian soil and limited the types of voter and civic educational materials that could be distributed to small brochures in the Croatian and Serbian languages 'in order not to provoke other nationalities' (Gallagher and Schowengerdt 1998: 202).

## 3. Host country agreements

The actors who help in the conduct of out-of-country voting programmes and the parties that sign formal agreements with the country conducting the election vary. Agreements can be signed with host governments, UN missions, local non-governmental organizations (NGOs) or third parties.

When external voting is taking place in multiple countries, host country agreements often vary from country to country. A certain level of standardization between agreements is critical to ensuring the transparency and integrity of the electoral process, particularly regarding sensitive issues such as elector eligibility and registration. However, when an election is conducted in multiple countries which are at varying levels of development, some procedural and logistical differences may be unavoidable.

Examples of host country agreements include those signed in connection with the 2004 presidential election in Afghanistan—the largest external voting programme to date in terms of numbers of registered electors and external turnout. The government of Afghanistan and the UN Assistance Mission in Afghanistan (UNAMA) signed two MOUs with the governments of Iran and Pakistan, respectively. These MOUs stipulated that the two host governments would provide widespread support for the external voting programme, including security for registration and polling centres, escorts for the transport of election material, and support for civic education and public information campaigns.

## 3.1. The role of third parties

Often, external voting can be arranged through agreements directly between the host country and the electoral management body that is conducting the election. However, in cases where the country of origin may only have a few democratic elections under its belt or may not have sufficient infrastructure, third parties can be contracted to help in implementing the external voting programme. The IOM has played this role in Bosnia and Herzegovina, East Timor, Kosovo and, most recently, Afghanistan and Iraq. Where a third party is involved, the agreement with the host country must provide for this participation. In addition to serving where there may be a gap in infrastructure, particularly when an election timetable is short, third parties can also be an important safeguard against any possible political or governmental influence from any host country. It is imperative that third parties serve as implementers only and ensure that all questions of a political nature are left to the appropriate governments. The use of third parties can add significantly to the costs of external voting programmes.

## 3.2. General guidelines for host country agreements

When negotiating host agreements to facilitate external voting programmes, there are a number of important criteria that must be recognized and protected.

First and foremost, all parties must ensure the secrecy, neutrality and transparency of the external voting programme, without local political or governmental influence or interference. Host country agreements must also protect the integrity of the constitution and electoral laws of the country holding the election. External voting programmes should be designed to mirror the administrative activities of the country of origin as closely as possible.

In addition, host country agreements should ensure that participation in external voting in no way affects the political, social or economic inclusion of participating persons within their country of residence. Some host country agreements from the January 2005 Iraqi elections state clearly that the eligibility of an individual living outside Iraq to vote, or the exercise of this right, in no way affected the individual's legal status in the host country.

As is mentioned above, it may also be necessary for some components of a host country agreement, particularly those that protect any data collected during the process, to remain in force after the expiry of any agreement or MOU. Such a clause would be particularly appropriate to protect against the sharing of any information gathered during the external voting programme for purposes other than facilitating the vote.

Where external electors are refugees, agreements can also ensure that electoral participation does not become a means of forced or premature repatriation of these populations before conditions to support their return are in place. Agreements can specify that the external voting programme will neither prevent nor delay the voluntary repatriation of refugees living in the host country. A number of MOUs between the IOM and countries hosting Iraqi refugees included language along these lines to ensure that the principle of non-refoulement—the principle enshrined in the 1951 Convention Relating to the Status of Refugees that no state shall expel or return a refugee to a territory where his or her life or freedom would be threatened on account of race, religion, nationality or political opinion—was respected. In contrast, in the case of Bosnia and Herzegovina, where external voting was largely by post, the Dayton Agreement stipulated refugee repatriation during the electoral period by stating that 'the exercise of a refugee's right to vote shall be interpreted as confirmation of his or her intention to return to Bosnia and Herzegovina. By election day, the return of refugees should already be under way, thus allowing many to participate in person'. When an electoral process defines the end of a peace agreement (and an end to corresponding humanitarian and refugee assistance programmes), there is a risk that obliging refugees to return to their country of origin in order to vote will violate the principle of non-refoulement.

### 3.3. External voting in consulates, in embassies or by post

Some host countries, such as Canada and some European countries, only allow external voting in embassies or consulates, or by post. When external voting takes place at a country's consulates or embassies, agreements with host countries are often not necessary. Similarly, when external polling is to take place by postal registration and voting, the need for agreements with host countries is less pressing. However, agreements can still be essential in ensuring critical host country support.

In the case of the 1996 Bosnia and Herzegovina elections, registration for external voting was carried out almost exclusively by post, and voting took place through a combination of postal and in-person polling, depending on the number of refugees within each host country. Coordination offices were set up in 17 countries and served to disseminate information and facilitate registration and voting. These offices were established through a serious of MOUs between the RESG and the major host governments. The nature of these agreements and the roles and responsibilities of each host country varied considerably. In the United Kingdom, refugee agencies were used to disseminate information. In the United States, an NGO, the League of Women Voters Education Fund, was used (Gallagher and Schowengerdt 1998: 206–7). In Germany, the government funded and administered an office that facilitated the registration and voting processes.

## 4. Costs

Past external voting programmes, particularly those in post-conflict contexts, have been funded through widely differing mechanisms. Chapter 5 discusses the general aspects of the cost of external voting, but these present particular problems where host countries are concerned. Many consider it important that the costs borne by host countries be kept to a minimum, for a number of reasons. First, minimizing the costs borne by host countries will contribute to ensuring that cost is not a factor in host countries' decisions on whether or not to allow foreigners to vote on their soil. Second, it will help to protect the electoral process itself from any potential interference by others who may have a stake in the outcome of the election.

Generally, countries that have a longer history of democratic elections and have a more established electoral process tend to fund external voting programmes themselves. In the cases of post-conflict societies, costs tend to be shouldered by the international community, either through direct assistance to the electoral commission or government conducting the election or by other means. For external voting in Bosnian elections, for example, host countries have both funded and administered electoral activities. For these elections in the United States, the US Department of State made a grant to the League of Women Voters Education Fund to facilitate absentee voting.

The majority of costs are borne by the country of origin or the international community. An important exception is that host countries typically assume the costs of providing security for the registration and polling activities. A second cost typically borne by host countries is the provision or loan of certain election materials, such as ballot boxes, for use in the election. External voting programmes can increase their appeal to host countries when implementing partners agree to purchase any materials and equipment from domestic markets wherever possible. This was a component of Syria's MOU with the IOM during the 2005 Iraq National Assembly elections.

For the January 2005 Iraqi elections, some host countries provided security at their own expense, while others did so only with the financial support of the IOM. For example, Turkey's MOU with the IOM for the Iraqi external voting programme stated that the government of Turkey would provide appropriate places for the establishment of election centres, but the costs of these locations would be borne by the IOM. It also specified that the IOM would pay in advance a specified amount per election centre for security (65,000 US dollars (USD)) and issue an additional advance for the transport of election materials (10,000 USD).

Where external electors are refugees under international protection, international law does provide some guidance regarding the costs of refugee assistance. It embodies a principle of 'equal burden-sharing', recognizing that all states have a duty to provide assistance to refugees. This principle is designed to prevent the 'burden' of refugees from falling disproportionately on states neighbouring a conflict, which could possibly cause them to close their borders. The principle of equal burden-sharing is also designed to prevent refugees from becoming a source of tension between states. (The use of the word 'burden-sharing' is unfortunate as there is a growing literature that explores essential contributions of refugees to their host countries, but the basic principle of the international community sharing responsibilities to minimize tension is an important one. See Bouchet-Saulnier 2002: 338–9.)

In the view of the present author, these costs of refugee assistance should be considered to include the facilitation of political participation. The application of this principle would prevent the costs of enfranchisement from falling disproportionately on less developed nations which tend to be those that host large populations of refugees who are potential external voters. The application of equal burden-sharing within the international community would prevent cost from being a source of disenfranchisement, contributing to greater overall political participation, and would remove a heavy financial burden on some less developed states.

## 5. Conclusions

Host country issues are challenging, complex and close charged. To complicate matters, external voting programmes are often conducted hastily to tight timetables. There is little clarity regarding who has the mandate to advocate, facilitate and evaluate external voting. There are no consistent policies, practices or standards guiding host governments' positions and responsibilities. Differences in political culture, administrative structure, infrastructure, and legal framework must be taken into consideration. However, there are a few components of external voting programmes that have begun to standardize.

• Any information on individuals that may come into the hands of the host country as a result of the external voting programme should be used exclusively for the external voting programme.

• The legality of an individual's residency, including a lack of documentation, does not affect an individual's eligibility to exercise his or her right to political participation.

• Participation in an external voting programme should not affect the political, economic or social inclusion of individuals within their host country in any way.

• While host countries may have a role in the registration process, usually through providing demographic data, it is important that protections are put in place to prevent foreign governments from influencing the electoral outcome through an engineered turnout by screening the registration process.

• It is critical that host countries facilitate and support the dissemination of information, including voter and civic education as well as political campaigns.

• Participation in an external voting programme should neither prevent nor delay the voluntary repatriation of refugees living in the host country.

• The political, financial and logistical obstacles to external voting programmes should be approached with the intention of overcoming them. The costs of not conducting external voting may, in the long run, be much greater.

# CHAPTER 7

# 7. The political rights of refugees and displaced persons: enfranchisement and participation

Jeff Fischer

## 1. Introduction

This chapter describes the processes of enfranchising refugees and internally displaced persons (IDPs) and allowing them to participate in the political processes of their home countries. It presents pertinent issues, lessons and principles that provide the basis for establishing an international policy framework on these issues. The involvement of refugees in electoral processes is particularly significant in elections that are held under international supervision as part of a post-conflict transition to democracy. In such situations electoral and political processes must be pluralistic and inclusive if they are to have credibility. To the extent that refugees are deprived of their political rights, an electoral process must be considered deficient.

Under the definition used for this Handbook, IDPs are not external electors, but they are considered together with refugees in this chapter because they present similar problems and in practice they can constitute a large group of external electors. The term 'refugee' is used here to connote both types of displacement.

### 1.1. Who is a 'refugee'?

International law recognizes four forms of individual displacement that are relevant to the kinds of election and political process under discussion.

The first of these is that of the *refugee*, defined under the 1951 United Nations Convention Relating to the Status of Refugees and the associated 1967 Protocol as a person who 'owing to a well-founded fear of being persecuted for reasons of race, religion, nationality, membership of a particular social group or political opinion, is outside the country of his nationality and is unable or, owing to such fear, is unwilling to avail himself of the protection of that country'. The 1967 Organization of African Unity (OAU) Convention Governing the Specific Aspects of Refugee Problems in Africa gives a wider definition, stating that the term 'shall also apply to every person who, owing to external aggression, occupation, foreign domination or events seriously disturbing public order in either part or the whole of his country of origin or nationality, is compelled to leave his place of habitual residence in order to seek refugee in another place outside his country of origin or nationality'.

The second form is that of *asylum seeker*, an individual whose application for asylum or recognition as a refugee under the conventions is pending and who fears persecution if returned home. The third is that of *internally displaced persons* who are refugees within their own country's borders, and the fourth is that of the *returnee*, an internally displaced person or refugee who has returned home but requires continued assistance for a period of time. For the purposes of this chapter, refugees and asylum seekers are the focus of attention because of their forced migration. The standards and best practices for enfranchisement for refugees are largely applicable to both displaced persons and returnees.

At the end of 2004, the United Nations High Commissioner for Refugees (UNHCR) estimated that the collective population of concern had reached 19.2 million individuals. Refugees represented the largest component of that figure (48 per cent), with 9.2 million people classified in that category. Ninety-three per cent of the refugees were in Asia, Africa and Europe, in that order by size of the refugee population. The rest of the Western hemisphere accounted for all but a fraction of the remaining 7 per cent. Of asylum seekers, 35 per cent were in North America, and another 32 per cent in Europe. The UNHCR estimates that women comprise roughly 49 per cent of the total population of concern (UN High Commissioner for Refugees 2004).

In a 1997 report, the Refugee Policy Group provided figures on the presence of refugee populations in some of these countries during election years (see table 7.1).

Demographics aside, the circumstances of refugees compel an examination of their political rights because these rights are often at issue. The political rights of refugees are defined in numerous international and regional conventions. These include the Universal Declaration of Human Rights (1948); the United Nations Convention Relating to the Status of Refugees (1951; entered into force 1954); the International Covenant on Civil and Political Rights (1966; entered into force 1976); the American Convention on Human Rights (1969; entered into force 1978); and the African Charter on Human and People's Rights (1981; entered into force 1986). These documents clearly demonstrate that refugees are afforded full rights of citizenship and political participation, including membership of political parties, the right to stand as candidates for election, access to election information, and enfranchisement.

In post-conflict situations, elections are frequently used as ways of facilitating the repatriation of refugees and their reintegration into the country of conflict. The election process serves to reunite a conflict-torn country into common institutions, incorporating former battlefield antagonists into the political arena. Registration to vote is also the first

Table 7.1: Refugee populations and electoral events

| Country | Year | Election type | Estimated no. of refugees at signing of peace accord | Refugees as % of total population |
|---|---|---|---|---|
| Angola | 1992 | Presidential | 350,000 | *3.5* |
| Bosnia and Herzegovina | 1996 | Presidential | 1.2 million | *27* |
| Cambodia | 1993 | Constituent Assembly | 360,000 | *4* |
| Eritrea | 1993 | Presidential | 900,000 | *28* |
| Liberia | 1997 | Presidential | 750,000 | *25* |
| Mozambique | 1994 | Presidential | 1.7 million | *10* |
| Namibia | 1989 | Presidential | 41,000 | *27* |
| Sierra Leone | 1996 | Presidential | 360,000 | *8* |

Source: Gallagher, Dennis and Schowengerdt, Anna, 'Refugees in Elections: A Separate Peace', Refugee Policy Group, October 1997.

step in the re-establishment of individual political identity. Because many refugees arrive in a country without identity documents, electoral registration activities that determine individual eligibility will result in a re-establishment of identity by providing a system for the recognition of both refugees' actual residence and their right to residence in their home country. In fact, registration as an elector can be seen as one of the first political rights afforded to refugees.

## 2. Obstacles to refugee enfranchisement

Despite these covenants, the refugee faces an array of the obstacles which must be surmounted before his or her political rights can be fully realized. Such obstacles include intimidation, illustrated among other things by the use of food relief as a tool to gain the political cooperation of groups of refugees; physical obstacles such as destroyed bridges or remote or impenetrable border crossings; and difficulty in accessing both election-specific information and more general reporting on civic life at home.

Refugees traditionally have been among the last of marginalized groups to become enfranchised. International practice on the promotion of the political rights of refugees has not yet been standardized. There is a lack consistency from region to region in terms of resource allocation, practice and institutional leadership. The range of policy differences is illustrated by a comparison of the examples of Bosnia and Herzegovina in 1996, where refugee enfranchisement was written into the 1995 General Framework Agreement for Peace in Bosnia and Herzegovina (the Dayton Agreement) and balloting was conducted for refugees in 55 countries (see the case study), and Liberia in 1997 where there were no out-of-country enfranchisement opportunities and no organized repatriation.

As the Refugee Policy Group study (Gallagher and Schowengerdt October 1997) points out, there are four models of political participation that can be identified in international practice. These models are:

- limited spontaneous repatriation;
- elections in asylum;
- full organized repatriation; and
- limited spontaneous and facilitated repatriation.

The application of consistent international standards takes on special significance in the case of refugees because, by definition, enfranchisement efforts are international: they involve cross-border agreements between the countries and international organizations charged with administrative responsibilities or the implementation of peace accords (see also section 4 below). The recognition of consistent international principles on refugee enfranchisement and participation would also act as a foil to the tactic of 'cleansing' a region or community to expel a population and eliminate its political interests. The political motives for displacing people would be reduced if the refugee populations produced by rogue regimes did not lose their political rights but continued to have a voice and to vote regardless of their temporary dislocation.

Not only are there obstacles for refugees to overcome in achieving their political rights, but the international organizations that are charged with implementing enfranchisement programmes and promoting participation by refugees face obstacles of their own. These include competing policy options, time constraints and resource limitations.

## 3. The regulatory framework

In order to manage programmes for the enfranchisement of refugees and plan for their participation, a regulatory framework must be established. Bilateral agreements for international organizations to conduct electoral registration programmes in host countries must be concluded. This framework will structure a political process that qualifies individuals to vote, produces elected representative bodies, and contributes to the establishment of post-conflict governments. There are several policy issues that must be resolved in the course of developing this regulatory framework.

### *3.1. Entitlement*

The regulatory framework must establish the rules for entitlement or the qualifications that someone must possess to be eligible to participate. The criteria to be considered in establishing entitlement include age; intention to return; date of expulsion from or last residence in the home country; and proof of identity and eligibility.

**Intent to return**

Although consistent standards must be applied, any enfranchisement of refugees must be considered a temporary arrangement and be organized on an election-by-election basis. Because the creation of suitable conditions that enable refugees to return must be the ultimate objective of a peace initiative, the organizers must assume an implicit intent to return on the part of the refugee. Implicit intent to return provides the demonstrable link that an individual maintains with a former community and forms the basis of the assumption of entitlement to vote.

**Residential option**

In recent electoral events, refugees have been offered three options as to the locations where their political rights can be exercised:

- from their original residence;
- if internally displaced, from their current residence; or
- from a future intended residence.

**Proof of identity and eligibility**

The procedures by which identity and eligibility are proved can determine the overall credibility of an election. The procedures employed must specify which documents will be recognized and must prevent counterfeiting. In cases where refugees lack personal documentation because of loss or confiscation, a form of 'social documentation' may be considered by which enquiries are made and people can witness to other individuals' identities and place of residence. However, although they are unavoidable in many situations, social documentation processes are difficult to control and police, and complex to administer.

## 3.2. The election cycle

The type of election for which refugees or IDPs may vote, and the sequencing of their voting, must be established in the regulatory framework. The timing of refugee voting may differ from that of in-country voting. Differential timing can be advantageous for the practical purposes of expediting the tabulation of the ballot and the announcement of the results.

## 3.3. Systems of representation

Systems of representation that nominally include refugees are often based on pre-conflict population patterns. The system should also permit refugees to stand as candidates.

## 3.4. Security

The refugees must feel secure when voting in asylum. If an election or referendum is conducted in a climate of intimidation, this will impair the legitimacy of the result. Security planning should include both people and objects. For people it should include voters, candidates, observers and the media; and for objects it should include facilities and commodities. Such security arrangements must be negotiated with the police and security forces of the host country.

## 4. Special political and logistical requirements

The political and logistical requirements of such undertakings pose complex policy questions for the organizers of an election. They also give rise to constellations of countries and organizations uniquely brought together for each such event.

### 4.1. Country and organizational constellations

Every effort or programme of refugee enfranchisement will naturally involve a constellation of countries, both the countries from which refugees have fled and the hosts for the refugee populations. On both sides, wide-ranging negotiations will be required (see also chapter 6, on host country issues). Topics for negotiation include transit agreements to facilitate visa-free travel (if refugees are to vote in the country of origin), Temporary Protection Status, and agreements on dual citizenship. Although standards can be established, there is no single model that can be employed for host country assistance and cooperation. Some parameters are specified by national law and will vary from country to country.

Although voter registration, political campaigning and balloting are conducted within another country's borders, there must be no violation of the host country's sovereignty. These events can also be costly for the host governments. Memoranda of understanding are useful tools for describing the roles of each partner in the enfranchisement initiative.

This constellation can also be defined to include the range of international and non-governmental organizations that are involved in the process. For example, the International Organization for Migration (IOM) managed the voting by refugees in the elections in Bosnia and Herzegovina in 1996–7, the Popular Consultation for East Timor in 1999, and the external voting in the election in Kosovo in 2000. The League of Women Voters conducted refugee balloting for Bosnian refugees residing in the United States in 1996.

In some cases, special administrative structures must be established. For example, in Bosnia and Herzegovina, under the terms of the Dayton Agreement, refugees were given the right to vote in the municipality where they were resident in 1991 or at some future intended municipality of residence. Refugees residing anywhere in the world were afforded the right to vote and the Organization for Security and Co-operation in Europe (OSCE) established the Refugee Elections Steering Group to oversee out-of-country voting. Another instrument required for the implementation of the Dayton Agreement is the Sub-Commission for Future Municipalities, established for the 1997 elections, which adjudicated all claims for future intended municipality registration. In Kosovo, the Joint Registration Taskforce (JRT) of the UN and OSCE has a unit that is devoted to out-of-Kosovo registration of electors. The IOM has two liaison officers working in the JRT facility.

## 4.2. Information

One particular challenge for a refugee information programme is finding sufficient resources to reach pockets of people in far-flung areas. The multidimensional politics associated with refugee voting is at once domestic, regional and international in scope. The information campaign should be scoped accordingly. It must be broadly based in order to reach all the different gender, age, language, regional and ethnic sub-populations that comprise the refugee populations.

## 4.3. The politics of displacement

New tactics in the politics of displacement can develop. This was the case with the displacement of people during the 1999 UN-sponsored Popular Consultation for East Timor. Under the usual scenario, a population is driven from its homes as a result of a conflict. After the conflict is resolved, a reconciliation election is held and the rules regarding their enfranchisement are decided. However, in the case of East Timor, these individuals were displaced for the purposes of the Popular Consultation ballot: they were unwillingly moved from their homes or were rounded up by militias and evicted. The estimates of the total number of internally displaced ranged from 30,000 to 50,000. On the basis of 450,000 registered electors, that could mean that as many as 10 per cent of the electors were displaced. Obviously, the enfranchisement of that percentage of the electorate was an important objective and essential to the credibility of the election outcome.

## 5. Conclusions

Elections will continue to follow conflicts as the means of reconstituting post-conflict governments. Refugees will be a factor in each of these election events. Although organizations such as the UNHCR have consistently supported refugee political rights, during the 1990s international responses were inconsistent as regards political will and resources to enfranchise refugees, and varied from event to event and from region to region. Obtaining consistency in the responses should involve the allocation of resources as well as the regulatory framework and practices in host countries.

Commensurate with the implementation of such consistent standards, the capacity to monitor their application must also be provided by the international community, and the responsibility for doing so must be assigned. A programme of focused observation of political processes involving refugee populations must be adopted for an international group to consider.

Finally, one motive for expelling a population—disenfranchising it—can be eliminated by maintaining consistent international responses to guarantee that elections provide for full political participation by refugees.

CASE STUDY: Afghanistan

# Afghanistan's 2004 presidential election: external voting for a large displaced population

Catinca Slavu

A large segment of the Afghan population was forced to migrate to the neighbouring countries as a result of Afghanistan's long history of humanitarian and political crisis. With the UN High Commissioner for Refugees (UNHCR) and host government sources estimating that approximately 2.5 million Afghans were still displaced in Pakistan and Iran at the time of preparations for the 2004 elections, the Transitional Islamic State of Afghanistan undertook to include these refugees in the nation-building process.

Afghans in Pakistan and Iran had previously been given the opportunity to vote in post-conflict Afghanistan for the election to the Emergency Loya Jirga in June 2002, followed by the election to the Constitutional Loya Jirga in December 2003. (A Loya Jirga, or 'grand council' in the Pashto language, is a consultative forum unique to Afghanistan in which, traditionally, tribal elders convene to settle affairs of the nation or rally behind a cause.) The Emergency Loya Jirga was elected to form a transitional government, and the Constitutional Loya Jirga was elected to adopt Afghanistan's first post-conflict constitution. Special procedures were used for both elections, which were indirect elections without universal suffrage.

## The legal and administrative framework

The franchise for the 2004 presidential election was regulated by the constitution of Afghanistan; by the Election Law (chapter IV); by decisions of the Afghan Joint Electoral Management Body (JEMB) in consultation with the UN Assistance Mission in Afghanistan (UNAMA) and the government of Afghanistan; and by individual memoranda of understanding on the conduct of the out-of-country elections signed by the government of Afghanistan with the governments of Pakistan and Iran. The decision to offer the franchise outside Afghanistan was taken by the JEMB following an assessment undertaken jointly with UNAMA and the United High Commissioner for Refugees (UNHCR), in consultation with the United Nations Development Programme (UNDP). The location and timing of external voting were the responsibility of the JEMB. Sizeable Afghan communities had also been displaced to Tajikistan, the USA and some European countries. The JEMB's decision to enfranchise only those displaced to Pakistan and Iran was taken for logistical reasons, as well as because the vast majority of expatriated Afghans were in those two countries.

The decision to provide the external vote to those displaced to Pakistan and Iran became highly political, as voting trends were expected to follow ethnic lines and the bulk of the refugees in Pakistan were Pashto, while those in Iran were Tajik and Hazara. Given its potential for politicization, the decision to conduct external voting was delayed several times; only when it became clear that both host countries would agree to allow and support the external franchise on their territories on conditions generally consistent with international standards was a final decision made by the JEMB.

Because the decision was made very late, the time available, including detailed negotiations with the host governments on the provision of support, was very limited. The International Organization for Migration (IOM) was finally contracted to undertake the operation only 69 days before election day, although it was contemplated much earlier that it would be chosen for the task. The conduct of the operation had to be outsourced, as the JEMB Secretariat had neither the logistical means nor the legal authority to operate outside Afghanistan. The IOM was chosen because of its previous experience in carrying out external voting operations in Bosnia and Herzegovina, East Timor and Kosovo. It contracted IFES (formerly the International Foundation for Election Systems) to provide technical management to the Out-of-Country Registration and Voting Programme.

Time limitations, in turn, meant that it was impossible to establish election facilities (registration and/or polling centres) in all areas where there were clusters of Afghan communities. The operation was therefore limited to the main centres where Afghan populations were concentrated: areas of high security concern in Pakistan and isolated refugee camps in both Pakistan and Iran could not be reached.

External voting operations outside embassy premises (which are the territory of the country they represent) require legal agreements with the host country governments. These establish the general parameters of cooperation between the election management body or the organization contracted to undertake the operation on its behalf. In the case of post-conflict elections or situations where security is a concern, special assistance is often needed from the host government to ensure that the transport of election material takes place without delays or security incidents, that security is provided at the election facilities, that refugees are allowed to move freely and so on. Given the security concerns associated with Afghan elections, the negotiations with the governments of Pakistan and Iran were initially protracted. However, once cooperation was secured, the two governments made all efforts to facilitate the IOM's mandate. This extended particularly to the provision of official security for the operations, without which registration and/or voting could not have taken place.

Although the government of Pakistan offered to become quite deeply involved in the electoral process and assist with the organization of the elections in the areas not reached by the IOM, this was not thought to be appropriate. The point at issue was the electorate's expectations of trust in the electoral process, which outweighed the undoubted value of Pakistan's electoral management infrastructure.

## Eligibility

According to the legal framework, Afghans living in Pakistan and Iran were entitled to participate in the election provided that they were 18 years of age by election day and could prove their Afghan nationality.

Inside Afghanistan, as there was no voter register in place for the 2004 presidential election, a voter registration exercise was also organized before the election. Gender-segregated registration (and, subsequently, polling) stations were established throughout the country from 1 December 2003 to 20 August 2004. Registration procedures established that upon the presentation in person of documentation proving eligibility according to the requirements set out by the JEMB (identity, age and Afghan nationality), Afghans would be registered. Each registered elector was then issued with a registration card containing address and identification information, including a photograph taken at the Registration Centre.

In Pakistan, under criteria determined by the JEMB, all Afghan citizens over the age of 18 at the time of election and who had arrived in Pakistan after 1979 were entitled to register to vote. In order to vote, all eligible electors had to undergo an advance registration process. In exceptional circumstances, where applicants did not have documents showing that they were from Afghanistan, a special interview procedure was put in place which was subject to a 'challenge' procedure at the time of voting. Electoral registration followed the same principles as applied to the in-country process—advance in-person registration; the issuing of an electoral registration card, in this instance without a photograph; arrangements for the voter lists to be on public display for a certain period before polling; and gender-segregated registration facilities.

In Iran, the JEMB decided to waive the advance registration requirements as the government authorities were able to make a refugee database available for election purposes. The Iranian Ministry of the Interior had set up a sophisticated documentation system since the refugee flow began, and this database and documentation system were used without further evidence of Afghan nationality being required. The JEMB decided to accept that the government-issued refugee card could be used as means of proving identity and eligibility to vote. The IOM negotiated with the Iranian authorities to extend the eligibility criteria from only those who participated in the 2003 refugee registration process to all Afghans legally residing in Iran. A skeleton electoral register was created on election day itself.

Additionally, Afghans who were on the registers in Afghanistan were allowed to vote from abroad in the election. This special procedure was introduced in response to security concerns, related mostly to geographical areas at the borders with Pakistan and Iran. The threat level here was higher, in the context of widespread cross-border migration between Afghanistan and its two neighbours, Pakistan in particular.

The personal registration and polling method was chosen as the postal infrastructure of the two host countries was deemed unable to support a postal voting option. Proxy registration and proxy voting were also not made available because of the specific cultural context in which the election was to take place and the ease with which identification documents could be forged.

## Implementation and turnout

To implement the Out-of-Country Registration and Voting Programme, the IOM established programme headquarters in Islamabad, Pakistan, and two regional offices in Islamabad and Tehran, Iran. Eight field offices were established in Pakistan and seven in Iran to coordinate registration, polling, voter outreach and counting activities.

Voter registration was organized over four days commencing on 1 October and ending on 4 October. (A three-day process was initially scheduled. However, a one-day extension was decided upon to ensure maximum participation.) A total of 1,657 registration stations in 630 centres, with equal numbers of stations for women and men, were established in eight urban and refugee camp clusters throughout Pakistan. Over the four days of the registration period, 737,976 Afghans registered in Pakistan, of whom 28 per cent were women. The low female turnout was expected given the very short period of time for voter education and registration. This turnout was also comparable with the approximately 33 per cent female turnout inside Afghanistan.

Given that sufficient time was not available for an adequate electoral registration process, the lack of adequate documentation of the refugee population became the most significant challenge to establishing a fraud free election. As voters were not able to be issued with photographic registration cards, an anti-fraud mechanism had to be put in place at the time of registration. Thus, in order to prevent duplication of names on the electoral register, a decision was made to apply voter marking ink at the time of registration as well as at the time of polling.

The election was held on 9 October 2004 both in-country and out-of-country. A total of 2,787 polling stations were established in Pakistan and Iran. In Pakistan, the number of stations was adjusted from 1,657 used during registration to 1,661 which were located in 630 polling centres. In Iran, 1,093 polling stations were opened in 125 polling centres. In total, 818,189 Afghans participated in the election from abroad (577,776 in Pakistan and 240,413 in Iran), which constituted 10.06 per cent of the total electorate (8,128,940 voters).

In Pakistan, 80 per cent of the registered electorate participated in the polls, whereas in Iran voter turnout represented half of the estimated eligible voters (estimated between 400,000 and 600,000). The overall high turnout in both Pakistan and Iran was achieved due to the extensive voter education campaigns conducted by the IOM Out-of-Country Registration and Voting Programme and also to the Afghan community's great interest in participating in their first-ever democratic election. Female turnout reached 32 per cent of the total electorate—29 per cent in Pakistan and 40 per cent in Iran. In Iran, women's participation was in proportion to their share in the population, largely due to high levels of literacy and the influence of Iranian society on the Afghan women. According to government data, women constitute approximately 40 per cent of the total Afghan population in Iran.

## Funding

There were no budgetary constraints on the decision-making process. Once the political decision had been made, funding was made available for voter registration and polling through the voluntary donation project budget. The multilateral Afghanistan

Reconstruction Trust Fund (ARTF) was set up in May 2002 to provide, among other things, support to Afghanistan in the area of recurrent costs of the government. In addition to the United States, 21 donors pledged 430 million US dollars (USD) to the fund. The Transitional Islamic State of Afghanistan maintains an inventory of donor-funded activities through the Afghan Assistance Coordination Unit, a subordinate office of the Ministry of Finance. The ARTF is jointly managed by the Asian Development Bank, the Islamic Development Bank, the UNDP and the World Bank, which also administers the fund. External election-specific fund-raising was coordinated by the UNDP, and 26.7 million USD were made available to the IOM on the basis of a cost estimate contained in its proposal to the JEMB. The total cost of the Out-of-Country Registration and Voting Programme amounted to 91 per cent of the initial estimate of 24,289,322 USD, or approximately 20 USD per voter in Iran and 32 USD per voter in Pakistan, where advance registration increased the cost per voter.

## The future of external voting in Afghanistan

Although repatriation exercises have been taking place from both Iran and Pakistan, over half a million Afghans remained displaced in Pakistan towards the end of 2005. If a political decision is made to continue to conduct external voting, similar future operations during the transitional period could probably be funded from the same sources and through the same mechanisms as those used for the 2004 presidential election.

For Afghanistan's elections to the legislature in September 2005, the candidate-centred Single Non-Transferable Vote (SNTV) system in use meant that a different ballot paper had to be used for every electoral district, and getting the correct ballot paper to all external electors would have been immensely costly and complex. The political decision made was not to provide the franchise abroad for these elections because of the high costs involved and because no consensus as to the system to be employed could be reached. However, special registration and polling centres, open until very late on election day, were set up close to the borders to allow migrants in neighbouring countries to come into Afghanistan to vote. This might be seen as a 'half-measure' designed to achieve the maximum extension of the franchise to nationals who were out of country at the time of the elections, short of actually introducing external voting. If it is decided in future to offer the option of external voting for parliamentary elections, changes to the legal framework governing external voting will need to be made to define the method by which external votes are to be translated into seats. Like some other countries, Afghanistan may decide to allow external voting only for presidential elections.

CASE STUDY: Bosnia and Herzegovina

# Bosnia and Herzegovina: post-war trends in external voting

Linda Edgeworth and Nada Hadzimehic

The devastating war that tore Bosnia and Herzegovina (BiH) apart in the early 1990s and divided the country's three constituent peoples ended with the signing of the General Framework Agreement for Peace in Bosnia and Herzegovina (the Dayton Agreement) in Paris on 14 December 1995. Prior to the war, Bosniac, Croat and Serb ethnic groups were interspersed with no specific concentrations of any group in any particular part of the country. (The term Bosniac has been generally used since the war to describe the Muslim population of Bosnia and Herzegovina.) The pattern of multi-ethnic integration was irretrievably altered as a result of the war. Ultimately, the Dayton Agreement was intended to ensure that BiH remained a single state, but under the terms for peace it was divided into two 'entities': the Muslim–Croat, known as the Federation of Bosnia and Herzegovina, and the Serb, known as the Serb Republic (Republika Srpska, RS). The agreement also outlined a national constitution that specified a basis for power sharing among the three ethnic groups for defined federal institutions, including a tripartite presidency, a shared central legislature, and separate governmental structures for the two entities. For the restructuring to begin, one of the key conditions of the Dayton Agreement was that elections be held throughout the country not later than nine months after its signing. The first post-war elections were held in September 1996. They were to include elections of officials at all levels of government, including municipal elections, taking into consideration the changes of municipal boundaries affected by the drawing of the Inter-entity Boundary Line dividing the Federation from the RS.

Although verifiable statistics have never been readily available, it has been estimated that approximately 2 million people, nearly half of the entire population, was displaced by the war, with about a quarter of the population taking refuge outside the country. The mass emigration caused by the war itself was exacerbated by the severe economic conditions that faced the country afterwards. The sheer numbers of refugees and the international interest in seeing them repatriated as quickly as reasonably possible made it imperative that they be fully enfranchised as participants in the elections that would greatly affect their futures, the stability of their country under the new governmental institutions and structures, and the possibilities for their safe and secure return.

Three factors, which have evolved concurrently, have shaped the process of external voting for BiH since the war and had significant impact on the procedures as they exist today. The first is the transition from a passive voter registration system to an affirmative registration system whereby every citizen must personally apply to register as an elector. The second is the progressive shift of responsibility out of the hands of the international supervisors and back into the hands of the BiH electoral authorities. Finally, the procedures set in place at the end of 2005 have been significantly affected by the dramatic decline in participation by voters living abroad which has been experienced in each successive election since 1997.

Prior to the war, inclusion on the electoral registers required no action on the part of an elector. Local officials compiled the registers on the basis of residency records maintained by the municipality. Because so many municipal records were lost or destroyed during the war, the Dayton Agreement declared that inclusion in the 1991 pre-war census, which identified each person's municipality of residence, would be the basis for establishing eligibility to participate in the elections. Furthermore, it provided that persons who were no longer living in the municipality in which they had resided at the time of the census would, as a general rule, be expected to vote in their pre-war municipalities. The exception to the rule covered people who had moved in the period between the 1991 census and the beginning of the war in April 1992 and who could substantiate that move with appropriate documentation. These general rules applied to all citizens abroad, including refugees (General Framework Agreement, annex 3, article IV).

A small loophole was provided in that a person could apply to the Provisional Election Commission to 'vote elsewhere'. Eventually, under rules and regulations adopted by the Provisional Election Commission working under the direction of the Organization for Security and Co-operation in Europe (OSCE), this was interpreted to mean that a displaced person could apply to vote in the municipality in which he or she currently resided, or in the case of an out-of-country elector in a 'future municipality' to which he or she declared an intention to return. In the latter case a stringent set of rules was adopted defining what documentation would be necessary to substantiate that declaration of intent. Documentation could include, for example, confirmation of a promise of employment, or residence with family members already resident in the intended municipality of future residence.

A significant number of refugees might reasonably have been expected to take advantage of the 'future municipality' option, given that in the post-war environment the three ethnic groups are more clearly concentrated in separate regions. It is estimated, for example, that as many as 300,000 people who formerly lived in the territory of today's Federation now live on the RS side of the Inter-entity Boundary Line; similarly 200,000 people who used to live in the RS now reside on the Federation side of the boundary line (Association of Election Officials of Bosnia and Herzegovina 2003). However, the stringent nature of the documentation, investigation and verification requirements put the future municipality option out of reach for the vast majority of refugees who might have been interested in exercising this option.

The use of the 1991 census as a basis for the electoral register for the 1996 elections, while expedient, failed to provide a sound basis for establishing a verifiable number of registered electors against which an auditable election result could be definitively and accurately compared. In addition, incidents of electoral fraud were suspected as ethnic groups sought to mobilize voters improperly to use the ballot box to regain territory lost in the war or to consolidate political influence over territory gained in the war. Due to concerns about how such instances could adversely affect the local elections, the municipal elections were postponed altogether and were not held until 1997.

It was in preparation for these municipal elections that a complete shift was made to establish an affirmative registration system whereby every citizen has had to apply to be registered as an elector and has had to provide supporting documentation to establish identity and voting residence. This shift had a particularly burdensome effect on refugee voters because of the time constraints involved in the two-way postal process, and the fact that access to the required documentation was often limited.

External voting procedures were also significantly affected by the step-by-step transition from an election process that was totally supervised by the international community, under the auspices of the Office of the High Representative and administered by the OSCE, to one totally managed by national authorities, specifically the Election Commission of Bosnia and Herzegovina and its secretariat. This transition was completed in August 2001.

Another factor that is seriously affecting the current approach to out-of-country voting in BiH is the continuing decline in both the number of potential voters remaining out of the country and their interest in participating in BiH elections. Both these circumstances have had a major impact on the facilitation of registration and voting by electors who have lived outside BiH since the 1996 external voting efforts began.

In 1996, reaching out effectively to the upwards of 800,000 citizens estimated to be living abroad taxed the logistics and manpower capacities of the OSCE's Sarajevo-based operations. The task of operating the programme within BiH was also hampered by the lack of a reliable postal service within the country. In preparation for the first post-war elections in 1996, the OSCE established an emergency Refugee Elections Steering Group (RESG) to oversee the registration and voting of eligible electors outside the country. The OSCE also entered into a memorandum of understanding with the International Organization for Migration (IOM) to serve as the operational arm of the RESG from its base in Vienna. Outreach to potential voters was accomplished through communications and coordination with refugee organizations, immigration offices, diplomatic missions and consular offices, as well as Bosnian social clubs that had emerged in countries hosting larger numbers of refugees, and through advertising in publications that targeted these refugees. Ultimately, 630,257 electors outside BiH were registered, of whom nearly 400,000 actually voted in the 1996 elections (International Organization for Migration, undated). External voters posted their ballot papers to the IOM's operations office in Vienna. Once verified, they were shipped to the counting centre in Sarajevo where they were counted and integrated into the countrywide results.

The RESG was disbanded for the 1997 elections, but a similar arrangement between the OSCE and the IOM was maintained. In addition to the postal voting services provided to voters scattered in 80 countries around the world, in-person registration centres and polling stations were established in the former Federal Republic of Yugoslavia (FRY) and in Croatia to serve the 156,000 refugees residing in those countries in nearly equal proportions. Regardless of whether he or she had participated in the 1996 elections, each external elector was required to register anew and submit a copy of an authorized identification document. Acceptable identification included identity documents issued by BiH authorities in either of the entities or by former Yugoslav authorities in the state, or a refugee document issued by a host government or international refugee agency. An applicant could also submit a copy of a passport granted by a host government which permitted dual citizenship. Upon proper registration each elector was sent a confirmation form that was posted to him or her well in advance of his or her ballot packet. This form was to be returned with the completed ballot papers, which were to be sealed in a special envelope to preserve the secrecy of the vote. In the event of a person returning to BiH before voting as an external voter, he or she had the opportunity to present the confirmation form in order to be assigned to a polling place within BiH.

In 1997 the number of out-of-country applications dropped to just under half a million, but turnout among them was over 80 per cent.

Through the 1998 elections the application rules remained the same for new registrants. However, those who had registered successfully in 1997 did not have to re-register. Rather, they were sent a confirmation form to confirm their continued interest in voting, to record any changes in personal status or address, or to change their voting option from their 1991 municipality to a future municipality of intended residence. The major change in the process in 1998 was the development of an external voting department within the OSCE Mission in Sarajevo. The transfer of operations to Sarajevo was deemed a critical step in preparing for the eventual takeover of responsibility for the conduct of elections by the Election Commission of Bosnia and Herzegovina and the inevitable pulling out of international supervisors. The department was supervised by international personnel but was fully staffed by local staff from both the Federation and the RS. The IOM was also retained, but in a much more limited capacity. It continued to arrange for the in-person registration and voting sites in the FRY and Croatia, and to serve as the repository for applications and votes cast by post before they were transported to Sarajevo for processing and counting.

Once again the number of voters abroad declined. Approximately 350,000 external electors received ballot papers. The postal turnout rate remained over 80 per cent, although participation in the FRY and Croatia fell significantly. The decline in these two countries was attributed to a great degree to voters' disappointment at the choices on the ballot paper, as parties continued to be ethnically based. A Croat voter residing in Croatia who had formerly lived in what was now the territory of the RS was likely to find only Serb parties on the ballot paper for his or her 1991 municipality, and Serb voters who had formerly resided in Federation territory would have found predominantly Croat and Bosniac parties to choose from on their ballot papers.

Two major changes in external voting procedures were implemented for the elections in 2000. Operations were managed solely out of Sarajevo, without the assistance of the IOM. In addition the establishment of in-person polling stations in the FRY or Croatia was abandoned, and BiH voters who chose to participate from those countries had to do so by post.

By the 2000 elections it became obvious that the number of registered external electors was decreasing with each election. In 2000 this number fell to 222,000.

In August 2001, the Election Law of Bosnia and Herzegovina was enacted and responsibility for organizing elections was finally transferred from the OSCE Mission to the Election Commission of Bosnia and Herzegovina. The procedure for registration and voting by external electors that had been established by the OSCE was generally maintained. However, under the new law, the eligibility of BiH citizens seeking to register could no longer be confirmed on the basis of their inclusion on the 1991 census. They had to substantiate their claim to citizenship with a copy of a citizenship certificate or a copy of a newly issued national ID card.

By 2002, the total number of successfully registered external electors had dropped to 58,000. The significant decline in external voting is attributed to two important factors. The first is reduced interest in participating in BiH elections as more and more refugees still living abroad have sought and received citizenship in their host countries. In addition, more stringent application and documentation requirements continue to hinder potential voters for whom accessing the proper documents is still burdensome. For the latest elections, in 2004, the total number of successful external registrants was 27,000, while an additional 30,000 applications were rejected due to the lack of acceptable supporting documentation.

The turnout among registered external electors remains high, however, at about 80 per cent—well above the turnout for in-country voters in 2004, which was about 52 per cent. However, some 20 per cent of ballot papers returned from voters abroad could not be counted because registrants had failed to follow the instructions that were sent with them. Those instructions indicated that a copy of an ID document and the confirmation of registration form had to be enclosed in the outer mailing envelope along with the secrecy envelope containing their marked ballot papers.

Given the significant decline in participation by Bosnians living abroad, it is anticipated that the Election Commission of BiH will soon approach the Parliamentary Assembly with proposed amendments to the election law to limit external voting to voting in person in BiH diplomatic offices abroad.

# CASE STUDY: Iraq

# Iraq: a large diaspora and security concerns

Judy Thompson

## Background

The Law of Administration for the State of Iraq for the Transitional Period (TAL) specified that elections were to occur no later than 31 January 2005. The date was set as 30 January 2005 for elections to the National Assembly, the Governorate councils and the Kurdistan National Assembly. Coalition Provisional Authority (CPA) Order no. 92 established an electoral commission—the Independent Electoral Commission of Iraq (IECI)—to be the exclusive electoral authority for Iraq. The commission is structured in such a way as to ensure its independence.

The IECI requested an assessment of external voting (out-of-country voting, or OCV), and this was undertaken in October 2004 by the International Organization for Migration (IOM). The objective was to provide a general overview of the options available and to ascertain the numbers of Iraqis in the diaspora. Demographic data were almost non-existent. The assessment report was presented to the IECI in late October 2004. It identified two options—one that could be implemented for the January 2005 election to take account of the tight time lines, and a more evolved system to be implemented for future electoral events. If an OCV programme were to be implemented for the January 2005 election, it was recommended that an experienced organization such as the IOM manage it.

## IECI decisions and legal provisions

The IECI recognized the problems and risks of the short time line but decided that it was important to give the diaspora the opportunity to participate. It decided that OCV would apply to the National Assembly elections only, since the voters did not live in a local jurisdiction. The electoral system for the National Assembly elections, under which Iraq is a single electoral district (with proportional representation), made it possible to use a single ballot paper for the out-of-country voters. The suggested threshold for the numbers of potential voters in the diaspora of one country was 10,000. However, of the 14 countries the IECI named to host the OCV programme, most had over 15,000 potential voters. The IECI included France (with only an estimated 6,000 Iraqi electors) and excluded Norway (which had 23,000). Since the numbers were rough estimates, it was difficult to set a firm threshold. OCV was to take place in Australia, Canada, Denmark, France, Germany, Iran, Jordan, the Netherlands, Sweden, Syria, Turkey, the United Arab Emirates, the United Kingdom and the United States. The estimated total number of eligible Iraqis in these countries was 1.2 million. Estimates of the total diaspora ranged up to 2 million or more but there was no way to confirm this number or even to establish a reasonable estimate of the worldwide total. (The estimated total number of electors in Iraq was 14.2 million.)

A memorandum of understanding (MOU) was signed by the IECI and the IOM on 11 November 2004, authorizing the IOM to conduct the OCV programme in the 14 countries. This gave them just over two months to complete the task. The IOM immediately started to negotiate MOUs for the programme with the various governments. It established cooperation with host countries, deployed staff, identified offices, developed materials and established polling and registration centres in an extremely short time. By 26 December 2004, 11 countries had signed agreements, with the other three signing shortly after. The concern over security issues had to be considered in each of the 14 agreements.

Two IECI regulations provided the legal basis for the OCV programme—10/2004 (Out-of-Country Registration and Voting) and 16/2005 (Polling and Counting Outside Iraq). The regulations outlined the procedures and clarified the counting process.

## Eligibility to vote

Iraq has had a series of wars, which has meant that displacement and migration have occurred over a long period, starting as early as 1968. It was therefore difficult to limit eligibility by time period or status for expatriate Iraqis. However, most Iraqis did retain their documents.

The Electoral Law and the TAL specify provisions for eligibility and citizenship that are broad enough to include OCV voters. In order to vote, a person must be deemed an Iraqi citizen, be entitled to reclaim citizenship or be eligible for Iraqi citizenship (which is established only through the paternal, and not through the maternal link); must be born on or before 31 December 1986; and must be registered to vote. According to the TAL, anyone who has Iraqi nationality is deemed an Iraqi citizen; an Iraqi can have more than one citizenship; and no Iraqi can have his/her citizenship withdrawn. This definition was very broad so that estimates of numbers of eligible expatriates included almost anyone who had left the country at any time for any reason.

## Registration procedures

There were no databases of Iraqis who would qualify for OCV, so each external elector had to provide proof of eligibility. This was not required in-country as the Public Distribution System (PDS) database was used as the basis for the electoral lists and only names to be added required proof.

Iraqi embassies were inadequate for the numbers of persons expected to register; moreover, not all the countries selected had an Iraqi embassy, so IOM staff in each country identified suitable premises. Security was an issue and security procedures were developed for each country.

The registration period was very close to the voting dates (17–25 January 2005). To accommodate the registrants, opening hours were extended and two days were added to the original registration period. A total of 279,785 Iraqis registered to vote at 74 registration centres in 36 cities (in the 14 countries). This represented some 25 per cent of the number for which the IOM had established registration capacity.

Registration procedures required applicants to present two documents to prove eligibility: this was in an attempt to prevent fraud, irrespective of whether one document, such as a passport, for instance, could prove all criteria. However, after the start of registration it became obvious that in some cases many Iraqis were in possession of only one document. The IOM then approached the IECI for permission to accept one legal document instead of two, and this was granted. There were a very small number of instances of malfeasance by registration staff, including accepting registration by proxy, registration without proper documents and intimidation. These were identified and dealt with by supervisors.

As the registration period was extended by two days, the last day coincided with a display period, during which challenges to the electoral list could be made. Because many Iraqis had to travel long distances to the registration and polling centres, especially at a time when many were attending the hajj, the Iraqi diaspora had requested that same-day registration and voting be allowed. However, the IECI decided, upon the recommendation of the IOM, that, in order to allow for a display period between registration and polling and to reduce the potential for fraud, no registration would be conducted during the polling period.

There was an intensive public information campaign using the media (radio, television and the printed press), distribution of posters and flyers, community meetings, a global information centre, a website, emails and text messaging. Thanks to the support provided by the host governments, there were no serious security incidents.

## Polling procedures

The three-day voting period, 28–30 January 2004, ended with a total of 265,148 Iraqis voting from out of country. This was 94.8 per cent of registered external electors or 22 per cent of the estimated expatriate population in the 14 countries. The voting had taken place in 358 polling stations located in 75 polling centres in 36 cities (in the 14 countries).

The personal voting option was chosen as it was deemed to be more credible than other approaches (such as postal voting). Procedures were similar to those for in-country voting, including the use of voter-marking ink to prevent double voting. There were no serious problems but there were reports of minor incidents such as campaigning near polling centres. There were two incidents related to demonstrations against the election. In Auburn, Australia, there was a brief interruption in the polling (for one hour) while the police dispersed disruptive demonstrators. One notable success was that at the polling station in Manchester, UK, there was no disruption in the polling.

Initially, it had been anticipated that all OCV ballot papers would be returned to Iraq and counted in a central location there, but a more practical approach was adopted and counting centres were established in each city where there was external voting. An exception was the case of the Netherlands where, for security reasons, the government had requested that counting take place in only one of the three cities where OCV voting took place.

Observers (and IECI monitors) were present throughout the programme, from registration to polling and counting, in all locations.

## Financing

It had been estimated that the OCV programme for Iraq would be the most expensive operation of its kind ever undertaken due to the security risks and the costs of addressing them. The figures suggested by the assessment report (including security costs) were in the range of 67–92 million US dollars (USD) in total. The actual expenditure was close to the upper limit of the range. The IECI paid the IOM in instalments according to the arrangements set out in the MOU.

## Conclusion

Given the time constraints and the complexity of the arrangements, it was generally agreed that the IOM had run a successful programme. It reported that it had identified the committed expatriates—those who wanted to participate and were interested in the democratic process in Iraq. The reasons suggested for large numbers of expatriates not registering included security fears, concern about the confidentiality of voter information, lack of interest due to the length of time out of Iraq, lack of documentation, and inconvenience for those living far from the voting centres. Since registering and voting required two visits to the location, it was a costly decision for those living a long distance from the designated cities (the IOM estimated that the selected cities were close to 60–70 per cent of the diaspora in each country). The Danish Government was unique in assisting with these transport costs.

The costs of the OCV programme were very high and questions were raised about the value in relation to the number of registrants. However, it was necessary to prepare for the possibility of over 1 million persons registering and the possible security threats.

As a result of the relatively low registration figures, the IECI is to review the parameters of future OCV programmes for Iraqi elections. Future electoral events will need to be assessed in the light of the security situation and the need for a comprehensive OCV programme. They will take into account expanding the operation to other countries and potentially changing the in-person registration and voting system to a postal system, at least in those countries where the postal infrastructure would allow this.

# CHAPTER 8

# 8. The political rights of migrant workers and external voting

Carlos Navarro

## 1. Introduction

According to estimates from a study of the International Organization for Migration (IOM), in 2005 around 190 million people (over 3 per cent of the world's population) lived in a country different from the one in which they were born. This figure barely hints at the magnitude and complexity of the international phenomenon of migration. This phenomenon has been present throughout the history of mankind, but there is no question that in recent decades it has reached proportions never seen before, and it is also presenting unprecedented challenges. In the same sense, although less recent, a study published in 1999 by the International Labour Organization (ILO) reported that at least 50 per cent of the 170 million people then estimated to be involved in international migration flows belonged to the category of economically active workers.

Experts believe that the main cause of or motivation for most large-scale international migration is still fundamentally economic. This is explained to a great extent by the fact that dominant and growing patterns of world development have accentuated regional asymmetries and the process of socio-economic polarization within most countries. Given this pattern, it is not surprising that an increasing number of people see international migration as a means of escaping unemployment, poverty and other socio-economic pressures.

In this context, a chapter devoted to the political rights of international migrant workers, and more specifically to the basic features of an external voting mechanism that seeks to benefit them, is particularly relevant to this Handbook.

Two factors operating on a global scale are creating a favourable context for defending the political rights of international migrants in general and migrant workers in particular. One has to do with an unprecedented extension and re-evaluation of institutions, rules and democratic practices, in which demands for universal suffrage are prominent, particularly because international migrants in general and migrant workers in particular have generally been excluded until recently. The other has to do with the existence of a series of international legal instruments that expressly recognize the political rights of migrant workers, and consequently provide a basis on which they can claim their political rights—at least the right to active participation, the right to cast their vote.

The available evidence suggests that in many cases, and especially in developing countries which are emerging or restored democracies, the majority of the potential beneficiaries of external voting are the migrant workers living temporarily or permanently abroad. They account for the majority of people in the diaspora. In some cases the majority of external voters may be other categories of people, such as refugees or exiled or displaced people, but there seems to be no doubt that the most recurrent and dominant pattern is for the majority of international migrants to be working people who move from the developing countries to regions and countries of higher economic growth and economic development.

Accordingly, this chapter identifies and examines some key questions for the design, implementation and evaluation of external voting mechanisms that face the great challenge of achieving the inclusion and participation of migrant workers as potential voters.

## 2. Awareness of migrant workers' political rights

In the past 50 years the international community has adopted several legal instruments that recognize and promote a group of legal rights that are relevant to, and in some cases specially targeted at, the people involved in international migration movements. Even so, it is interesting to note that practically until the 1970s the political rights of immigrants in their country of origin, and in particular the rights of migrant workers, and the exercise of those rights had no place and were given no priority either in the scholarly literature or on the international political agenda. Up to that time no initiatives or concrete state policies were aimed at migrant workers.

The first important change came in the late 1970s as a result of the debate over an initiative that arose from a renewed interest within the Council of Europe member countries. In 1977 the member countries subscribed to the European Convention on the Legal Status of Migrant Workers, which was the first international legal instrument specifically to recognize the political rights of migrant workers and their right to vote and to stand for election in their country of origin. These rules were restricted to citizens of the Council of Europe member countries and were conditional on the principle of reciprocity being maintained. The convention came into force in 1983 and was to motivate some of the countries in the region to start recognizing the political rights of certain foreigners or migrants. Above all, the question of the political rights of migrants began to take on more importance and become more visible on the international political agenda and in the corresponding debate.

The greatest achievement in this area was the International Convention on the Protection of the Rights of All Migrant Workers and Members of Their Families, adopted in December 1990 by the United Nations General Assembly. This convention, which entered into force in July 2003, constitutes a more rigorous effort to create an international legal instrument that is expressly directed at migrant workers and their families and respect for their human rights. However, it is important to underline two issues. First, the convention states that a group of civil, economic, social and cultural rights of non-documented migrant workers must be recognized at an international level, although the right to vote and to stand for election is not included. Second, on the other hand, it recognizes a series of additional rights only for migrant workers and their families 'who are documented or in a regular situation in the State of employment' (articles 35 and 41). Among these rights are those which concern the right to participate in public matters in the country of origin, including the right to vote and stand for election in the country of origin, but also to exercise political rights in the country of employment if that country grants them this right in the exercise of its sovereignty.

From the perspective of international law and from the point of view of some host countries, it may be relevant and even necessary to distinguish between documented or legal migrant workers and those who do not have the proper documentation, or illegal migrants. However, from the point of view of countries which are interested in promoting external voting initiatives in order to benefit all those of their citizens who are living abroad, this distinction should not govern the conception and formal design of the external voting mechanism.

It is important to keep in mind that these international legal instruments are aimed at promoting the political rights of migrant workers on two qualitatively different and even contradictory levels. They are advocating at one and the same time the recognition of political rights *by the host countries* (which is clearly not related to external voting as defined for the purpose of this Handbook) and *by the countries of origin* (which clearly places the debate in the field of external voting). While one trend aims to promote and facilitate the process of integration of migrant workers into their new political community, the other seeks to restore their ties with the political community of origin. However, this dual aspect only emphasizes the ambiguity that underlies the current issue of migrant workers' political rights and the vulnerability of those rights, which sometimes are neither recognized by the host country nor protected by the country of origin.

## 3. The challenges of designing an external voting mechanism that includes migrant workers

Almost by definition, the dilemmas and the level of complexity faced by those designing and implementing a mechanism for external voting differ widely from one context to another. They depend on the specific conditions, demands and expectations of every country and are related to legal, institutional and socio-political factors, as well as financial, technical and operational issues. Developing a model that tries to incorporate migrant workers residing abroad will therefore undoubtedly create some additional challenges and complexities.

It must be borne in mind that, even though the concept of migrant workers refers to a real phenomenon, in the end it represents an analytical category that is very difficult to translate literally when designing the details of an external voting mechanism. The most suitable way to determine the extent to which a mechanism can really include migrant workers will therefore be first to identify some common elements of the phenomenon of international migration for working purposes and then from those elements to identify the requirements the external voting mechanism needs to fulfil in order to promote or guarantee the inclusion of migrant workers.

From this perspective, in general terms, we can say that there are four factors which characterize the phenomenon of international migration for economic or work reasons.

1. The first is its massive scale, that is, the fact that it involves a significant proportion of the population from the countries where the flow originates. This normally means that the share of the population that would be entitled to vote but is resident out of the country represents a significant percentage of the national whole. Consequently, the size of the diaspora not only presents a number of challenges in terms of organization and electoral logistics if an important segment of potential voters is to be enfranchised; it also means that the candidates can speculate on the possible influence of the diaspora on the outcome of an election. Even if the available comparative statistics seem to prove the contrary, in the countries that are discussing or trying external voting for the first time, it is common for different political forces to think that the potential universe of the population residing out of the country and eligible to vote will fulfil the requirements needed to register as a voter and will actually vote.

2. This phenomenon usually involves less developed countries. Persistent or recurrent problems related to economic growth may impose certain budget restrictions on the choice of a mechanism for external voting, or at least limit the potential range of available options.

3. Even if the natural destinations of the flows of international labour migration are the most economically developed regions or countries, the dynamics of the flows can easily combine patterns of geographical concentration and dispersion. Even though there are instances of international migration that is highly focused (such as Mexican workers migrating to the United States, where over 95 per cent of the labour migrants from Mexico are concentrated) and there are certain strongholds with the highest concentrations (for example, a large proportion of migrant workers from the Dominican Republic are in New York), usually those host regions or countries are more or less diversified. Once again, this factor may pose financial, organizational and logistical challenges regarding the design and coverage of an external voting mechanism.

4. Because of the predominant migration policies in the main countries of destination, an increasing proportion of migrant workers are illegal (or non-documented) workers. This issue requires two important clarifications. First, although the distinction between legal and illegal migrants may be important from the point of view of the host country, from the perspective of the home state that is interested in promoting an external voting initiative that will benefit all its citizens abroad, such a distinction should not be applicable to the conception and formal design of an external voting mechanism, which would place the state in the unacceptable position of discriminating against its own nationals depending on their migratory status abroad. Second, on the other hand, the fact that a fair proportion of the potential electorate abroad is made up of illegal migrant workers cannot be overlooked when designing and operating an external voting mechanism which aims to incorporate them. The situation of non-documented migrant workers can have an important effect on their ability to fulfil the requirements for registering as electors or their ability to vote. The irregular situation in which these people live in the host country normally makes them reluctant to approach the authorities of their country of origin in order to follow any official procedure, even those related to the protection and defence of their fundamental rights, since they fear that to do so would expose their position and lead to sanctions or reprisals. It is by no means certain that the opportunity to exercise their voting rights is a sufficient incentive in itself to overcome such reluctance and fear.

Under these conditions, it is clear that an external voting mechanism of which the main objective is the effective incorporation of migrant workers who are living temporarily or permanently out of their country of origin poses challenges and requires additional effort in terms of its conceptual design and operational characteristics. Ideally speaking, the mechanism must provide the largest possible coverage in order to take account of a massive number of electors in a diaspora which combines patterns of geographical concentration and dispersion. It also needs to offer flexible and accessible options for the registration of electors and the casting of votes, taking into account prevailing conditions as well as the perceptions and expectations of illegal migrants. Both the law and comparative experience indicate that there are models and variants that can be adjusted to practically every need.

In this sense, a first problem is that, if specific needs or exigencies are to be accommodated, the available options are often constrained by budgetary limitations. Undoubtedly the existing technological models and options may make it possible to design an external voting mechanism that is able to incorporate tens or hundreds of thousands of potential voters in the regions or countries concerned (and not always concentrated in the main urban areas) and to offer them broad facilities or options for registration and voting. However, it is clear that the design and operation of such a mechanism would be very costly and even beyond the means of many of the emerging or restored democracies.

Another determining factor may relate to the ability to reform or renew the electoral system applied *within* the country when the external voting mechanism is being shaped. This ability to reform or innovate does not mean budgetary issues related to the design or operation of the external voting mechanism but the *political* ability to pass the necessary legal changes to support and provide a legal basis for the mechanism. Furthermore, it is practically impossible to replicate electoral procedures and mechanisms that are normally used within the country when shaping an external voting mechanism. This is linked partly to the principles of international law regarding the extraterritorial enforcement of the law and partly to practical restrictions. Thus, the very design of an external voting mechanism must take into account the need to consider and make possible the review, modification and reform of the electoral mechanisms and procedures currently used in the country.

If the current electoral system enjoys a high level of confidence on the part of political forces and public opinion, and has credibility, it can be easier to introduce the reforms required for external voting on the understanding that this will almost always imply some kind of changes, for example, to the rules, procedures and timetabling. On the other hand, if the internal electoral system is a source of controversy or if it lacks credibility, the debate on external voting can be a new source of controversy, and therefore complicate the process required to negotiate and pass the required reforms.

Finally, it is worthwhile mentioning that international law recognizes the right of states to adopt juridical norms with extraterritorial range provided that those juridical norms regulate acts taking place within their own territory. From this perspective, the ability to regulate issues related to external voting is clearly delimited. A country can regulate external voting whenever its regulations do not have extraterritorial effects and are subject to the limitations imposed by the laws of the host countries.

This principle, although generally valid, has to be qualified, however, when it is considered in the light of the framework of relations among states that are heavily involved in the international migration phenomenon: an external voting initiative can have practical effects within these relations, not necessarily at a formal level, but especially and fundamentally as regards the construction of a favourable context to guarantee its viability and efficacy. In this regard, it might be relevant to take into account the perceptions and attitudes of public opinion in the host country towards migrants in general, and especially towards migrant workers. If migrant workers are believed or perceived to be the group that will benefit most from the opportunity to vote from abroad, the matter can become highly complex, particularly if an important or a majority migrant sector happens to be in an irregular or undocumented situation. There is a big difference between an initiative that is not aimed expressly at migrant workers, or addresses them only marginally, and one that is expressly intended to benefit them, particularly if they are perceived as a problem by important sectors of public opinion in the host country. Whatever the reason for it (and the causes can be very different), prejudice on the part of public opinion against migrant populations (and not only against migrant workers or people in irregular situations) could seriously reduce the host country's willingness to offer the required support and facilities. At the same time, it could also seriously affect the potential beneficiaries' motivation to participate in elections because of fear of reprisals.

Other aspects related to the nature of the legal and political system of the host country, which could impede or help an external voting initiative, also have to be considered. As a general rule, the more democratic, open-minded and plural that political system is, the smaller the obstacles or difficulties will be to its allowing and even cooperating in the organization of elections of another country within its national territory.

## 4. Alternatives for design and implementation

Obviously, it is impossible to even think about the possibility of an ideal model for external voting that would guarantee the effective inclusion of working migrants. There are neither standard flows of working migrants nor standard mechanisms for the casting of votes abroad. In this case as in any other one, the most appropriate model will be the one that will fit the prevailing conditions and fulfil the specific requirements of a particular context.

Nevertheless, this does not exclude the possibility that some different approaches and experiences can be identified and assessed that could be useful when designing a mechanism bearing in mind an electorate abroad that is predominantly made up of working migrants, and in this way facing some of the complexities that this challenge implies. With this objective in mind, this chapter analyses briefly the experience of a series of countries where emigration for work is the predominant component in their pattern of international migration, and which are therefore potentially able to adopt an external voting mechanism that allows the incorporation of working migrants. Although there are no conventional parameters to clearly identify the countries with such a profile, among the 114 countries and territories that currently allow their citizens to vote abroad, we have selected four which, according to basic indicators, are characterized by strong international migration mainly for work opportunities—the Philippines, India, Mexico and the Dominican Republic.

According to available estimates, the population from these countries that is entitled to vote and residing abroad is not only made up mostly of working migrants (and the members of their families); it also represents an important percentage of the total number of electors registered within the country. For instance (and taking into consideration the fact that precise data are not available for all cases), the population that would be entitled to vote in the Dominican Republic and is resident out of the country may represent up to 25 per cent of the 5 million electors registered in the country, whereas Mexicans abroad may represent about 15 per cent of the 70 million electors registered at the beginning of 2006.

To define how the specific external voting mechanisms of this group of countries are able to accommodate migrants working abroad, we will analyse and compare three of their main components: (a) the entitlement to vote as an external voter; (b) the requirements and procedures established for the registration of external voters; and (c) the procedure used for actual voting. In the light of the factors analysed in the sections above, the degree of inclusiveness of these three components can show how effectively the mechanisms adopted by these four countries include and integrate working migrants abroad. These three components also offer a framework within which to identify and assess the complexities and challenges that could face other countries that are considering making provision for external voting for migrant workers.

The mechanism adopted by India does not allow generalized access for working migrants abroad, since only those persons who are carrying out official duties and military personnel may be recognized as external voters. In the Philippines, Mexico and the Dominican Republic there are no restrictions of this kind, and they are therefore at least willing to include working migrants. These three countries also share two features that it is important to emphasize: (a) they only adopted mechanisms for external voting very recently (it was applied for the first time in the Philippines and Dominican Republic in 2004, and in Mexico in 2006); and (b) their adoption was to a great extent the result of pressure exerted by organized groups of migrants residing abroad.

Examination of the requirements and procedures for registration in these three countries reveals some filters that may restrict the access of migrant workers, particularly those whose stay in the host country is irregular. For the purposes of the present study, the most evident barrier is seen in Mexico and the Dominican Republic, where in order to be able to register as an elector the interested person must have an identification document which can only be obtained in the home country. If the citizen does not have this document and is unable to travel to the home country in order to obtain it within the time limits set for the registration process (a requirement that can sometimes be insurmountable), his or her ability to vote from abroad is in practical terms annulled.

It is also important to consider the procedures for registration and polling, which are very often interrelated: personal voting reduces the options for registration as an elector, whereas remote voting or mixed options extend the options. The three countries analysed clearly show the range of these variables. In the Dominican Republic the option has been personal voting, but only to be applied abroad in five countries (Canada, the United States, Spain, Puerto Rico and Venezuela) where the population resident abroad is concentrated. In this case it is possible to speak of a selective approach regarding the geographical coverage of external voting. This applies where most migrants, particularly workers, do not reside in large cities and do not have easy access to urban centres. In order to promote the registration of citizens in those five countries, the Dominican electoral registry had to send out staff to suburban areas around selected cities.

Mexico, where at the time of writing the country's first experience of external voting was about to happen, in the presidential election of July 2006, surprisingly opted for a postal voting procedure. In principle, this could expand the possibilities of coverage and access to all potential electors, notwithstanding their place of residence or their location. However, as is mentioned above, the fact that an official identification document is required and is only obtainable in person within the country contributes to limiting the potential coverage and therefore to excluding certain migrant workers abroad.

The Philippines wisely opted for a mixed procedure. At first registration centres were established in all countries where there was a diplomatic or consular representation already in place, and in some cases the authorities used mobile units to promote and facilitate the registration of interested citizens. Later on, the general rule applied was that of personal voting in the same facilities, but voters living in countries with efficient postal services were also allowed to vote by post. The system for external voting in the Philippines embodies the most appropriate elements that have to be taken into account when a country's external voters are mainly migrant workers.

## 5. Concluding comments

In the past few years, issues related to the political rights of international migrants in general, and those of migrant workers in particular, have begun to acquire relevance on the academic agenda as well as the international political agenda. This development has already been translated into the adoption of various international legal instruments that specifically provide for this type of right, as indicated by the International Convention on the Protection of the Rights of All Migrant Workers and Members of their Families.

Although the debate and regulations on external voting are not necessarily related specifically to the questions of migrant workers' political rights, there is no doubt that the concurrence of the globalization and democratization processes at the same time as international migration is growing is creating a clear demand for the full recognition of their political rights in many developing countries. The most general and visible expression of this demand is the guarantee of their right to vote. Through the exercise of this right, migrant workers seek not only to maintain or reinforce their sense of belonging to their original national political community but also to redefine the terms of their relations with the country they feel to be their own.

The design and instrumentation of mechanisms for external voting in countries which have large numbers of migrant workers abroad can face three fundamental challenges.

First, the category of migrant worker is difficult to translate into a mechanism for external voting. Above all, how reasonable or feasible is it to isolate or privilege the migrant worker category over other categories of migrants? If it is reasonable or feasible, how can migrant workers be distinguished or identified in a legal and procedural way within the whole community of migrants abroad? In contrast to mechanisms that may be specifically designed for a certain type of voter or resident abroad (e.g. only those carrying out official duties, students or refugees), there is unlikely to be strong support for distinguishing migrant workers from other kinds of potential voters.

The second great challenge is that international migration for work is often a large-scale phenomenon that exhibits diverse geographical distribution patterns, that is, it regularly involves thousands of persons (potential voters) distributed according to heterogeneous patterns (sometimes concentrated, sometimes dispersed) not only across one or several countries of destination but also within every one of them. This means that we must make a careful assessment of the most suitable options for registering them and conducting the voting, as well as running electoral information campaigns. This assessment must take into account not only the advantages and disadvantages offered by the different models but also, and fundamentally, the administrative and financial capacities of the country or the electoral authority involved.

The third challenge lies in making the electoral regulations and procedures more flexible, and innovating or adjusting them, in order to genuinely and positively include migrant workers. On this subject, it is important to keep in mind that the regulation and control of campaign activities and the administration of electoral justice are usually very sensitive topics in developing democracies, while the opportunity to duplicate abroad certain characteristic guarantees or attributes of the domestic system will be limited. Clearly, without full confidence in the accountability and impartiality of the domestic electoral system it will be very difficult to accept adjustments or innovations abroad since as a general rule the mechanisms of control and security are likely to be weaker for the external vote.

In favourable conditions, the creation of an external voting mechanism that seeks to include migrant workers can present a good opportunity to introduce interesting innovations to several components of the electoral system, and even to try out different methods of voter registration, as well as different procedures for the conduct of the actual voting. Under adverse conditions, however, the design of the mechanism could be problematic for all those involved, and especially for the authorities responsible for organizing, conducting and overseeing elections. In any case, even if the mechanism for external voting is sufficiently flexible and well-intentioned in trying to include migrant workers overseas, the migrants' juridical, socio-economic, political and cultural conditions are likely to work against the initial intentions and expectations.

One conclusion that can be drawn at this point is that any mechanism for external voting entails a range of alternatives and variants which can be adapted to specific conditions and requirements. A universe of potential voters abroad made up mainly of migrant workers presents a series of challenges and complexities that can be addressed by a limited set of options. It is clear that from a conceptual and legal point of view it is neither possible nor desirable to design an external voting mechanism that is aimed exclusively at migrant workers, but it is also true that the legal and procedural options chosen regarding a set of basic aspects of the characteristics and reach of an external voting mechanism (Who is eligible to vote? What are the requirements and procedures for registration and voting?) will largely determine its ability to effectively include migrant workers.

CASE STUDY: Dominican Repulic

# The Dominican Republic: political agreement in response to demands for the right to vote from abroad

Luis Arias Núñez

As a result of a wide-ranging agreement reached between the main political and social forces on a thorough reform of the political and electoral system, as well as to correct the fraud that was widely believed to have characterized the general elections of 1994, the electoral law of the Dominican Republic, Law no. 275-97, was promulgated in December 1997. It incorporated significant changes and innovations, and article 82 made it possible for Dominican citizens who were resident abroad to vote—although only in elections for the presidency and vice-presidency of the republic.

Two main factors assisted the recognition of the right to vote from abroad. First, establishing it in the electoral legislation did not require any constitutional reform: the constitutional norms relating to the ownership and exercise of political rights do not require the vote to be cast within the national territory or in any determined electoral district. Second, it was a justifiable demand made by the different organized groups of Dominican residents abroad to which the main political forces of the country were very sensitive.

To realize this right, article 83 of Law no. 275 of 1997 authorized the electoral authority, the Central Electoral Board (CEB), to put in place the necessary measures to guarantee the implementation of external voting, and article 84 regulated its form and the related procedures. The law specified that its implementation would be considered for the presidential election of 2000 but it was up to the electoral authority to decide when it would come into effect. The CEB decided that it would not be in a position to regulate and guarantee the application of the right to vote abroad in time for the 2000 presidential election, but that it would do everything necessary to ensure its implementation for the presidential election of 2004.

With the electoral process of 2000 concluded, one of the first and main initiatives the CEB took to fulfil its commitment was to set up a commission to study voting by Dominicans from abroad. The commission was charged not only with examining the subject exhaustively, including organizing discussion forums and consultation processes with the political parties, interested sectors and so on, but also with establishing coordination mechanisms with the executive agencies the participation of which was indispensable to running the voting abroad—especially the Ministry of Foreign Relations and its consular offices.

From the different opinions expressed in these forums and consultation processes it was clear that in order to guarantee broad participation by potential voters abroad—almost all of them migrant workers—it was essential for the legal regulation to include three basic principles—the total security of the vote, the freedom of the vote, and total respect for the integrity of voters abroad.

On this basis, in June 2001 the CEB approved the Regulation for the Registration of Electors Residing Abroad, which stipulated that registration centres would be established in the countries where Dominicans were resident and where there were consular or diplomatic offices of the Foreign Ministry, and previous consultation with the legally recognized political parties. Under this regulation, and working from the results of the consultation process with the political parties and the available information on the numbers and locations of the Dominican population abroad, the countries and cities where efforts would be focused for the registration and voting abroad were gradually defined, on the basis that there would be personal voting only.

Although the regulation emphasized that all electors had the right to vote in the 2004 presidential elections, the exceptions to this should be also emphasized. They include, for example, Dominicans found guilty of a criminal offence in the country of residence until they are rehabilitated. It is also important to note that the regulation provides specifically for persons with dual citizenship, so that Dominicans who have acquired another nationality can exercise the right to vote in Dominican elections so long as they fulfil the legal requirements, and so long as the country whose nationality they have adopted does not specifically ban the exercise of this right within its territory.

Finally, in January 2004, the CEB issued the Regulation on the Suffrage of the Dominican Abroad, which affirmed the requirements for voters abroad as well as the precise arrangements for the organization and logistics of the electoral process abroad.

## Registration of electors and the implementation of voting from abroad

Essentially, to be able to vote from abroad, the citizen must (a) be in possession of a current identity and electoral card (which is issued by the electoral authority, but only within the national territory, although an update or replacement may be requested abroad); and (b) register within the correct time period for the register of electors abroad, for which electoral registry abroad offices (ERAOs) were set up.

In October 2001 the first ERAO opened in New York City, which is the foreign city with the largest number of Dominican residents. During 2002 registration offices opened in two other US cities (Miami and Boston), Canada (Montreal), Spain (Barcelona and Madrid), Puerto Rico (San Juan) and Venezuela (Caracas), and in 2003 the last two were opened in the United States (New Jersey and Lawrence). The countries and cities where the great majority of Dominican residents abroad lived were now covered. At the same time, and in order to direct, coordinate and follow up the plans and necessary programmes for the implementation of external voting, in October 2002 the Central Electoral Board set up the Division for the Vote of the Dominican Abroad. Although in principle the CEB anticipated closing the period for registration abroad in mid-

December 2003, it finally decided to extend it until 26 January 2004—less than four months before the date set for the election—in order to give Dominicans abroad greater opportunity to process their registration. At the end of this period, 52,431 electors were registered abroad.

Dominican citizens who were enrolled in the definitive register of electors residing abroad were disqualified from voting inside the Dominican Republic in the 2004 presidential election, but once that election was over they were again qualified to vote in the legislative and municipal elections to be held in 2006, in which voting from abroad was not to be allowed.

On the other hand, the 2004 Regulation on the Suffrage for the Dominican Abroad confirms that only those Dominicans who have registered at the ERAO in time and appear in the definitive register of electors residing abroad can take part in presidential elections.

For organizing the voting abroad, the regulation stipulated the creation of logistic coordination offices (LCOs), which were in charge, along with the Division for the Vote of the Dominican Abroad and after consultation with the political parties, of identifying the premises where the electoral logistical plan would be carried out—receiving, keeping and sending out election material such as the ballot papers and ballot boxes—as well as those where the polling stations would be located. The LCOs were also responsible for identifying, recruiting, training and selecting the people who would actually manage the polling stations abroad.

It is important to note that, by agreement of the electoral authority and the political parties, the polling stations abroad were installed not on the premises of diplomatic and consular representations but in nearby and easily accessible locations. The polling stations were organized in the same way as they were in-country and their staff had to meet the same requirements as are demanded in the Dominican Republic, but in addition they had be enrolled in the registry of the district where they would carry out their functions. For the promotional and informational tasks of the registry, as well as for the identification and negotiation of the locations where the registration centres and polling stations were to be placed, the support offered by organized groups of Dominicans abroad was very important.

For election day, 16 May 2004, the CEB issued a resolution regarding the schedules for the voting from abroad. After consultation with the political parties, it decided to define a special voting schedule for the cities of Barcelona and Madrid: the polling stations would open at 09.00 hours and close at 20.00 hours local time. In other countries and cities voting would be according to the same schedule as in the Dominican Republic, from 06.00 to 16.00 hours (always local time). Except for this variation, the voting abroad was carried out according to the same principles and on the basis of the same organization as in the national territory: Dominicans abroad who were properly authorized to participate in the presidential election would go to their corresponding polling stations and mark their preference on the ballot paper by means of the free and secret suffrage. Once the voting was concluded, polling station staff, in the presence of delegates of the political parties, carried out the counting of the ballot papers and the results were set down in formal protocols which were then taken to the LCOs. Each of these offices received the protocols of the polling stations under their jurisdiction and counted the results from all of them to transmit them to the CEB central offices in the Dominican Republic, where the final count was done.

Thus, for the presidential elections of 16 May 2004, 101 polling stations were installed in 11 cities, seven of them in the United States, and 35,042 of the 52,431 registered electors voted—a participation rate of 66.8 per cent, as the table shows.

**Table: External voting in the Dominican Republic presidential election of 16 May 2004**

| City | No. of registered citizens | No. of valid votes | No. of votes cast | Turnout (%) |
| --- | --- | --- | --- | --- |
| Barcelona | 2,989 | 1,329 | 1,336 | 44.70 |
| Boston | 4,202 | 3,491 | 3,536 | 84.15 |
| Madrid | 5,944 | 2,913 | 2,913 | 49.01 |
| Miami | 2,399 | 1,745 | 1,776 | 74.03 |
| Montreal | 404 | 303 | 306 | 75.74 |
| New Jersey | 6,418 | 4,439 | 4,502 | 70.15 |
| New York | 24,343 | 16,369 | 16,608 | 68.22 |
| Orlando | 282 | 190 | 191 | 67.73 |
| Puerto Rico | 4,622 | 3,225 | 3,300 | 71.40 |
| Tampa | 261 | 203 | 205 | 78.54 |
| Caracas | 567 | 369 | 369 | 64.06 |
| Total | 52,431 | 34,576 | 35,042 | 66.83 |

Source: <http://www.jce.do/stor/boletines/2004/Boletines2004/BExterior.asp>.

To meet the expenses that the electoral process abroad implied, the CEB produced a budget which was submitted for consideration and approval to the executive branch and the two chambers of the legislature. The budget approved for the elections abroad was 114,581,115 Dominican pesos (DOP—c. 2.6 million US dollars (USD)).

In this, the country's first experience of voting from abroad, the main difficulties involved in organizing the voting by citizens abroad related to the logistical aspects, and specifically the shipment and distribution of election material to all the registration and voting sites. Another difficulty was linked to the need to consider the legislation of the countries where the voting abroad was carried out, and to introduce the necessary adjustments to facilitate the organization of the voting abroad.

After the 2004 external voting experience, Dominicans abroad and political parties are still interested in improving this mechanism in order to allow more citizens to participate in the 2008 presidential election. The ERAO continues to register Dominicans in the register of electors residing abroad, but there are many citizens interested in voting who do not have the necessary identity and electoral cards which, as is mentioned above, can only be obtained for the first time within the national territory. As a compensatory measure, currently Dominicans abroad can register on the national territory and receive photographic proof of identity which they can take to the ERAO in the city where they reside to obtain their ID and electoral card. Nevertheless this subject continues to be debated, and the electoral authority has worked on a new project that proposes to modify the procedures for obtaining an identity card. This project, which must be approved by the plenary of the CEB, aims to increase to almost 300,000 the total number of citizens registered by 2008. After the 2004 elections and as of 4 December 2006, 7,027 additional citizens had registered on the list of Dominicans abroad.

Finally, it is important to note that there is currently no debate on the political agenda about modifying or improving the current arrangements.

CASE STUDY: Mexico

# Mexico: safeguarding the integrity of the electoral process

Carlos Navarro and Manuel Carrillo

In June 2005, following controversy and debate lasting almost ten years, the Mexican Congress finally approved a reform to the electoral law allowing Mexicans to vote from abroad. This was to be possible for the first time during the national elections of July 2006. External voting applied only to presidential elections and was by post only.

## Historical background

The need to give citizens the right to exercise their right to vote from abroad and make it possible for them to do so cannot be explained without taking into account the existence of one of the largest, most persistent and most focused international migrant movements in the world—that of the millions of Mexicans who go to the United States, mainly to work. Certainly, not all the Mexicans residing permanently or temporarily abroad have migrated for work, nor are they concentrated in the United States only, but, not surprisingly, one of the main drivers for achieving the right to vote abroad has been the organization and mobilization capacity of several groups of Mexicans living in the USA, who were gradually joined by political forces, social movements and opinion leaders from Mexico.

For many years different voices had been asking for a debate about and for the introduction of a law to give Mexicans living abroad the right to an external vote, but it was only in 1996 that this demand was really met and the first juridical and institutional steps were taken to allow for this possibility to be realized. That year, as part of a large package of electoral reforms, a provision in the constitution which prevented voting from abroad was removed and a series of requirements were established in order for the Congress to provide the final ruling on this matter. Defining the arrangements for external voting took almost a decade.

## The subject of heated debate

The decision-making process was very complex and lengthy. Although the electoral authority and different stakeholders worked hard and well to promote an informed debate on the basis of sound facts and figures (including holding the first international seminars to assess the issue in comparative perspective), it was not easy for the political parties represented in the parliament to reach the agreements needed in order to pass a bill. The debate evolved in different stages. At first, the appropriateness of allowing citizens to vote when they were not resident in the country was the subject of controversy. Once the main objections in this regard had been overcome, the debate centred on evaluating the available alternative mechanisms and defining the most suitable method to guarantee that voting from abroad would preserve the essential attributes of the electoral regime that has been built up and strengthened in Mexico in recent years. Finally, the assessments focused on the cost-effectiveness of the operational options available.

The debate about preserving the main attributes of the electoral system when designing any external voting mechanism was critical. A fundamental reform process had taken place in Mexico during the late 1980s in order to deal with the serious lack of public confidence in elections and their credibility. This reform radically changed both the characteristics of the electoral organization and the conditions of the electoral contest. The legislation gradually incorporated several devices to guarantee the integrity and transparency of the organization and management of the electoral process, as well as equity and accountability in the electoral contest. During the debates over external voting, it was agreed that these were essential features of the Mexican electoral system that would be extremely difficult to replicate abroad.

There was also the question of the numbers of Mexicans residing abroad who would be entitled to an external vote. In late 1998, a commission of experts set up by the Federal Electoral Institute (Instituto Federal Electoral, or IFE, the autonomous organization responsible for managing federal elections) presented a report on this issue which made proposals for external voting by Mexicans. According to the report, an estimated 9.9 million Mexicans residing abroad would be entitled to vote—at the time equivalent to 15 per cent of the total number of citizens registered to vote in the country. Of those 9.9 million, 98.7 per cent, or almost 9.8 million, were in the United States. These estimates showed clearly the extent of the challenge, which up to this point had been the subject of much speculation. But they also provided some candidates with fuel for speculation about the possible effects of the external vote on the outcome of elections.

Although the 1996 reform of external voting was brought in with the intention of having it in place for the presidential elections of 2000, lack of agreement between the main political forces with parliamentary representation prevented the Congress from making any decision on the regulation and implementation of external voting before these elections. Nevertheless, the issue had then been settled as a priority item on the agenda of the political and legislative debate. Between 1998 and 2004, the executive branch along with legislators from different parliamentary groups presented almost 20 bills on external voting to the Congress. Some of the bills presented in the framework of the mid-term elections of 2003 advocated extending external voting to elections for deputies and senators, as well as presidential elections, and even the creation of a special electoral district that would guarantee parliamentary representation for citizens residing abroad. Again, lack of agreement among the different parliamentary forces prevented any final definition, and the target date for implementation was put back to the federal elections of July 2006.

By the end of June 2005, just before the deadline for approving legal reforms that would be implemented during the July 2006 federal elections, the Congress finally approved a mechanism enabling Mexicans residing abroad to vote, but only for presidential elections. After assessing different alternatives, the Congress opted for postal voting, which is a major innovation for the Mexican electoral system, since every election that takes place within the country entails the voter's appearing in person at the polling site.

## Voter registration

To be able to cast a vote from abroad, Mexican citizens residing in a foreign country must have a photographic voting card, which is issued free of charge by the IFE in Mexico, and then send a written request by registered post to be included in a special register of Mexican voters abroad. The photographic voting card requirement became the target for all the criticism of the external voting arrangements, since many Mexicans residing abroad do not have it, and it is only possible to get one in person within the national territory. For citizens who fulfilled this requirement, a period of three and a half months was established during which they could request registration, by post, using the official forms designed by the IFE (for the July 2006 election this period was from 1 October 2005 to 15 January 2006). An additional term of one month (up to 15 February) was established before the register of external electors was closed, in order to allow all applications in transit to be received or to allow the interested parties to correct any omission or error in requests that had been sent at the proper time.

To promote the external vote, the IFE worked with the collaboration of the Secretariat of Foreign Affairs, by means of its 139 diplomatic representations, and also with the assistance of a wide array of social organizations of Mexicans abroad, to inform citizens abroad of their right to an external vote and of the mechanisms for registering and polling. All voters enrolled abroad are temporarily removed from the national electoral register but are automatically reinstated when the relevant election is over.

## The voting and the election campaign

External voting is by post only. The IFE has to send (by registered post) the documents required to cast a vote to all citizens fulfilling the requirements to be registered as voters abroad, no later than 20 May of the election year.

The counting of all votes cast abroad is carried out in one national centre in Mexico, simultaneously with the counting of the votes cast within the country, that is, starting at 18:00 on polling day. In order for the postal votes cast abroad to be included in the count, the electoral authority must receive them one day before the beginning of polling.

To guarantee equity during the electoral process and to protect the control mechanisms for the funding and financial oversight of political parties and campaigns, the mechanism approved by the Congress bans any kind of campaign activity abroad by the parties and candidates. Therefore, and in order to enable voters abroad to cast an informed and reasoned vote, the IFE agreed with the different parties on the creation of a comprehensive electoral kit that included detailed information on the platforms and programmes of the different presidential candidates, and this was distributed to all registered voters abroad along with the official documents required to vote.

## Take-up and costs of external voting

For the preliminary arrangements and the initial setting up of the external voting mechanism, the IFE invested around 119.3 million pesos (MXN—c. 10.8 million US dollars (USD) at a rate of exchange of 11 MXN = 1 USD) during 2005. For the implementation phase throughout 2006, it devoted another 186 million MXN (16.9 million USD), making an estimated overall cost of 305 million MXN (c. 27.7 million USD).

According to reliable estimates, the voting-age Mexican population residing abroad on a permanent basis is currently up to 11 million. Moreover, the IFE estimates that around 4.2 million Mexicans residing abroad have a valid photographic voting card. The combination of these two factors created high expectations that the register of external electors would be massive. However, only 40,876 Mexicans abroad finally registered for the July 2006 elections. Of those, only 32,632 (80 per cent) returned the envelopes with their marked ballot papers in time to be included in the official count of votes cast abroad. Certainly, time constraints, the inherent difficulty of reaching all Mexicans abroad who were entitled to vote and get information to them on time, the innovative approach adopted to registration and voting from abroad, and the strict eligibility criteria established all help to explain this low figure.

Accordingly, and because the external voting mechanisms have to be reviewed and improved, the first Mexican experience, like that of many other countries, indicates the need for more detailed research and a more integrated assessment in order to determine the factors that underlie its political culture and which can in turn be helpful to efforts to encourage voter turnout.

CASE STUDY: Philippines

# The Philippines: the first experience of external voting

Philippines Committee on Overseas Absentee Voting

In the Philippines, the right of suffrage 'may be exercised by all citizens of the Philippines not otherwise disqualified by law who are at least 18 years of age and who shall have resided in the Philippines for at least one year and in the place wherein they propose to vote for at least six months immediately preceding the election' (Philippine Constitution, 1987, article V: Suffrage, section 1, para. 1). Case law, meanwhile, has established that a person's 'intent to return' and not his actual physical presence needs to be established to satisfy the residency requirement of the constitution.

The enactment of the Overseas Absentee Voting Law (Republic Act (RA) no. 9189) on 17 February 2003 gave life and meaning to article V, section 2, of the constitution, which mandated the Congress to provide a 'system for absentee voting by qualified Filipinos abroad'. Its primary aim is to ensure equal opportunity for all eligible citizens of the Philippines who are living or staying abroad to exercise their fundamental right to vote. This provision of the constitution specifically recognized the role played in nation-building by Filipino overseas workers, both land-based and sea-based, who have to leave the country mainly for economic reason in order to offer a better life for their families back home. The same law also provided that Filipino citizens who are immigrants or permanent residents of other countries may exercise their right of suffrage on condition that they sign an affidavit of intent to return within three years from the approval of their application as overseas absentee voters (OAVs). The affidavit should also contain a declaration that they are not applying for citizenship in the host country.

The immigrant or permanent resident who voted in the 2004 national elections should return to the Philippines within three years after his application was approved. Should he or she fail to return to the Philippines within that period and vote again in the next national elections, they will be perpetually barred from voting in absentia and may be imprisoned for one year.

A flurry of activity followed that saw a partnership between the Commission on Elections (COMELEC) and the Department of Foreign Affairs (DFA). A Committee on Overseas Absentee Voting (COAV) was created within COMELEC, while an Overseas Absentee Voting Secretariat (DFA-OAVS) was formed at the DFA. In essence, COMELEC is to supervise the whole overseas voting process, while the embassies, consulates and other diplomatic missions run it. COMELEC formulated the implementation rules and regulations on registration, voting, counting and the tabulation of the count ('canvassing' is the term for tabulation that is used in the Philippines law), while the different posts abroad saw to it that these were implemented in the 2004 national elections, and will do so in future elections. Training modules for the members of the Foreign Service Corps were prepared and eventually handled by COMELEC.

On 17 September 2003, the Citizenship and Re-acquisition Act (RA no. 9225) was passed. It granted natural-born citizens of the Philippines the right to regain and retain their Philippine citizenship provided they swear the Oath of Allegiance and without requiring that they give up their naturalized citizenship. This law also provided full restoration of their civil and political rights, such as (but not limited to) the exercise of their right of suffrage provided they also sign the affidavit of intent to return. As the next national elections were to be held in May 2004, the one-year residency requirement was deemed not to have been met by those who availed themselves of RA 9225. Hence, even if naturalized citizens were able to re-acquire or retain their Philippine citizenship, and even if the names of those approved for registration were included in the National Registry of Overseas Absentee Voters, COMELEC did not allow them to vote.

Based on government records and figures of the International Organization for Migration (IOM), the usual estimate of the number of Filipinos abroad is about 7 million. More than 1 million live in the USA and Canada.

## Electoral registration

For the first time in Philippine history, Filipinos abroad were able to vote for the president, the vice-president, members of the Senate and the party list members of the House of Representatives in the 2004 national elections. The electoral registration period was short—from 1 August to 30 September 2003. A standard application form was provided by COMELEC.

There were two kinds of registration. Applicants had to apply for registration if they were not registered as electors anywhere in the Philippines, while those already registered as voters in the Philippines could apply for certification as OAVs.

As required by the OAV law, registrants went in person to the different posts abroad armed with their Philippine passport and other documents proving their identity. Their biometric data were captured live: their photographs, thumbprints and signatures were taken digitally. From these data, COMELEC produced the National Registry of Overseas Absentee Voters, the Certified List of Overseas Absentee Voters for each diplomatic post, and the applicant's identity document.

Field registration was also conducted outside the diplomatic missions, as not all Filipinos abroad are concentrated in the areas where missions are situated. In the Philippines, registration was conducted at the offices of the election officers in the different municipalities and cities all over the archipelago. Seafarers also filed their applications at COMELEC. Registration of Filipinos in countries where there are no Philippine diplomatic missions had to be done personally at the embassy or consulate which had consular jurisdiction over the place where they reside.

After initial verification by the diplomatic posts, all application forms were sent to the COAV in Manila and turned over to the local election registration boards (ERBs) in the different cities and municipalities all over the Philippines for the addresses given by the applicants to be verified. The applications for registration/certification were either approved by the ERBs on the basis that the applicants were indeed resident at the place claimed before leaving for abroad, or refused. Thereafter, the processed forms were returned to the COAV in Manila where the COMELEC central office is located. These approved forms became the basis of the Certified List of Overseas Absentee Voters.

Unfortunately, this cumbersome and tedious procedure proved to be a major bottleneck in the implementation of the OAV law, and eventually the DFA-OAVS and the COAV produced different statistics for the actual number of registered Filipino overseas electors.

The DFA, through the Philippine posts abroad, generated 364,187 registrants, of whom 361,884 were classified as regular OAVs. This figure is at least one-third of the estimated number of registrants submitted by the DFA prior to the start of the registration period. Of the applications received, 2,020 came from persons with dual citizenship, while 567 requested transfer from external voting back to the Philippines. Of these latter, 520 applications were granted and 47 were refused. Hence the final figure of 359,297 in the Certified List of Overseas Absentee Voters. Of the 359,297 who registered, only 2,302 were seamen.

The ERBs rejected 397 applications on the grounds that the applicant was not a resident of the city or municipality, or that the person had used an assumed name, or that he or she was unknown in the city or municipality. Due to time constraints, these applicants were not notified of the rejection of their application in time for them to file petitions for inclusion in the Certified List of Overseas Absentee Voters.

Reports from the missions confirmed that, compared to the first week of the registration period (1–10 August 2004), the number of those registering during the last week (21–30 September 2004) jumped by 643 per cent, showing the tendency of the Filipinos to act at the last minute.

By geographical area, the Asia–Pacific and Middle East regions accounted for 86 per cent of the total numbers of registrants, with almost equal number of registrants for each. Europe accounted for 10 per cent, and the Americas a modest 4 per cent. A profile of the registrants would show that most are Filipino overseas workers employed as domestic help in the Asia–Pacific region or as skilled workers in the Middle East.

The Certified List of Overseas Absentee Voters was posted on the websites of both COMELEC and the DFA-OAVS some time in February 2004, and corresponding hard and soft copies were sent to the diplomatic posts.

## The voting

External voting was held in 81 Philippine embassies and consulates, three Manila economic and cultural offices (MECOs) in Taiwan, three satellite voting centres, and 18 field voting precincts. For diplomatic posts with registered seafarers, the voting was held over a 60-day period, starting on 12 March 2004, while those which had only land-based voters started voting on 11 April 2004. The deadline for voting was 10 May 2004 at 15.00, Philippine time, as required by the OAV law (which was also the close of the one-day voting in the Philippines).

The OAV law provides for the overseas absentee voter to vote in two ways. The first is *personal voting:* the registered elector has to present him- or herself before the Special Board of Election Inspectors (SBEI) at the diplomatic post where he or she is registered as an elector in order to vote. In 2004 voters trooped to the posts to cast their votes in person by writing the names of their chosen candidates in the spaces provided on the ballot papers prepared and sent by COMELEC. For each day of the voting period, the posts allotted one cardboard ballot box which had to be sealed at the end of the day regardless of whether it contained a ballot paper. (This meant 60 ballot boxes at missions where there were registered seafarers and 30 ballot boxes at missions were there were only land-based registrants.) The other method is *postal voting:* the registered voter will receive an envelope containing the ballot paper which he has to fill in and send by mail to the post where he/she is registered as an elector. This method was adopted in Canada, Japan and the United Kingdom where the postal systems are efficient and reliable.

Only 4 per cent of overseas registrants were covered by postal voting. On the other hand, personal voting was conducted in 70 countries, covering 245,627 OAVs.

## The counting and tabulation of votes

Of the 359,297 registered and approved overseas absentee voters, 233,092 (65 per cent) voted in the May 2004 national and local elections. This is a considerable turnout under the circumstances and similar to the national turnout in previous national elections.

The Philippine Embassy in Havana in Cuba was the first mission to finish counting and tabulating the votes, while it took the Consulate General in Hong Kong almost 100 hours, or four days, to finish counting as each SBEI or election precinct counted more than 800 ballot papers. Counting was done manually, with the contents of the ballot papers being read aloud and individually tallied. Each precinct would then tabulate the result in the election returns provided by COMELEC. Tabulating and summing up the election returns on a per-country basis took longest—six days—in the Embassy in Riyadh, where the election returns coming from Consulate General in Jeddah and the Philippine Overseas Labor Office in al-Khobar had to be accounted for.

Geographically, the Asia–Pacific and Middle East countries posted the highest turnout by OAVs. In the Middle East, turnout would have been much higher had it not been for the security problems which plagued the region during the voting period. Most OAVs voted during the weekend in Asia–Pacific, Europe and the Americas, while in the Middle East countries most voters came on Thursdays and Fridays, which are considered weekends by most Muslims.

In countries where postal voting was adopted, turnout was only 48 per cent. Factors that affected the turnout were mail being returned to the sender because the addresses provided by the voters were insufficient, addresses as encoded at the COAV being misspelled and therefore incorrect, and a postal strike in the UK. In some instances, mail intended for a particular diplomatic post was misrouted to the COAV.

The respective chairpersons of the Board of Canvassers for each country flew in to the Philippines in time for the overseas votes to be included in the national tally.

## Problems most frequently encountered

The implementation of the OAV law was a success in many ways but, as so often when new arrangements are implemented for the first time, the conduct of the voting and the implementation of the OAV law were not without problems.

1. The tasks allocated to the members of the Foreign Service Corps by the OAV law are over and above their consular duties and required special training. Registration itself took place too soon and the period of registration was too brief to enable the missions to prepare fully for the new task. Hence, the time they spent on the whole electoral process meant less time for their given functions at the posts.

2. The ERBs were not given sufficient time to be informed about the overseas absentee voting process. This led to their decisions on applications being submitted late or in some instances not submitted at all. This may explain the reason why the COAV reported a lower number of registrants compared with the figure submitted by the DFA-OAVS.

3. Misspelling and incorrect inputting or wrong data in the voters' records and IDs were attributed to the complicated application form for registration as an OAV. Most registrants complained about the numerous items to be filled in. As a result, complaints ranged from the issuing of defective IDs to names not appearing in the Certified List of Overseas Absentee Voters, although the COAV did not have any record that the applications concerned had been rejected.

4. The affidavit of intent to return, also called the 'killer clause', discouraged immigrants, permanent residents abroad and persons with dual citizenship from registering as OAVs. They cannot be sure when they will return to the Philippines, so it is difficult to say that they will return within three years of the approval of their application. Moreover, they would not risk being penalized by imprisonment if they failed to return to the Philippines as mandated by the law and voted again in the next national elections as OAVs.

Under the OAV Law, COMELEC would have to set up a monitoring mechanism to enforce this provision of the law. To date, however, it has yet to finalize the procedural rules to implement this provision of RA no. 9189 as the rules and regulations of 2003 dealt primarily with the requirements and procedures for registration, voting, vote-counting and tabulation.

5. The voting period was too long. Some posts which opened as early as 12 March 2004 did not have a single voter until the first day of voting for the land-based OAVs, as not all who had registered decided to vote. Even the 30-day voting period was perceived to be long.

6. Voter education was a particular concern for the diplomatic posts. Most OAVs, including members of the Foreign Service Corps, have been away for several years already. They had problems identifying the candidates and some were not known to them. This resulted in people voting by 'name recall', or voting for those whose names were familiar as few candidates campaigned at the different posts due to cost constraints.

The party list elections were another source of confusion. Most voters asked if they should vote for a particular category of candidate (i.e. migrants or labourers) or for the party list.

7. The low turnout at some posts was attributable to the fact that field registration was not translated into actual field voting. Hence, those registered in the field were not able to vote by reason of distance and cost.

8. The voting, counting and tabulation procedures and the corresponding forms were mostly adopted for overseas absentee voting from the local electoral process. The electoral management bodies found most of them tedious, repetitive and impractical.

9. As most voters were excited about having the chance to exercise their right of suffrage, the ballot papers were usually filled in to the last item. To this was added the problem of electors understanding ('appreciation' is the word used in the election code) of the ballot papers—for example, correctly interpreting similar-sounding names—and of election officials interpreting them and deciding which were spoiled or invalid. Although the SBEIs were trained and taught how to 'appreciate' the ballot papers, they were still apprehensive when the counting of ballot papers came. Hence, counting took time, especially as each SBEI for counting was assigned at least 500 ballot papers, if not more.

## The cost of external voting

COMELEC was allotted 600 million pesos (PHP—c. 11 million US dollars (USD)) for the implementation of the OAV law while the DFA was given a budget of 200 million PHP (c. 3.7 million USD) for the year 2003 and during the 2004 national elections. For the forthcoming registration, both government agencies would be operating on the excess funds from the previous year.

The estimated average cost per registrant was 847.89 PHP (15.42 USD) while the estimated average cost per voter was 1,306.96 PHP (23.77 USD). The difference is understandable as only 65 per cent of the registrants actually voted. Overseas voting is most expensive in Havana, Cuba, while the MECO in Kaohsiung, Taiwan, had the lowest estimated cost per registrant (11.29 USD) and the embassy in Muscat, Oman, had the lowest estimated cost per voter (14.92 USD).

## Recommendations for the improvement of the law

Given the problems and issues which confronted COMELEC in the implementation of the first OAV law, recommendations for its improvement have already been submitted to the Senate and the House of Representatives.

Amendments to the OAV law should be attuned to the proposed revisions of the constitutional requirement on residency and the modernized election laws of the land.

If the constitutional requirement of residency could be relaxed or even abolished because of the mere fact that OAVs are living and working abroad, the provisions on the affidavit of intent to return and the approval of the local ERB would not be necessary. If the residency requirement for OAVs could be relaxed, the election laws should also then be able to recognize the peculiarities and intricacies involved in overseas voting so that it would not be tied to the local scenario of the electoral process.

To date, COMELEC has submitted various amendments to the 1985 Omnibus Election Code for the consideration of the legislature. Suggestions from stakeholders already include automating registration and electronic voting, but the present election laws do not allow this. A more realistic alternative is expanded postal voting. The reason for the low turnout of seafarers, who easily comprise more than 200,000 overseas workers, was the requirement that they had to register and vote in person. Understandably as well, not all overseas Filipinos live near an embassy or consulate. As long as the law requires paper ballot papers and a 'paper trail' to avoid suspicions of cheating during elections, external voting in the Philippines will continue to entail personal registration and voting.

## Registration in 2005

At the time of writing, as amendments to the law were not yet in place, COMELEC is set to usher in a new, continuing registration for OAVs, beginning on 1 October 2005 and lasting until 31 August 2006, that is, for a period of 11 months. This is in response to the demand that the registration period should be longer than the mere two months of the last time.

To address the situation of having to send application forms to the local ERBs, COMELEC was to establish a Resident Election Registration Board (RERB) which would process and act upon all applications for registration at the central office of COMELEC in Manila.

Recognizing the nature of seafarers' work, COMELEC would now allow them to register at any Philippine embassy or consulate abroad. COMELEC would thereafter explore the possibility of expanding the coverage of postal voting to include other countries where there is a limited concentration of Filipinos.

The approved applications for registration/certification were to be considered as applications to vote in absentia, so that registered OAVs do not need to apply anew. COMELEC assumes that for so long as the voter does not apply for transfer of his registration records from his original post of registration to another place, whether in the Philippines or in another country, he is still residing at the same place.

Given that only a modest proportion of the people entitled to do so actually registered as OAVs during the 2003 registration, the natural reaction would be either to scrap or to suspend the implementation of the law. Some observers have attributed the low rate of registration to the perceived apathy of overseas Filipinos who cut all political ties with the country long ago. However, no one can deny the economic contribution they make to the country by way of remittances sent to their families in the Philippines. The task now is to convert this apathy into intelligent and informed votes. To deny the right of suffrage once so fiercely fought for does not seem to be the right response. Hence, if the Filipinos overseas can be made fully aware of their rights and of the potential impact of a consolidated overseas vote in the country's socio-political setting, perhaps their contribution to the political life of the country will be even greater than their economic contribution to nation-building.

CASE STUDY: Cape Verde

# Cape Verde: a large diaspora and low turnout by external voters

Nuias Silva and Arlinda Chantre

The Republic of Cape Verde is a small island country with a strong tradition of emigration which goes back to the 19th century, the result of hard living conditions. Despite the citizens' need to emigrate, however, they have never abandoned the bonds that tie them to their home country, and their currency remittances are an important source of wealth for the national economy.

In the light of this evidence, at the time of the first democratic elections held in Cape Verde, in 1991, Cape Verdeans residing abroad were immediately called upon to participate. In 1992, when a new constitution was adopted, the right of Cape Verdeans living abroad to vote was specified in the constitution. However, they can only participate in elections to the legislature under certain conditions:

(a) they emigrated from Cape Verde not more than five years prior to the date of the beginning of voter registration; or
(b) they have and are providing for a child or children under 18 years of age or handicapped, or a spouse or older relative habitually residing in the national territory, at the date of the beginning of voter registration; or
(c) they are serving in a state mission or a public service position recognized as such by the competent authority, or residing outside the national territory as the spouse of a person in that position; or
(d) if they have been resident abroad for more than five years, they have visited Cape Verde within the past three years.

It should be emphasized that the electoral law did not include any additional requirement for citizens to prove their bonds to the national territory. Cape Verdean nationality is enough, and entitlement is not affected if a person has dual or multiple nationality, even if the other nationality is that of the country where the citizen is resident at the time. It is, however, noticeable that the lawmakers were concerned to provide the suffrage only to those Cape Verdeans living abroad who retain some bonds with the country.

Citizens resident abroad were divided into three electoral districts in accordance with their residency—Africa; the Americas; and Europe and the rest of the world—each electoral district abroad electing one representative.

Those living abroad have the right to vote in presidential as well as legislative elections. Even so, because there were as many Cape Verdean citizens living abroad as were living in the national territory at the time, a solution was chosen that should not compromise national independence—otherwise the votes of citizens resident abroad could have decided the election of a president, whatever the choice of the residents in the national territory. The compromise solution was a system of weighting, as follows. Each citizen residing abroad is entitled to one vote, but these votes must not amount to more than one-fifth at most of the total votes counted in the national territory. If the total number of votes from electors registered abroad exceeds this limit, it is converted into a number equal to that limit and the number of votes cast abroad for each candidate is adjusted proportionately.

Citizens resident abroad can stand for election to the National Assembly (the parliament) but not presidential elections. Candidates for the presidency must have been resident in the national territory for three years prior to the election and cannot have dual or multiple nationality.

For elections to the National Assembly, the provisions in force in 1991 were preserved in the 1992 constitution, but the number of representatives elected by citizens residing abroad was increased, entitling those registered abroad to elect six representatives. The definition of electoral districts abroad and the distribution of seats between electoral districts was left to be determined by legislation, and this was done by the Electoral Law for the Election of the President and the Electoral Law for Elections to the National Assembly, both of 1994. The latter (Law no. 116/IV/94 of 30 December 1994) retained the definition of the electoral districts abroad provided for by the 1991 electoral legislation—Africa; the Americas; and Europe and the rest of the world. Each electoral district abroad now elects two representatives, out of 72, and has as headquarters the city of Praia, the capital of Cape Verde.

The extraordinary constitutional revision of 1995 and the ordinary revision of 1999 kept the established principles unaltered.

Having defined the current constitutional framework, let us analyse how it works in practice.

## Registration

A citizen must be registered in the electoral registers in order to vote, and the electoral code establishes specific arrangements for citizens residing abroad. During the annual registration period, which abroad is from April to June (in the national territory it is from June to July), registration takes place in electoral registration commissions functioning at the country's consulates, embassies or diplomatic missions. It is worth noting that during the registration period the electoral registration commissions may, as happens in the national territory, set up mobile teams to promote the registration of citizens as close as possible to their place of residence. Outside this registration period, the consulates, embassies or diplomatic missions promote the registration of every elector residing within the geographical unit for registration who seeks any other consular services. It can even be said that a citizen residing abroad is in a privileged position compared to a citizen residing in the national territory, since the former can register throughout the year, while a citizen residing in the national territory can do it only from June to July each year.

## The management of external voting

The electoral legislation also sets down specific rules for the organization and conduct of the electoral process abroad.

As many polling stations as necessary are organized so that the number of electors for each polling station does not exceed 800. The polling stations are not confined to consulates and embassies; their number and location are determined by the individual in charge of the consular services, in accordance with the rule of the closest proximity to the voter.

The voting process is similar in all aspects to the process on the national territory. There is no postal voting for external electors.

After the polls close, each polling station board proceeds to determine the partial results. These results, together with the other electoral materials, are sent to the respective consular services, which collect all the electoral material from the polling stations under their jurisdiction. The officers in charge of the consular services then send all the elements they have received to the National Elections Commission headquarters in Cape Verde, so that it can proceed to determine the results for the three electoral constituencies abroad.

There is no separate budget for external voting.

## Turnout

Despite all the efforts made to engage every citizen abroad in the major decisions affecting the country, few Cape Verdeans living abroad are registered to vote, and few participated in the legislative and presidential elections held in 2001. In 2001, a total of 28,022 citizens residing abroad were registered to vote, distributed as follows for the three electoral districts: Africa 5,720; the Americas 8,120; and Europe and the rest of the world 14,182. Only 7,558 of these registered citizens, or 27 per cent, exercised their right to vote, as follows: in Africa 2,486; in the Americas 2,812; and in Europe and the rest of the world 2,260.

According to available data from 2004, 33,998 citizens residing abroad are properly registered—5,694 in Africa, 8,152 in the Americas and 20,152 in Europe and the rest of the world. The population in the national territory was 434,625, according to the most recent census (in 2000), and projections suggest that it would have risen to 475,947 in 2005. The size of the diaspora is estimated at 500,000, including 265,000 in the USA; 80,000 in Portugal; 45,000 in Angola; 25,000 in Senegal; 25,000 in France; and 5,000 in Argentina. Of these some 50–60 per cent may be eligible to register as electors. The main challenges for the Cape Verdean electoral management bodies is therefore to achieve a higher rate of registration and a higher turnout.

# CHAPTER 9

# 9. Observation of external voting

Kåre Vollan

## 1. Observing elections: general background

Observation of elections in transitional or post-conflict democracies became increasingly common during the 1990s. In the early 1990s it had something of the character of a 'guided tour' rather than an assessment against agreed standards that follows a solid methodology. During the 1990s, however, more precise standards for elections were developed by regional organizations—including the Organization for Security and Co-operation in Europe (OSCE) Office for Democratic Institutions and Human Rights (ODIHR), the European Union (EU), the Southern African Development Community (SADC) Parliamentary Forum and the African Union (AU)—based on interpretations of international conventions and declarations, and observation methodologies were developed by regional organizations and by the United Nations (UN). As regards guidelines for election observation, International IDEA together with the UN built on regional standards and developed codes of conduct in the mid-1990s. More recently, the Carter Center, the United Nations Electoral Assistance Division (UNEAD) and the US-based National Democratic Institute brought together global and regional organizations, culminating in the signature of a Declaration of Principles for International Election Observation and Code of Conduct for International Election Observers in October 2005.

International election observation was initially conceived as necessary for a transitional period until general trust in electoral processes had increased and observation would no longer be needed. However, in the past five years it has become more common to send international teams to assess or observe even the elections of 'old' democracies. Such countries have developed processes and legislation over a long period of time which are to a large extent a result of tradition rather than an effort to meet objective standards. While no formal global standards for electoral processes exist, there is a broad common understanding of what constitutes an acceptable election. This understanding has, however, been developed on the basis of the needs of new democracies, implying standards which are meant to create trust between parties who have had little reason to trust each other in the past. Assessments of the electoral processes of traditional democracies against such new standards may therefore add to the electoral process, provide more comparative data and prepare even old democracies for new challenges both in their political environment and regarding new elections technology.

External voting is implemented in many of the older democracies, and the security and secrecy aspects have not been maintained to the same degree as they have for personal voting at in-country in polling stations. The postal voting system used in the United Kingdom (UK) in 2004—not only to accommodate external voters—was a system based on trust, and it was not designed in such a way that it could prevent wilful fraud or the perception of wilful fraud. In 2005 the OSCE/ODIHR launched an election assessment mission to the UK where not least the postal voting came under scrutiny.

However, even though elections in established democracies are sometimes the target of election observation missions, post-conflict countries and fledgling democracies are still receiving most of the attention from observers. Many of the challenges of observing external voting operations are linked to elections in these countries. There is often pressure in these situations to observe the operations due to the perception that the eligibility criteria can be easily manipulated or twisted outside the host country.

## 2. Types of observation and their purpose

Election observation has two main purposes: to assess the election against agreed or accepted standards, and to provide a presence and visibility which will provide fewer opportunities for irregularities and deter fraud. The first purpose can be achieved with a limited number of observers, since conclusions may be drawn from samples. The second objective is likely to require a much larger presence.

Election observation can be carried out by domestic non-governmental organizations (NGOs), or by intergovernmental organizations or international NGOs. While both domestic and international observation can produce effective assessments of elections, domestic observation is usually the only practical way to achieve widespread presence and visibility. Domestic observation is thus—together with the participation of the parties and the review of a critical press—the main instrument for transparency in electoral processes. Even if the electoral process has little or no credibility in the country concerned, domestic observation can contribute to a long-term process of improving the elections. In addition such observation may secure a good electoral process beyond the point when elections have gained general credibility.

Observation reports have a number of targets. These include the domestic electorate and key domestic stakeholders—legislators, the electoral management body (EMB), political parties, the media and commentators. At the same time, donors, intergovernmental organizations and the international public may also be important audiences.

The checks and balances in older democracies are normally taken care of either by appointing representatives of political parties or candidates (party agents) who may observe all parts of the process (which is carried out by independent bureaucrats), or by ensuring that the staff of electoral bodies at all levels are non-partisan, or at least represent a balance of political party sympathies. In new democracies it has become common to allow civil society to observe elections on a more neutral (non-partisan) basis and such practice may prove useful even in older democracies. In addition, international organizations such as the UN, the SADC, the OSCE, the Council of Europe, the AU and the EU, as well as governments and international NGOs, may be invited to observe elections.

## 3. The assessment prior to observation

It is now better understood that it is not worthwhile for all elections to be observed by international organizations, in particular the intergovernmental organizations. It may be the case that elections are run under conditions where the overall conclusions of observation are inevitable from the outset. If, for example, the conditions for standing as a candidate are so exclusive that much or all of the real opposition is eliminated before the elections start, the rest of the electoral process may have limited significance, as in the presidential election in Iran in 2005. Iran is also an example of a case of elected bodies being overshadowed by the powers of the non-elected Council of Guardians, and where international observation, if conducted, could have had the effect of rubber-stamping a result in a situation where even a correctly conducted election did not support a multiparty democracy.

However, even though the conditions for an election are such that an assessment of the legal framework may conclude that the playing field cannot be level, observation may still be organized, not least to show the civil society of the country concerned that there is a focus on the elections, and there may be a long-term objective in building up capacity for the conduct of fair elections in the country. It has therefore been seen to be worthwhile to observe elections in Belarus, Pakistan or Zimbabwe, even though the conditions at the outset might have been assessed to be far from ideal.

## 4. When should external voting be observed?

External voting can often be controversial. For example, opposition parties may claim that it is being used by the incumbents in support of the governing parties, either by allowing (or not allowing) the external vote, or because in the way the process is implemented, which may not be seen to be sufficiently transparent.

If an election is being observed, an assessment of the external voting is an integral part of the process. That does not, however, mean that the process needs to be assessed by observers at every step, even if this is practically possible. One example would be the external voting in Croatia. Shortly before the legislative elections in 1995 the election law was amended to include 12 members of the parliament to be elected by Croatians living abroad. The citizenship law permitted any ethnic Croat to obtain Croatian citizenship without having a family or territorial connection to the Republic of Croatia and without having any intention to move to Croatia. The only condition was that the person issued a written statement stating 'that he or she considers himself or herself to be a Croatian citizen'. The result and intention of the rule were that more than 300,000 Croats from neighbouring Bosnia and Herzegovina acquired Croatian citizenship and were given the right to vote. The opposition claimed that the incumbents allowed this trusting that the Croats in Herzegovina would vote in favour of nationalistic parties. The political and legal conditions for the external voting were therefore more important than the technical conduct of the election.

For the Croatian presidential elections in 1997, the OSCE/ODIHR decided not to observe the external voting. The voting took place in polling stations across Herzegovina and some other cities in Bosnia and Herzegovina and, with an OSCE mission well established in Bosnia and Herzegovina, a high-quality observation operation would have been possible to organize. Given the general framework and the unusual (and, seen from Bosnia and Herzegovina, one would argue, unfriendly) citizenship rules, the main issue was not how the elections were carried out, but rather that they were allowed to happen at all.

For the Croatian legislative elections in 2000, the external voting was observed by the OSCE/ODIHR, partly because there was some development in the discussions between Croatia and Bosnia and Herzegovina regarding the citizenship issue, and partly because the parties to the discussions wanted this part of the process to be observed as well.

Even if there is general agreement on allowing external voting, the process itself may be difficult to observe. External votes are often not cast in person, and the arrangements can cover a large geographical area. The considerations regarding the observation of external voting would therefore involve logistical and practical issues. In the end it is important that an observation mission does not draw conclusions that cannot be substantiated by the evidence that has been collected from the process.

## 5. External voting: controlled and uncontrolled environments

In transitional democracies, where trust in the electoral processes is low, there has been some reluctance to offer citizens living abroad a possibility to vote without returning to the country to cast their vote in person. However, post-conflict countries have been an exception to this rule, as it has often been important to allow those who fled the war the right to vote. The idea would be that those who fled would have an intention of returning and they should be given the right to participate in the democratic process of rebuilding. The 1995 Dayton Agreement which ended the war in Bosnia and Herzegovina specified the right of the refugees to vote (see the case study).

For the first elections in Bosnia and Herzegovina in 1996, the external votes were cast in person. In 23 countries the external voting was observed by the OSCE. In later elections, the external voting was by post, and the observation was limited to the counting in centres inside the country. In the first presidential election held in Afghanistan (2004) refugees in Pakistan and Iran were allowed to vote (although they were not in the legislative elections in 2005), and during the first elections in Iraq (2005) after the 2003 war there were extensive arrangements for external voting (see the case study). However, for the Palestinian elections in 1996 and 2005, the diaspora were not allowed to vote, partly for practical reasons and partly because of the lack of Palestinian citizenship and clear documentation to show who is a 'Palestinian'.

The types of external voting observers will have to assess include:

- voting in a controlled environment, that is, in a place where the secrecy of the ballot is guaranteed by the presence of election staff, and where the vote can be cast without undue influence or intimidation. This means personal voting in the embassies or diplomatic missions of the home country; and
- voting in an uncontrolled environment, without supervision by election staff, and where the secrecy and security of the vote cannot be guaranteed. This voting can include: (a) postal voting, where the voter will be issued with a ballot paper and accompanying documentation which is to be returned by post; (b) electronic voting (e-voting), for example, over the Internet: after a person's identification and right to vote electronically have been verified, the vote is submitted via a computer program to a central computer for counting; and (c) voting by proxy.

Postal voting is the most common method for uncontrolled voting: although voting over the Internet may become common in future (see chapter 10), it is not in use for external voting anywhere yet. Voting in an uncontrolled environment may be vulnerable to impersonation, intimidation and fraud, and observation of the process needs to take such possibilities into account. Voting by proxy is used in some countries, such as the UK. Most countries, however, regard the vote as a personal matter. All votes cast in an uncontrolled environment raise important and controversial issues regarding the secrecy and security of the vote; see chapter 3 for a more extensive discussion.

If the external votes are cast in person, how far voting can be observed is basically a question of resources. If voting is done by post or electronically via the Internet, observation becomes more difficult.

## 6. Data collection

Election observation methodologies describe how information is collected, how to analyse it and how to assess it against agreed standards. The data collection includes:

- the legal framework;
- the procedures and instructions;
- interviews with main stakeholders such as election administrators and representatives of candidates and civil society; and
- first-hand information from the actual processes.

The first three points can always be covered provided there is a free flow of information and possibilities for meeting all involved. The collection of first-hand information is dependent on the transparency of the process and the manner in which the voting is implemented. The purpose is to assess whether the processes are implemented according to their descriptions and intentions. In order for the first-hand observation to be reliable, the evidence needs to be collected according to a plan which will provide a representative sample of information covering all parts of the processes.

## 7. The observation process: possibilities and limitations

Observing external voting may be difficult as a result of the reduced transparency of the process and the costs involved. Collection of first-hand representative evidence from all steps of the process may be impossible. In principle the observation should take the following steps:

- an assessment of the political environment in which external voting is implemented. Is there a general agreement on the terms for external voting and is there general confidence in the process?;
- assessment of the legal framework and the checks and balances worked into the system;
- assessment of the pre-election campaign. The election laws of the country will not apply, but it would still be of interest to assess what is being done to help voters make an informed choice from abroad;
- if the voting is done in person, observing the voting, reconciliation, packing and sealing of the voting material on the basis of a reasonable sample. The assessment of how big the sample needs to be would depend on whether one wants to draw conclusions about the external voting as a separate process in its own right, which would require good coverage, or whether the external voting is only a small part of the overall assessment of the elections;
- if the voting is done by post, observing the verification of the lists of external electors, the distribution of voting material, the reception and verification of the same, and the count; and
- if the voting is electronic, assessment of the process of implementing the system, including the rules for verifying the identity of the voters, audit trails, and the validation performed by the EMB.

All external voting constitutes a challenge from an observation point of view. Domestic observation is often based on wide coverage rather than sampling, and local NGOs may therefore want to cover all polling places. However, domestic observer organizations may not have the resources needed for proper observation of voting in embassies and consular offices (although a worldwide network of Indonesians, mainly students, succeeded in achieving wide-ranging coverage of voting at Indonesian embassies in the 1999 transitional elections). International missions may have an easier task in terms of resources to observe external voting if it takes place in a controlled environment, not least because the sample may be more limited.

Postal and Internet voting would be more complicated to observe. The first problem is the identity of the voter. In Bosnia and Herzegovina a number of attempts to impersonate postal voters allegedly living abroad were exposed in 1998 and 2000. In the case of Internet voting some of the security problems may be solved in the future, but the basic paper trail—the ballot paper—will be missing. In paper-based voting it is always possible to order a recount, and the actual voting will have been followed by observers and party agents.

The most important condition for reliable voting in an uncontrolled environment is general trust in the EMB. Even external voting in a controlled environment requires such trust, since full observation is difficult for parties and NGOs.

## 7.1. The political environment

External voting in transitional democracies is often controversial, either for political or for technical reasons, as discussed above in relation to Croatia. In Zimbabwe, the opposition sought a more liberal ruling for external voting, possibly believing that President Robert Mugabe would have less support among those who have left the country. On the other hand, the same opposition criticized the implementation of the rather limited external voting for its lack of transparency and control.

The key issues for observers to assess are the political environment under which external voting is being conducted and the independence and integrity of the EMB. In particular the arrangements for external voting should be subject to a high degree of consensus, since the transparency of external voting will almost inevitably be less than that of in-country voting. Any dictate from a political majority is likely to attract charges of fraud and manipulation unless the administrators' integrity is beyond doubt.

## 7.2. Personal voting in a controlled environment

External voting may be difficult to observe at all stages. If the voting is done in person in a controlled environment (such as embassies or consular offices), observation may be possible but will be expensive. If the resources are available, the observation of this kind of voting will be rather similar to the observation of in-country voting, where a sample is chosen for collection of first-hand evidence and the process is observed, from the opening to the close of voting to the reconciliation and sealing of the ballot material. However, there may be significant differences from the observation of in-country voting. Observers may stay in the same polling station throughout the voting, rather than moving from one polling station to another during election day. If the count does not take place in the polling station but in counting centres in the country itself, questions of the integrity of votes in transit arise. In such cases it becomes a task for observers to follow the processes of packing and sealing, reconciliation, and reception at the counting centre, as well as the count itself.

### 7.3. Postal voting

If voting is done by post, the actual voting may not be observed, but other processes such as the maintenance of the registers of external electors, the form of the letters sent out to the voters, the documentation required to accompany the ballot paper on its return, the checking of whether ballot papers are genuine and the count may be observed. However, the process may be spread over a period of time and may therefore be difficult to observe throughout.

### 7.4. Electronic voting

If the external voting is done electronically, for example over the Internet, it will be an even bigger challenge to observe all steps of the process. Confidence in the process will depend on the level of trust in the IT system, which in turn to a great extent is dependent on confidence in the EMB.

IT systems should meet a number of criteria, such as being reliable, user-friendly, secure (meaning that they can resist deliberate attacks from outside and inside at all times) and verifiable (meaning that they can be checked). IT systems may be manipulated from inside and from outside. Insiders may build in functions which may change the result in a certain direction. Such manipulation may in theory be conducted by the election administration itself. In transitional democracies, if the general trust in the election administration is low, an electronic voting system may add to the lack of confidence in the electoral process.

Full validation will be next to impossible for any observation mission to perform. One should therefore be very careful not to give the impression that an independent validation of the system has been carried out even though IT experts may have assessed parts of the process. Bringing in such expertise may give a false impression that the systems have been validated against international standards.

In particular, manipulation from inside is in practice almost impossible for an observation mission to assess. Even if the observation mission has IT expertise available, the experts should concentrate on the process which the EMB has carried out when acquiring the systems, rather that pretending to carry out an independent validation of the system. Such assessment of the process should include:

- the choice of supplier, including the requirements for certification against recognized standards for quality and security;
- the validation of the requirements specification and overall design;
- the use of quality auditing during implementation; and
- the strategies for testing the system.

In addition, the audit trails and all possibilities for recovering data in the event of a failure should be assessed. However, the main audit trail in traditional elections, namely the ballot paper, will be missing. It will therefore not be possible to reconstruct the results on the basis of a 'paper trail'. This is why observers need to put much emphasis on the assessment of whether there is a general consensus on the introduction of Internet-based voting and on the integrity of the EMB. A prototype of the IT system may have been validated by the EMB, and it is only the EMB which can ensure that the system being used for the elections is actually the validated system, without any manipulation from election administrators.

## 8. Conclusions

Observing external voting may be difficult both because of lack of transparency in the process and because of lack of resources to be able to collect first-hand information from a wide geographical area. Observation may therefore in some cases be limited to the overall assessment of the conditions for external voting, or to parts of the processes.

The political conditions for external voting should always be assessed. If the very fact that external voting is permitted is controversial, it is likely that general trust in its implementation will be low.

External voting will always be less transparent than in-country personal voting in polling stations. Voting outside controlled environments will be less easy to observe than voting in controlled areas, and e-voting will produce fewer audit trails (such as ballot papers). Therefore general confidence in the EMB and the election administrators is the first criterion for observers to assess when observing external voting.

Should such confidence not be in place, it is difficult to create it by observing the elections. Even if part of the process can be checked, it is difficult to ensure that the process cannot be manipulated by insiders. However, if there is general trust in the intentions of the election administrators, some parts of the process are possible to check and can be observed. They include:

- the registers of external electors;
- the validation of the voters;
- the content of the ballot material used for postal votes, and the manner in which the return of voting material is checked for correctness and against impersonation;

- the way an e-voting system is procured and validated by the EMB;
- the available audit trails; and
- security measures taken against attacks from outside and against technical failure in the case of electronic voting.

In addition, the issues regarding the secrecy of the vote and the possibility of systematic intimidation of voters should be assessed.

# CHAPTER 10

# 10. "E-voting" and external voting*

Nadja Braun

## 1. Introduction

Electronic voting—'e-voting'—is the option of using electronic means to vote in referendums and elections. Different systems exist, such as direct recording electronic (DRE) voting machines that record the vote directly without that vote being transmitted over the Internet or another network: for example, the interface of a DRE machine can be a touch screen, or the voter can fill out the ballot paper and then scan it into the system. Most commonly, e-voting refers to voting over the Internet using a personal computer (PC) with an Internet connection. There are also other means, such as personal digital assistants (PDAs), telephones or mobile phones, that could be used to cast a vote electronically.

It is useful to distinguish between two concepts of e-voting: 'polling place e-voting', and 'remote e-voting'. 'Polling place e-voting' refers to systems where a voter casts his or her vote inside a polling station or similar premises controlled by electoral staff; 'remote e-voting' is used to describe those systems where a voter casts his or her vote at any place outside the polling station. Both could be relevant for the purposes of this Handbook. There are different ways in which electronic means can be used to facilitate external voting. The most challenging would be to allow voters who are abroad to transmit a vote using electronic means, for example, casting a vote at a PC and transmitting it to the electronic ballot box over the Internet. E-voting could also be carried out in the supervised environment of a diplomatic or consular mission. However, in the course of the research for this paper, no instances of the latter solution being considered were found. Only remote e-voting seems to be an option for external voting.

---

*The views expressed in this chapter are those of the author and do not necessarily reflect those of the Swiss Federal Chancellery.

Section 2 of this chapter looks into examples where the use of remote e-voting is being considered as a channel for external voting. Section 3 analyses the arguments in favour and against remote e-voting for external voters, and section 4 gives an overview of the most important security challenges and possible approaches to solutions. Apart from the use of electronic means to vote in referendums and elections, electronic means can also be used to support single steps of the external voting process. Section 5 provides some examples of how new information and communications technologies, especially the Internet, can assist an elector abroad. Finally, section 6 draws conclusions from the research.

This survey is based on some examples of what is being done in the field of e-voting and external voting, collected by the Swiss Federal Chancellery. The research is by no means comprehensive and does not take into account each and every country that is practising e-voting or thinking of introducing it. Nor does the chapter look into the discussion about pros and cons of e-voting in general. The list of references and further reading in annex C gives some indications as to where further information about e-voting in general and the discussion about pros and cons can be obtained.

There are very few overviews of e-voting projects worldwide. An overview dating from the summer of 2004 is available on the website of the ACE project at <http://aceproject.org/ace-en/focus/e-voting/>; see also Buchsbaum 2005.

## 2. Remote e-voting and external voting

Some countries are testing and considering the introduction of remote e-voting especially, and sometimes even exclusively, for their citizens who are living or staying abroad. However, only a few countries allow external voters to cast their votes electronically. Furthermore, there are a few experiments with remote e-voting for external electors, and sometimes expressions of political intentions to consider the question of remote e-voting for external electors. This section highlights some examples of countries that are considering remote e-voting for their citizens abroad.

### Austria

In Austria, e-voting is not a top priority for the government. Nevertheless, the Austrian Federal Council of Ministers approved an e-government strategy in May 2003, in which e-voting is listed as a project in the annex, and in the spring of 2004 the Federal Ministry of Interior established a working group on e-voting in order to study and report on various aspects of e-voting (Federal Chancellery 2003; and <http://www.bmaa.gv.at/view.php3?f_id=6016&LNG=de&version>). The working group was not dealing with the question of e-voting for external electors. However, the explanatory memorandum to the Austrian Federal Act on Provisions Facilitating Electronic Communication with Public Bodies (the e-Government Act, available in English at <http://www.ris.bka.gv.at/erv/erv_2004_1_10.pdf>), which came into force on 1 March 2004, explains the provision for setting up a supplementary electronic register as 'a first step towards enabling Austrian expatriates in future for example to be given the possibility of casting votes at Austrian elections in electronic form' (Explanatory memorandum to the act, in German). In early 2007, the Federal Council of Ministers affirmed its willingness to look into remote e-voting as an additional means of voting as part of a bigger reform of democracy (see <http://www.wienerzeitung.at/DesktopDefault.aspx?TabID=3858&Alias=wzo&cob=274850>).

### Estonia

Discussions on remote e-voting started in Estonia in 2001 and one year later, the legal provisions for it were put in place. During summer 2003 the National Electoral Committee started the e-voting project. The system includes the use of smart cards and electronic signatures (see National Election Committee 2005). The first tests of the remote e-voting system were held in late 2004 and 2005 during local referendums and elections. In March 2007 Estonia held the world's first national Internet election. A total of 30,275 citizens (3.4 per cent) used remote e-voting which was available to Estonian voters in Estonia as well as abroad (see National Election Committee, 'E-voting Project').

### France

On 1 June 2003, French citizens residing in the USA were given the possibility of electing their representatives to the Council of French Citizens Abroad (Conseil supérieur des Français de l'étranger, CSFE; since 2004 the Assemblée des Français de l'étranger, AFE) by remote e-voting. The AFE is a public law body that is allowed to elect 12 members of the upper house of the French Parliament, the Senate. In 2003, the Forum des droits sur l'internet (Internet Rights Forum), a private body supported by the French Government, published recommendations on the future of e-voting in France. It recommended that remote e-voting should not be introduced, except for French citizens abroad who should be able to elect the CSFE by voting over the Internet (see Internet Rights Forum 2003). For the elections of 18 June 2006 all French citizens abroad were able to choose between three voting channels—personal voting, postal voting or electronic voting (Ministry of Foreign Affairs March 2006).

### The Netherlands

In most districts in the Netherlands, voting is done electronically at polling stations. The Dutch Government is also considering and testing remote e-voting (<http://www.minbzk.nl/uk/different_government/remote_e-voting_in>; and Caarls 2004). Dutch nationals resident abroad are entitled to vote in elections to the House of Representatives and the European Parliament (Hupkes 2005). They have to register with the municipality of The Hague for each individual legislative or European election. Dutch electors resident abroad are considered to be an ideal test group for an experiment with e-voting and telephone voting because they are already permitted to vote by post. The purpose of the e-voting project was to ease access for electors abroad and to encourage their participation in elections. The evaluation of the use of e-voting during the elections to the European Parliament in June 2004 showed that e-voting had an added value and made voting more accessible. Subsequently, in the legislative elections in November 2006, Internet voting was made available again as an experiment and an alternative to postal voting for Dutch voters abroad. A total of 19,815 valid ballots were cast in this way (see <http://www.minbzk.nl/bzk2006uk/subjects/constitution_and/internet_elections>).

## Spain

Since 1995, the Generalitat de Catalunya, the government of the autonomous region of Catalonia in north-eastern Spain, has run several pilot projects in parallel with public elections using electronic voting machines inside polling stations. In November 2003, a non-binding remote e-voting pilot was held in parallel with elections to the Catalan Parliament. Over 23,000 Catalans resident in Argentina, Belgium, the United States, Mexico and Chile were invited to participate using any computer connected to the Internet. The Generalitat de Catalunya sponsored this pilot to examine the use of secure electronic voting in the future (see <http://www.gencat.net/governacio-ap/eleccions/e-votacio.htm>).

## Switzerland

In August 2000 the Swiss Government gave the Federal Chancellery the task of examining the feasibility of remote e-voting. An interim report of the Swiss Federal Chancellery on remote e-voting called Swiss living or staying abroad 'the most suitable target group' because remote e-voting could save them time, increase effectiveness and save costs (Federal Chancellery August 2004). Since 2002, a variety of legally binding tests of remote e-voting have been carried out in the cantons of Geneva (see <http://www.ge.ch/evoting>), Neuchâtel (see <http://www.guichetunique.ch>) and Zurich (see <http://www.statistik.zh.ch/produkte/evoting/index.php?p=5>), including between 2004 and 2006 seven remote e-voting trials on the occasion of national referendums. The pilot projects were evaluated in 2005 for a number of different aspects, including the potential of remote e-voting to increase voter turnout, the security risks and its cost-effectiveness. The evaluation has shown that remote e-voting is feasible in Switzerland (see Federal Chancellery, <http://www.bk.admin.ch/themen/pore/evoting/00776>). In March 2007 the Swiss Parliament adopted the legal basis for harmonizing the voter registers for Swiss voters abroad. This is the first step towards the offering the Swiss abroad the possibility of remote e-voting, for which there is a strong demand (see <http://www.aso.ch>).

## The USA

The USA built an Internet-based electronic voting system for the US Department of Defense's Federal Voting Assistance Program (FVAP). The SERVE voting system, as it was called (Secure Electronic Registration and Voting Experiment), was planned for deployment in the 2004 primary and general elections, and would have allowed the electors overseas and military personnel to vote entirely electronically via the Internet from anywhere in the world. It was expected that up to 100,000 votes would be cast electronically. However, SERVE was stopped in the spring of 2004 following a report by four members of a review group financed by the Department of Defense. They recommended that the development of SERVE be shut down immediately because they considered the Internet and the PC not to be sufficiently secure (Jefferson et al. 2004).

# 3. Arguments in favour of and against remote e-voting for external electors

## 3.1. In favour

The common denominator in the seven countries mentioned above is the fact that they wish to make it easier for their citizens abroad to participate in national elections and referendums. In that respect, external electors are considered to be one of the most suitable target groups for remote e-voting, since there is no comparable voting channel fully available for them that would be as comfortable and as accessible. Postal voting—the channel that is probably most comparable to remote e-voting—does not offer the same benefits, since postal services are sometimes too slow for delivering the ballot paper before voting day and thus some external electors are prevented from voting. Other voting channels, such as voting at an embassy or diplomatic mission, are not as convenient for the voter, since he or she needs to go to a certain place during certain hours. The overall thought behind making it easier for external electors to vote in elections and referendums is, of course, to increase voter participation and thus strengthen democratic legitimacy.

Apart from convenience to external electors, there are other reasons in favour of remote e-voting.

1. In some cases, citizens living or staying abroad are considered to be an ideal test group for remote e-voting, while the real intention is to introduce this new method for electors inside the country as well.

2. In some cases, citizens abroad are well organized—even better organized than interest groups inside a country—and capable of formulating their needs and putting them onto the agenda.

3. Depending on the circumstances and the other voting channels available for external electors, remote e-voting might save costs.

## 3.2. Against

Because by and large only those countries that are considering the introduction of remote e-voting provide information on the subject, there are only a few arguments to be found against the introduction of remote e-voting for external electors. These reasons include:

1. *Security concerns*. However, there are no special security concerns with specific regard to remote e-voting for external electors. Rather, it is remote e-voting as such that is considered to be not secure. The security concerns include doubts about the Internet as a means of transmission of confidential information, fear of hacker attacks—both by insiders (e.g. software programmers) and by outsiders (e.g. political parties, terrorists or other states)—and anxiety about the possibility of undue influence being exerted on the voter during the voting process (e.g. 'family voting').

2. *Financial aspects.* It may be costly to build the infrastructure for providing remote e-voting only to a limited number of electors. The expensive items can be the building of a digitized, harmonized register of external electors or the maintenance of security of the system.

3. *Equal treatment of all electors (external and internal).* In Switzerland for instance, the government says that if remote e-voting is introduced it has to be done on a step-by-step basis. It should be introduced for 'internal' electors first and only after that for external electors. The reason behind this is that there is no centralized electoral register for external electors (see the case study). External electors from one canton should not be able to vote electronically while those from another canton do not have this opportunity.

The Australian Electoral Commission (AEC) answers the question 'Can I vote via the Internet?' on its website (<http://www.aec.gov.au/_content/What/enrolment/faq_os.htm>) as follows:

> The introduction of internet or computerised voting is not a feasible proposition at this time, as a number of security, technical, financial, access and equity issues have to be solved before it could become a fact of electoral life.
> - There is no appropriate software technology for use in full preferential voting system.
> - Many voters, especially the elderly and those with poor literacy and numeracy skills may have difficulty with using the internet.
> - There is a risk of fraud and errors occurring in software without the safeguard of paper ballots to recount.
> - Start up costs would be significant.
> - The AEC would need to continue to provide traditional voting facilities for those with no internet access.

However, Australian electors in Australia have been able to use polling place e-voting for elections to the Australian Capital Territory Legislative Assembly. In 2001 and 2004, e-voting was available at four pre-polling voting centres over a two- to three-week period and at eight polling places on polling day itself (see <http://www.elections.act.gov.au/Elecvote.html>).

## 4. Some security challenges for remote e-voting and possible solutions

Before remote e-voting is introduced, several security challenges have to be faced. Table 10.1 gives a first idea of the most important of them. However, each country has different legal conditions and different technical infrastructure available. These should be taken into account as well.

## Table 10.1: Security challenges for remote voting and possible solutions

| Challenges | Possible solutions |
|---|---|
| *Unambiguous identification*<br>The participant in a vote or election must be clearly identified and authorized. | • Individual code in order to gain access to the system<br>• Indication of date of birth and the place of origin for the purpose of identity validation and prevention of systematic fraud<br>• Use of a digital signature<br>• Further personal data could be required. |
| *Authenticity of the e-voting servers*<br>Citizens must have the guarantee that their votes are sent to the official servers. | • The server certificate should be reviewable by the citizens (fingerprint control).<br>• Authenticity could also be demonstrated by an answer code or symbol (image) which can be verified, e.g. on a polling card sent to the elector by post. |
| Unique and universal voting<br>Citizens are allowed to cast one vote. The casting of two or more votes must be prevented. | • As soon as an advance vote (postal or electronic) is cast, the voter could be marked in the electronic electoral register.<br>• Unambiguous features on the polling card (e.g. any tampering with the metallic field or seal covering individual ID codes) could indicate that a citizen has probably already cast a vote. |
| *Protection of voting secrecy/protection of privacy*<br>The intention of citizens must remain secret and must not be seen by a third party. | • Separate and divided storing of personal data and vote.<br>• Random mixing of votes in the electronic ballot box so that it is impossible to gather knowledge of how someone has voted by comparing the sequence of casting votes and time flags in the electronic electoral register |
| *Hacker attacks to:*<br>(a) voting devices (private computers, etc.): possible interception and modification of votes, e.g. by Trojan horses (the weakest point of any e-voting system)<br><br>(b) vote transaction from client to server: possible interception and modification of votes (e.g. man-in-the-middle attack, domain name server (DNS)-hacking).<br><br>(c) central server platform (heart of the e-voting system), e.g. denial-of-service attack. | • Firewall protection<br>• Code voting<br>• Virus scans<br><br>• Vote encryption<br>• Verification by the voter: vote is transmitted as an image, not as text information<br>• In the transaction dialogue all packages should be check-sum tested (hash code) to prove their integrity<br><br>• Several redundant servers<br>• Collaboration with major providers |

| Challenges | Possible solutions |
|---|---|
| *Force majeure*<br>Thunderstorms, earthquakes, terrorist attacks etc. | • Several servers at different locations<br>• Housed in highly secure rooms (access control, fire protection, emergency power supply) |
| *Traceability, recounting*<br>Electronic votes must be recounted if appealed. | • Voter gets a receipt when his or her vote has been cast<br>• Audit trail journal of the counting of conventional and electronic votes signed by the public servants and controllers in charge<br>• Separate storage (CD-ROM) of electronic votes and log files (encrypted) |
| *Confidence*<br>The system and its components must be trustworthy. External experts must be able to review source codes. | • Training of controllers<br>• Use of open-source software (operating system)<br>• Disclosure of proprietary applications |

## 5. Other support through new information and communication technologies

There are also other, less far-reaching ways in which electronic means—among them the Internet—can be used to facilitate voting from abroad. The range goes from providing information to facilitating different steps of the voting process without going so far as to allow voters to cast their ballot electronically. This section highlights some examples.

### Australia

Electors abroad can do different things by fax: enrol to vote; apply to become an 'eligible overseas elector'; enrol as spouse or child of an eligible overseas elector; enrol as an 'itinerant elector'; or apply for a postal vote.

### New Zealand

Overseas electors can download their ballot paper, declaration and supporting documentation from the Internet starting three weeks before election day. However, they cannot return the ballot papers electronically or vote by email, as the website of Elections New Zealand (<http://www.elections.org.nz/voting/how_vote_overseas.html>) emphasizes. Only overseas electors are allowed to download the ballot paper. Completed ballot papers can be returned by fax or ordinary post. Only voters abroad are allowed to fax their ballot papers; if a ballot paper is faxed from within New Zealand, the vote will not be counted.

**Singapore**

Singapore offers overseas electors the possibility of filling out a registration form online. However, the form cannot be transmitted over the Internet, but has to be printed out, signed and sent to the Elections Department or any overseas registration centre by registered post. Registered overseas electors are assigned to vote at one of the overseas polling stations (located within Singapore's high commissions, embassies or consulates). If the elector does not remember which his polling station is, he can find out online (<http://www.elections.gov.sg/overseasvoting.htm>).

## 6. Conclusion

Electors abroad are clearly a focus group that is of particular interest for those countries that are considering the introduction of e-voting in a general manner. At the same time, they are a target group that can be difficult to include in e-voting for practical reasons. Other countries see a need to introduce e-voting for their external electors but do not see the same urgency for introducing e-voting for the internal electors. However, there is no definite trend towards the introduction of remote e-voting, not even in the countries where the first steps towards it have been taken.

CASE STUDY: Estonia

# Estonia: more options for external voting

Epp Maaten

The Republic of Estonia re-established its independence on 20 August 1991 on the basis of legal continuity of statehood. The legislative body in which the supreme power of the state is vested is the parliament, which is elected by proportional representation (PR). The first fully free and democratic national legislative and presidential elections were held on 20 September 1992.

According to the constitution, a citizen who has attained 18 years of age has the right to vote. Participation in voting may be restricted for citizens who have been legally incapacitated or have been convicted by a court and are serving sentences in penal institutions. In legislative elections, every Estonian citizen with the right to vote who has attained 21 years of age has the right to stand for election (paragraphs 56–58 and 60 of the constitution).

The parliament is elected in free, general, uniform and direct elections on the principle of proportionality.

## Entitlement of external electors

Since independence was regained, Estonian citizens with foreign residency have been granted the right to vote in legislative elections and referendums. However, external voting is not possible in elections to local government councils. External voting was practised for the first time during the constitutional referendum in June 1992.

In legislative elections, voters who are *permanently* resident abroad vote in the electoral district in Estonia where they or their parents, or grandparents, were last permanently resident. Citizens who are staying abroad temporarily vote in the electoral district in which they are entered on the electoral register, according to their residence (paragraphs 50 and 54 of the Riigikogu Election Act 2002). External electors, both temporarily and permanently resident abroad, may choose whether to vote at a foreign mission in person or by post.

## The organization of the external vote

Estonia's foreign diplomatic missions organize external voting. The leader of each mission must appoint one of the officials working there to organize the voting. Their work is coordinated by the Ministry of Foreign Affairs, which is also responsible for training and for delivering voting materials such as the electoral registers, ballot papers and envelopes.

Since the late 1990s, with increased volumes of travel and migration, external voting has become more significant. There were major changes in the electoral law concerning external voting in 1998. Estonia is a small country and does not have many diplomatic missions (there were 35 at the time of the 2004 elections). In earlier elections many Estonians were not able to vote because they were living a long distance away from the diplomatic mission. To overcome this problem, in 1999 a procedure for advance postal voting was introduced. The option of personal voting at diplomatic missions still remains.

Since 1999 citizens who are staying abroad *temporarily* have also been able to vote externally, either at Estonian diplomatic missions or by post. Additionally, according to the amended election laws, electors who are permanently resident abroad and who have not voted in the country of residence have the option of casting their vote in Estonia.

To ensure the principle of one person, one vote, external voting takes place in advance. At the diplomatic missions, voting is organized on at least two days in the period between 15 days and ten days before election day. All external voters' ballot papers should be received by the National Election Committee not later than the fourth day before election day. The National Election Committee then sorts them and delivers them to the appropriate electoral district. The right to vote is checked again in the voter's electoral district to ensure that no one has voted more than once. The votes are counted on election day itself.

To improve the checking of their eligibility, all electors, including those living permanently abroad, are registered in a central population register. Before the start of the external voting period, the lists of electors are sent to the diplomatic missions. In certain cases these may be amended by the diplomatic missions.

To ensure the secrecy of the vote, ballot papers are sent in two envelopes. The inner envelope is anonymous, and the outer envelope shows the voter's name and the number of the electoral district. Once the voter's eligibility has been checked against the electoral registers, the outer envelope is removed and the ballot paper in the anonymous inner envelope is put in the ballot box.

For postal voting the voter submits a request to the diplomatic mission of his or her country of residence. If there is no mission in that country the voter addresses the request to the nearest mission. This must be done not later than 45 days before election day. Not later than 35 days before election day, the diplomatic mission sends the voter a ballot paper, the list of candidates and two envelopes. The voter completes the ballot paper and places it in the two envelopes. On the outer envelope he or she writes his or her name and the number of the electoral district. The voter who is staying abroad temporarily also indicates his or her address in Estonia. He or she then sends the envelope back to the diplomatic mission, which collects all the ballot papers and forwards them to the National Election Committee (paragraphs 50–52 of the Riigikogu Election Act 2002).

## Trends in voting turnout

World War II and related events created the Estonian diaspora, with Estonians scattered all over the world. After independence former Estonian citizens and their descendants living abroad had the right to practically automatic Estonian citizenship, and many people have taken citizenship in this way. These are the majority of the electors living permanently abroad. Currently, some 14 per cent of all Estonians—160,000 persons (Kulu 1997)—live outside the country, but the number of electors is significantly smaller. For the 2004 elections, according to the population register about 15,000 Estonians permanently abroad had the right to vote.

In the first legislative elections, in 1992 and 1995, external voting was greatly valued by Estonian citizens living permanently abroad, perhaps because this was the first time in many years they had had the opportunity to take part in the political life of the newly independent Estonia. However, the number of participating voters living permanently abroad has fallen steadily (although in recent elections the share of permanent external voters among all participating voters has increased). An exception to the general trend was the referendum on joining the European Union, in 2003, when total turnout was relatively high and the turnout of voters living permanently abroad also increased.

In contrast, the turnout of citizens temporarily abroad increased over the period 1999–2003.

Exceptionally, in the 2004 elections to the European Parliament turnout was very low in Estonia, as it was in many other European Union countries.

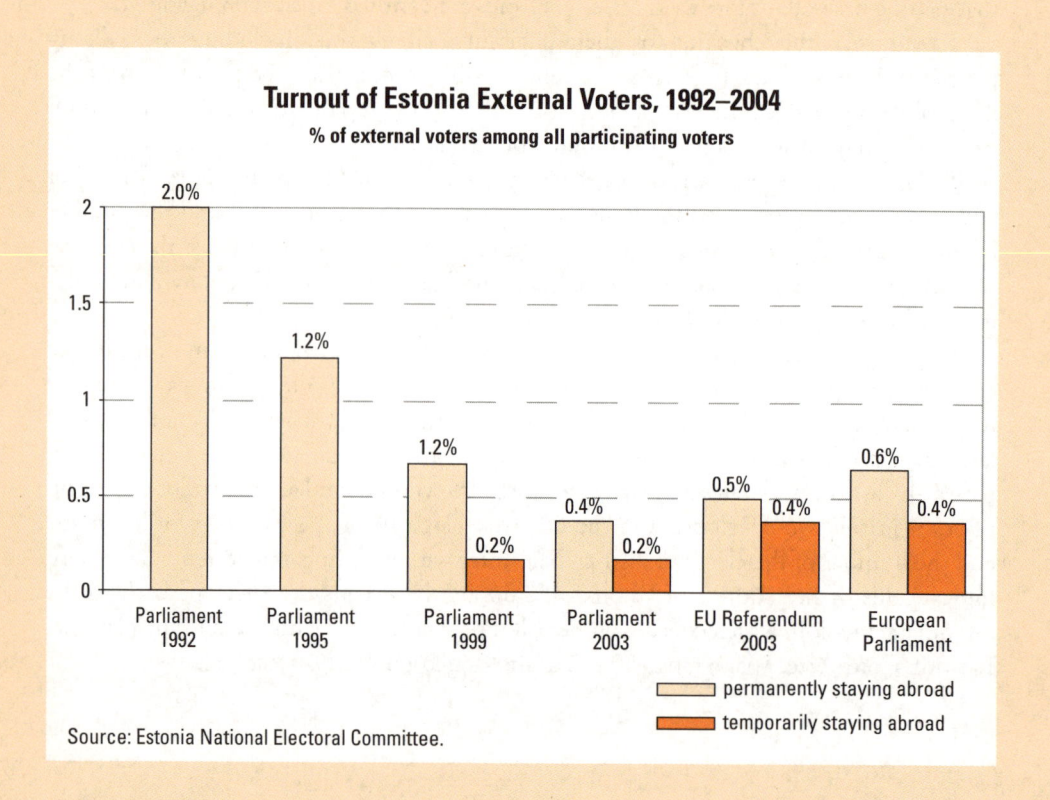

**Turnout of Estonia External Voters, 1992–2004**
% of external voters among all participating voters

| Election | Permanently staying abroad | Temporarily staying abroad |
|---|---|---|
| Parliament 1992 | 2.0% | — |
| Parliament 1995 | 1.2% | — |
| Parliament 1999 | 1.2% | 0.2% |
| Parliament 2003 | 0.4% | 0.2% |
| EU Referendum 2003 | 0.5% | 0.4% |
| European Parliament | 0.6% | 0.4% |

Source: Estonia National Electoral Committee.

## E-voting and external voting

In 2002 the legislative basis for electronic voting was created. The Riigikogu Election Act, the Local Government Council Election Act, the Referendum Act and the European Parliament Election Act all cover e-voting. The main object of e-voting is to give voters an additional option for casting their vote and thereby increase participation. It allows people to vote via the Internet using a digital signature and 'smart' ID cards for identification purposes. The first e-voting pilots were conducted in 2004 and 2005 during local referendums and elections, and in March 2007, in the world's first national Internet election, remote e-voting was available to Estonian voters abroad as well as in Estonia (see National Election Committee, 'E-voting Project').

There is still a concern that people who are permanently resident abroad need a new kind of document—the ID card—in order to vote electronically. The ID card is a compulsory domestic identification document, but not many citizens who are resident abroad have applied for it. On the other hand, for voters who are abroad temporarily, voting will become easy even in local elections (in which external voting organized by diplomatic missions is not foreseen).

If e-voting succeeds and people get used to this method of voting, it may affect external voting. Personal voting at diplomatic missions in foreign countries and postal voting are among the most expensive forms of voting. In future, therefore, consideration may be given to replacing some paper-based ballot procedures with electronic ballot papers, in particular in connection with external voting.

CASE STUDY: Switzerland

# Switzerland: external voting in a federal state with direct democracy

Nadja Braun

Switzerland is well known for its direct democracy and federal structure. All Swiss citizens over the age of 18 except for those who have been incapacitated on grounds of mental illness or mental disability (article 136, §1 of the federal constitution) may take part in elections to the National Council (the main chamber of the federal parliament) both by voting and by standing for election. They may also vote in popular votes (article 136, §2 of the federal constitution). A referendum is compulsory for all amendments to the constitution and for membership of some international organizations (article 140 of the federal constitution). In addition, electors have the right to initiative and referendum, that is, they can request a popular vote by collecting the requisite number of signatures (articles 138, 139 and 141). At present Swiss voters go to the polls on polling weekends. In many places, depending on the local regulations, they can also cast a postal vote, that is, fill out their ballot paper before the polling weekend at any place outside the polling station and send it by ordinary mail. There are no preconditions for postal voting: every voter can choose freely whether to cast a postal vote or to go to the polling station on polling day.

Switzerland is a federal state with 26 cantons and around 3,000 communes. At least four times per year there are popular votes in Switzerland on the national, cantonal and communal level. The four voting weekends and the intense political discussion on the issues that are put to a vote are a particular feature of the Swiss political and electoral tradition.

## Historical background (national level)

Swiss electors who are resident or staying abroad have been allowed to exercise their political rights since 1977. At first, they were only allowed to cast their vote on Swiss territory: they had to travel back to Switzerland in order to vote. This provision has to be seen in close relation with the practice of the Federal Council (the government) with regard to the politically relevant behaviour of foreigners inside Switzerland. Foreigners were not allowed to vote in their own national elections or referendums while on Swiss territory because of issues surrounding Swiss sovereignty. In the light of this fact,

Switzerland could not expect any other state to allow Swiss citizens abroad to cast a vote on its territory. In fact, Switzerland would not even have asked for this, because, if it had been granted Switzerland would have had to grant the same rights to foreigners in Switzerland. In 1989, however, the Federal Council changed its practice. Since then, foreigners have been allowed to take part in the elections and referendums of their own state on Swiss territory. At the same time, the postal vote for Swiss voters abroad was introduced.

Postal voting can be done from anywhere in the world. There are no restrictions whatsoever, except for slow postal services in some countries.

## Voting rights of Swiss citizens resident or staying abroad (national level)

Swiss citizens resident or staying abroad who are eligible to vote are able to take part at the national level in referendums and elections, as well as giving their signatures to initiatives and referendums (article 3, §1 of the Bundesgesetz über die politischen Rechte der Auslandschweizer (BPRAS), the federal law on the political rights of Swiss citizens resident or staying abroad). They have the right not only to vote in elections for the National Council (the 'active voting' right) but also to stand for election to the National Council, the Federal Council or the Federal Court. However, they may only take part in elections for the Council of States (the upper chamber of the federal parliament) if the law of the canton to which they are attached provides the right to vote for Swiss citizens resident or staying abroad.

In the Swiss federal system, those citizens who are resident or staying abroad do not constitute a distinct voting area or electoral district; instead they choose one commune as their 'voting commune'. This could be the commune in which they were born, or one in which they have been previously resident (article 5, §1 of the BPRAS). Eligible expatriates who wish to exercise their political rights must notify the local electoral office of their chosen voting commune where they intend to vote. The notification must be renewed every four years (article 5a of the BPRAS). Eligible Swiss resident or staying abroad can submit their vote either personally at the voting commune in Switzerland (according to the same rules as Swiss voters resident in Switzerland) or by post (article 1 of the BPRAS).

These are the only two options for Swiss voters abroad. There is no provision for voting in diplomatic representations abroad.

Switzerland is currently considering introducing remote e-voting. If it is introduced for Swiss nationals in Switzerland, then the next step would be to make it available to external electors as well. Currently, there are provisions allowing only for the testing of remote e-voting for Swiss voters abroad (article 1 of the BPRAS; see also chapter 10).

## Voting rights of Swiss citizens resident or staying abroad (cantonal level)

Because of the federal structure of Switzerland, voting rights at cantonal level may differ from voting rights at the national level. At the national level, Swiss voters may exercise the same political rights as Swiss voters in Switzerland, but the picture is different at the cantonal level. Only 11 cantons out of 26 (as of 1 October 2004 these were Basel-Land,

Bern, Fribourg, Geneva, Graubünden, Jura, Neuchâtel, Schwyz, Solothurn, Ticino and Zurich) allow electors abroad who are registered in the canton to exercise their political rights at cantonal level. However, the number of cantons that allow external voting is growing slowly but steadily. Usually, the reasons behind the introduction of external voting are of a political nature. If a political party thinks that the voters abroad will support its politics, it is in favour of introducing external voting.

## Some figures

At the end of 2006 there were some 645,010 Swiss citizens resident abroad, of whom about 494,802 were potentially eligible to vote (i.e. they were 18 or over and were not disqualified by reason of mental illness). At the end of December 2006, around 107,600 persons were entered in the electoral register of a Swiss commune and were therefore eligible to vote. These 107,600 electors represented 2.2 per cent of all eligible Swiss electors (4.9 million as of the end of November 2006).

## The costs of external voting

There are no specific data available on the costs of external voting. However, it is possible to make a rough estimate of the additional costs of external voting in comparison to voting in Switzerland. Given that there are some 110,000 external electors, and estimating that about 80 per cent of them live in Europe, the costs can be estimated as follows.

Table 1: The costs of external voting in Switzerland

| Element of expenditure | Cost per voter (CHF) | No. of voters | Total (CHF) | Total (EUR) |
|---|---|---|---|---|
| Postal charges within Europe (priority mail, 101–250 g) | 6.50 | 88,000 | 572,000 | 381,300 |
| Postal charge outside Europe (priority mail, 101–250 g) | 8.80 | 22,000 | 193,600 | 129,000 |
| Personnel costs (packing and advance sending of material) | 2.00 | | 220,000 | 146,700 |
| Total | | 110,000 | 985,600 | 657,000 |

CHF = Swiss francs. EUR = euro.

## The voting behaviour of Swiss citizens resident or staying abroad

A survey carried out in 2003 by the Organisation of the Swiss Abroad (ASO) and swissinfo/Swiss Radio International (see GfS Forschungsinstitut June 2003) revealed that Swiss citizens resident or staying abroad have a very distinctive voting profile, formed far less by their political opinions than by such values as modernity of outlook, cosmopolitanism, openness to change, tolerance towards foreigners and belief in the free market.

## Representation of Swiss abroad in the parliament

In the National Council elections of 19 October 2003, the Swiss People's Party (Schweizerische Volkspartei, SVP) in the canton of Zurich came up with a list of candidates for Swiss external voters (List 21: SVP-Union of Swiss Abroad). To date, no overseas candidate has ever been elected to the federal parliament. One reason for this may lie in the fact that the electoral potential of the Swiss abroad is diffused. Since they do not form their own constituency, their votes are distributed among the 26 cantons. However, the election in the spring of 2004 of the Swiss military attaché in Stockholm, Beat Eberle, to the parliament of the canton of St Gallen demonstrates that it is possible for Swiss citizens resident abroad to be elected.

# Annex A

# External voting: a world survey of 214 countries and territories*

- ☐ Countries with provisions for external voting
- ☐ Countries without provisions for external voting
- ☐ Countries in transition
- ☐ Countries with no provisions for direct elections

|   | Country or territory | Type of election | Voting method | First year implemented | Notes/comments |
|---|---|---|---|---|---|
| 1 | AFGHANISTAN | Presidential | Personal | 2004 | Applied for the Loya Jirga and constitutional Loya Jirga elections in 2002 and 2003, and then the presidential election in 2004, but not to the legislative elections in 2005. |
| 2 | ALBANIA | No external voting | No external voting | | |
| 3 | ALGERIA | Presidential, legislative, sub-national, referendums | Mixed (personal, proxy) | 1976 | Implemented in the referendum of 1976, for legislative elections 1977. |
| 4 | ANDORRA | No external voting | No external voting | | |
| 5 | ANGOLA | Legislative | Personal | Not applicable | External voting is still to be implemented. A decision by the EMB is needed, agreeing among other things that that the material conditions for an election are met. Once this happens, the citizens residing abroad will form one electoral district and will elect three representatives. |
| 6 | ANGUILLA | No external voting | No external voting | | |
| 7 | ANTIGUA AND BARBUDA | No external voting | No external voting | | |

* The survey corresponds to May, 2007.

|  | Country or territory | Type of election | Voting method | First year implemented | Notes/comments |
|---|---|---|---|---|---|
| 8 | ARGENTINA | Presidential, legislative | Personal | 1993 | |
| 9 | ARMENIA | No external voting | No external voting | Not applicable | External voting was abolished in 2007. |
| 10 | ARUBA | No external voting | No external voting | | |
| 11 | AUSTRALIA | Legislative | Mixed (personal, postal, fax) | 1902 | |
| 12 | AUSTRIA | Presidential, legislative, referendums | Postal | 1990 | |
| 13 | AZERBAIJAN | Legislative | Personal | 2000 | |
| 14 | BAHAMAS | No external voting | No external voting | | |
| 15 | BAHRAIN | No external voting | No external voting | | |
| 16 | BANGLADESH | Legislative | Postal | Not available | |
| 17 | BARBADOS | No external voting | No external voting | | |
| 18 | BELARUS | Presidential, legislative, sub-national, referendums | Personal | 1994 | |
| 19 | BELGIUM | Legislative | Mixed (personal, postal, proxy) | 1999 | |
| 20 | BELIZE | No external voting | No external voting | | |
| 21 | BENIN | Presidential | Mixed (personal, proxy) | Not available | |
| 22 | BERMUDA | No external voting | No external voting | | |
| 23 | BHUTAN | No provisions for direct elections | No provisions for direct elections | | |
| 24 | BOLIVIA | Presidential | Not yet decided | Not applicable | Not yet implemented. A law including external provisions was passed by the lower chamber of the parliament on 6 December 2005. It is now being discussed in the upper chamber. |
| 25 | BOSNIA AND HERZEGOVINA | Presidential, legislative, sub-national | Postal | 1996 | |

## VOTING FROM ABROAD

| | Country or territory | Type of election | Voting method | First year implemented | Notes/comments |
|---|---|---|---|---|---|
| 26 | BOTSWANA | Legislative | Personal | 1997 | |
| 27 | BRAZIL | Presidential | Personal | 1989 | |
| 28 | BRUNEI DARUS-SALAM | No provisions for direct elections | No provisions for direct elections | | |
| 29 | BULGARIA | Presidential, legislative | Personal | 1990 | |
| 30 | BURKINA FASO | No external voting | No external voting | | |
| 31 | BURMA[1] | No external voting | No external voting | | |
| 32 | BURUNDI | No external voting | No external voting | | |
| 33 | CAMBODIA | See comments | See comments | | Special practice at elections to the Constituent Assembly in 1993 |
| 34 | CAMEROON | No external voting | No external voting | | |
| 35 | CANADA | Legislative, referendums | Postal | 1944 | |
| 36 | CAPE VERDE | Presidential, legislative | Personal | 1991 | |
| 37 | CAYMAN ISLANDS | No external voting | No external voting | | |
| 38 | CENTRAL AFRICAN REPUBLIC | Presidential | Personal | Not available | |
| 39 | CHAD | Presidential | Mixed (personal, proxy) | 2001 | |
| 40 | CHILE | No external voting | No external voting | | A legislative proposal is being discussed and was approved by one of the commissions of the Law Chamber on 4 October 2006 (the Commission on Human Rights, Nationality and Citizenship). It has been suggested that external voting be applied for presidential elections and plebiscites at the next presidential election in 2010. |
| 41 | CHINA | No provisions for direct elections | No provisions for direct elections | | |

[1] The UN name is Myanmar.

|    | Country or territory | Type of election | Voting method | First year implemented | Notes/comments |
|----|---------------------|------------------|---------------|------------------------|----------------|
| 42 | COLOMBIA | Presidential, legislative | Personal | 1962 | In the most recent presidential election (March 2006), Colombians abroad also participated in the primary elections for presidential candidates of two political parties (Partido Liberal and Polo Democrático Alternativo). |
| 43 | COMOROS | No external voting | No external voting | | There is an Electoral Code reform draft before the Congress, article 4 of which would provide for the possibility of voting in referendums from abroad. |
| 44 | CONGO (BRAZZAVILLE) | No external voting | No external voting | | |
| 45 | CONGO (KINSHASA), DEMOCRATIC REPUBLIC | No external voting | No external voting | | |
| 46 | COOK ISLANDS | Legislative, referendums | Mixed (personal, postal) | 1981 | The reserved seat for external voters was abolished in 2004. |
| 47 | COSTA RICA | No external voting | No external voting | | An Electoral Code draft handed to the Congress outlines the possibilities for introducing external voting. A draft chapter on external voting was handed to the lower chamber in May 2006 to be added to the Electoral Code. It suggests that citizens abroad can vote for presidential and legislative elections at diplomatic offices/personal voting. If external voting is approved it may be implemented for the 2010 national elections. |
| 48 | CÔTE D'IVOIRE | Presidential | Personal | 1995 | |
| 49 | CROATIA | Presidential, legislative | Personal | 1992 | |
| 50 | CUBA | No provisions for direct elections | No provisions for direct elections | | |
| 51 | CYPRUS | No external voting | No external voting | | |
| 52 | CYPRUS (NORTH) | No external voting | No external voting | | |

| | Country or territory | Type of election | Voting method | First year implemented | Notes/comments |
|---|---|---|---|---|---|
| 53 | CZECH REPUBLIC | Legislative | Personal | 2002 | |
| 54 | DENMARK | Legislative, sub-national, referendums | Postal | 1980 | |
| 55 | DJIBOUTI | Presidential, legislative | Personal | Not available | |
| 56 | DOMINICA | No external voting | No external voting | | |
| 57 | DOMINICAN REPUBLIC | Presidential | Personal | 2004 | Legislated in 1997. Discussions going ongoing about how the Dominican voters abroad can obtain their ID/voting card. |
| 58 | ECUADOR | Presidential | Personal | 2006 | |
| 59 | EGYPT | No external voting | No external voting | | Discussions in progress about the possibility of introducing external voting. |
| 60 | EL SALVADOR | No external voting | No external voting | | |
| 61 | EQUATORIAL GUINEA | Presidential, legislative | Personal | Not available | |
| 62 | ERITREA | Country in transition | Country in transition | | External voting allowed in the referendum on independence in 1993. Eritrean Referendum Proclamation (no. 22/1992) |
| 63 | ESTONIA | Legilsative, referendum | Mixed (personal, postal, e-voting) | 1992 | |
| 64 | ETHIOPIA | No external voting | No external voting | | |
| 65 | FALKLAND ISLANDS | Legislative, sub-national | Postal | Not available | |
| 66 | FIJI | Legislative | Postal | Not available | |
| 67 | FINLAND | Presidential, legislative, sub-national | Personal | 1958 | |
| 68 | FRANCE | Presidential, referendums (and 12 seats in the Senate) | Mixed (personal, proxy) | 1976 | External voting implemented for the first time in 1924 for French administrators posted to the occupied Rhineland. Postal voting. |
| 69 | GABON | Presidential, referendums | Mixed (personal, proxy) | Not available | |
| 70 | GAMBIA | No external voting | No external voting | | |
| 71 | GEORGIA | Presidential, legislative | Personal | 1995 | |

| | Country or territory | Type of election | Voting method | First year implemented | Notes/comments |
|---|---|---|---|---|---|
| 72 | GERMANY | Legislative | Postal | 1985 | |
| 73 | GHANA | Presidential, legislative | Personal | 2008 | |
| 74 | GIBRALTAR | Legislative | Postal | Not available | |
| 75 | GREECE | Legislative | Not yet implemented | Not applicable | |
| 76 | GRENADA | No external voting | No external voting | | |
| 77 | GUATEMALA | No external voting | No external voting | | |
| 78 | GUERNSEY | Legislative | Postal | Not available | |
| 79 | GUINEA | Presidential, legislative | Mixed (personal, proxy) | 1993 | |
| 80 | GUINEA-BISSAU | Legislative | Personal | Not available | |
| 81 | GUYANA | Legislative | Personal | 1993 | |
| 82 | HAITI | No external voting | No external voting | | |
| 83 | HOLY SEE (VATICAN CITY STATE) | No provisions for direct elections | No provisions for direct elections | | |
| 84 | HONDURAS | Presidential | Personal | 2001 | |
| 85 | HUNGARY | Legislative, referendums | Personal | 2004 | |
| 86 | ICELAND | Presidential, legislative, sub-national | Personal | 1949 | |
| 87 | INDIA | Legislative | Mixed (postal, proxy) | 2004 | |
| 88 | INDONESIA | Presidential, legislative | Mixed (personal, postal) | 1955 | |
| 89 | IRAN, ISLAMIC REPUBLIC OF | Presidential, referendums, sub-national | Personal | 1980 | |
| 90 | IRAQ | Legislative | Personal | 2004 | |
| 91 | IRELAND | Presidential, legislative, sub-national, referendums | Postal | 1992 | |
| 92 | ISRAEL | Presidential, legislative | Personal | Not available | |
| 93 | ITALY | Legislative, referendums | Postal | 2003 | |
| 94 | JAMAICA | No external voting | No external voting | | |

| | Country or territory | Type of election | Voting method | First year implemented | Notes/comments |
|---|---|---|---|---|---|
| 95 | JAPAN | Legislative | Mixed (personal, postal) | 2002 | |
| 96 | JERSEY | Legislative | Postal | Not available | |
| 97 | JORDAN | No external voting | No external voting | | |
| 98 | KAZAKHSTAN | Presidential, legislative, sub-national | Personal | 1994 | |
| 99 | KENYA | No external voting | No external voting | | |
| 100 | KIRIBATI | No external voting | No external voting | | |
| 101 | KOREA, DEMOCRATIC PEOPLE'S REPUBLIC OF | No external voting | No external voting | | |
| 102 | KOREA, REPUBLIC OF | No external voting | No external voting | | Discussions in process about the possibility of introducing external voting. |
| 103 | KUWAIT | No external voting | No external voting | | |
| 104 | KYRGYZSTAN | Presidential, referendums | Personal | 2000 | |
| 105 | LAO PEOPLE'S DEMOCRATIC REPUBLIC | Legislative | Personal | 2006 | |
| 106 | LATVIA | Legislative, referendums | Mixed (personal, postal) | 1992 | |
| 107 | LEBANON | No external voting | No external voting | | |
| 108 | LESOTHO | Legislative | Postal | Not available | |
| 109 | LIBERIA | No external voting | No external voting | | |
| 110 | LIBYAN ARAB JAMAHIRIYA | No provisions for direct elections | No provisions for direct elections | | |
| 111 | LIECHTENSTEIN | Legislative, sub-national, referendums | Postal | 2004 | |
| 112 | LITHUANIA | Presidential, referendums | Mixed (personal, postal) | 1992 | |
| 113 | LUXEMBOURG | Legislative | Postal | 1984 | |
| 114 | MACEDONIA, THE FORMER YUGOSLAV REPUBLIC OF | No external voting | No external voting | | |
| 115 | MADAGASCAR | No external voting | No external voting | | |

|  | Country or territory | Type of election | Voting method | First year implemented | Notes/comments |
|---|---|---|---|---|---|
| 116 | MALAWI | No external voting | No external voting | | |
| 117 | MALAYSIA | Legislative, sub-national | Postal | Not available | |
| 118 | MALDIVES | No external voting | No external voting | | |
| 119 | MALI | Presidential, referendums | Mixed (personal, proxy) | 1992 | |
| 120 | MALTA | No external voting | No external voting | | |
| 121 | MAN, ISLE OF | Legislative, sub-national | Postal | 1976 | |
| 122 | MARSHALL ISLANDS | Legislative | Postal | Not available | |
| 123 | MAURITANIA | No external voting | No external voting | | |
| 124 | MAURITIUS | Legislative, sub-national | Proxy | Not available | |
| 125 | MEXICO | Presidential | Postal | 2006 | |
| 126 | MICRONESIA, FEDERATED STATES OF | Legislative, sub-national | Mixed (personal, postal) | Not available | |
| 127 | MOLDOVA, REPUBLIC OF | Presidential, legislative, referendums | Personal | 1993 | |
| 128 | MONACO | No external voting | No external voting | 2007 | |
| 129 | MONGOLIA | No external voting | No external voting | | |
| 130 | MONTENEGRO | No external voting | No external voting | | |
| 131 | MONTSERRAT | No external voting | No external voting | | |
| 132 | MOROCCO | No external voting | No external voting | | |
| 133 | MOZAMBIQUE | Presidential, legislative | Personal | 2004 | |
| 134 | NAMIBIA | Presidential, legislative | Personal | 1994 | |
| 135 | NAURU | Legislative | Proxy | 2004 | |
| 136 | NEPAL | No external voting | No external voting | | |
| 137 | NETHERLANDS | Legislative | Mixed (postal, proxy, e-voting) | 1989 | |
| 138 | NETHERLANDS ANTILLES | No external voting | No external voting | | |

| | Country or territory | Type of election | Voting method | First year implemented | Notes/comments |
|---|---|---|---|---|---|
| 139 | NEW ZEALAND | Legislative, sub-national, referendums | Mixed (personal, postal, fax) | 1957 | |
| 140 | NICARAGUA | Presidential, legislative | N/A (most likely to be personal) | Not applicable | There is a law but the EMB needs to decide six months prior to the election that external voting will take place. This has not yet happened. |
| 141 | NIGER | Presidential, referendum | Personal | Not available | |
| 142 | NIGERIA | No external voting | No external voting | | Discussions in progress about the possibility of introducing external voting. |
| 143 | NIUE | No external voting | No external voting | | |
| 144 | NORWAY | Legislative, sub-national | Postal | 1921 | |
| 145 | OMAN | Legislative | N/A | Not available | |
| 146 | PAKISTAN | No external voting | No external voting | | |
| 147 | PALAU | Legislative, sub-national, referendums | Personal, postal | 1981 | |
| 148 | PALESTINE | No external voting | No external voting | | |
| 149 | PANAMA | Presidential | Postal | | A decision by the Panamanian Congress in 2006 and a following decision by the Electoral Tribunal in 2007 allows for External Voting. |
| 150 | PAPUA NEW GUINEA | No external voting | No external voting | | |
| 151 | PARAGUAY | No external voting | No external voting | | |
| 152 | PERU | Presidential, legislative, referendums | Personal | 1980 | |
| 153 | PHILIPPINES | Presidential, legislative | Mixed (personal, postal) | 2004 | |
| 154 | PITCAIRN ISLANDS | Legislative | Personal | 2001 | |
| 155 | POLAND | Presidential, legislative, referendums | Personal | 1990 | |
| 156 | PORTUGAL | Presidential, legislative, referendums | Mixed (personal, postal) | 1976 | |

|  | Country or territory | Type of election | Voting method | First year implemented | Notes/comments |
|---|---|---|---|---|---|
| 157 | QATAR | No provisions for direct elections | No provisions for direct elections | | |
| 158 | ROMANIA | Presidential, legislative | Personal | 1990 | |
| 159 | RUSSIAN FEDERATION | Legislative, presidential, sub-national, referendums | Personal | Not available | |
| 160 | RWANDA | Presidential, legislative, referendums | Personal | 2003 | |
| 161 | SAINT HELENA | No external voting | No external voting | | |
| 162 | SAINT KITTS AND NEVIS | No external voting | No external voting | | |
| 163 | SAINT LUCIA | No external voting | No external voting | | |
| 164 | SAINT VINCENT AND THE GRENADINES | No external voting | No external voting | | |
| 165 | SAMOA | No external voting | No external voting | | |
| 166 | SAN MARINO | No external voting | No external voting | | |
| 167 | SAO TOME AND PRINCIPE | Presidential, legislative | Personal | Not available | |
| 168 | SAUDI ARABIA | No provisions for direct elections | No provisions for direct elections | | |
| 169 | SENEGAL | Presidential, legislative | Personal | 1993 | |
| 170 | SERBIA | No external voting | No external voting | | |
| 171 | SEYCHELLES | No external voting | No external voting | | |
| 172 | SIERRA LEONE | No external voting | No external voting | | Voters may register but not vote from another country. |
| 173 | SINGAPORE | Presidential, legislative | Personal | 2006 | |
| 174 | SLOVAKIA | No external voting | No external voting | N/A | |
| 175 | SLOVENIA | Presidential, legislative, referendums | Mixed (personal, postal) | 1992 | |
| 176 | SOLOMON ISLANDS | No external voting | No external voting | | |

|  | Country or territory | Type of election | Voting method | First year implemented | Notes/comments |
|---|---|---|---|---|---|
| 177 | SOMALIA | Transitional | Transitional | | |
| 178 | SOUTH AFRICA | Legislative | Personal | 1994 | |
| 179 | SPAIN | Legislative, sub-national, referendums | Mixed (personal, postal) | 1985 | |
| 180 | SRI LANKA | No external voting | No external voting | | |
| 181 | SUDAN | Presidential, referendums | Personal | 1986 | |
| 182 | SURINAME | No external voting | No external voting | | |
| 183 | SWAZILAND | No external voting | No external voting | | |
| 184 | SWEDEN | Legislative, referendums | Mixed (personal, postal, proxy) | 1968 | |
| 185 | SWITZERLAND | Legislative, sub-national, referendums | Postal | 1977 | |
| 186 | SYRIAN ARAB REPUBLIC | Presidential, legislative | Personal | Not available | |
| 187 | TAIWAN | No external voting | No external voting | | |
| 188 | TAJIKISTAN | Presidential, legislative, referendums | Postal | 1994 | |
| 189 | TANZANIA, UNITED REPUBLIC OF | No external voting | No external voting | | |
| 190 | THAILAND | Legislative | Mixed (personal, postal) | 2000 | |
| 191 | TIMOR-LESTE | See comments | See comments | | External voting used in the 1999 referendum only. |
| 192 | TOGO | Presidential, legislative, sub-national, referendums | Proxy | Not available | |
| 193 | TOKELAU | Country in transition | Country in transition | | External voting used in the 2006 referendum on independence only. |
| 194 | TONGA | No external voting | No external voting | | |
| 195 | TRINIDAD AND TOBAGO | No external voting | No external voting | | |
| 196 | TUNISIA | Presidential | Personal | 2004 | |
| 197 | TURKEY | Legislative | Personal | Not available | |

|  | Country or territory | Type of election | Voting method | First year implemented | Notes/comments |
|---|---|---|---|---|---|
| 198 | TURKMENISTAN | No external voting | No external voting | | |
| 199 | TURKS AND CAICOS ISLANDS | No external voting | No external voting | | |
| 200 | TUVALU | No external voting | No external voting | | |
| 201 | UGANDA | No external voting | No external voting | | |
| 202 | UKRAINE | Presidential, legislative, referendums | Personal | 1994 | |
| 203 | UNITED ARAB EMIRATES | No provisions for direct elections | No provisions for direct elections | | |
| 204 | UNITED KINGDOM OF GREAT BRITAIN AND NORTHERN IRELAND | Legislative | Mixed (postal, proxy) | 1918 | |
| 205 | UNITED STATES OF AMERICA | Presidential, legislative, sub-national, referendums | Primarily postal | 1942 | The voting method in the United States of America varies by state as external voting processes in this federal system are mainly managed on state level. |
| 206 | URUGUAY | No external voting | No external voting | | |
| 207 | UZBEKISTAN | Presidential, legislative, referendums | Personal | 1994 | |
| 208 | VANUATU | Legislative, sub-national | Proxy | 1980 | |
| 209 | VENEZUELA | Presidential | Personal | 1998 | External voting applies for referendums on presidential recall. |
| 210 | VIETNAM | No external voting | No external voting | | |
| 211 | VIRGIN ISLANDS, BRITISH | No external voting | No external voting | | |
| 212 | YEMEN | Presidential, referendums | Personal | Not available | |
| 213 | ZAMBIA | No external voting | No external voting | | |
| 214 | ZIMBABWE | Legislative | Postal | 1980 | |

# Annex B

# Glossary of terms

This glossary defines the use of words within this Handbook. Some words may have specific definitions within the legislation and regulations of a particular country (note particularly in this context *citizenship, immigrant, naturalization* and *resident*).

**Advance voting** – The opportunity for *elector*s to cast their vote before election day. There are a variety of ways in which this can be done, including *postal voting* and voting at determined *polling sites*.

**Asylum seeker** – A person whose application for asylum in or recognition as a *refugee* by a country of which he or she is not a citizen is pending, and who claims to fear persecution if returned home.

**Attendance voting** – See *Personal voting*.

**Boundary delimitation** – The process by which a country, local authority area or area of a supranational institution is divided into *electoral districts*.

**Campaign** – The political activity, including meetings, rallies, speeches, demonstrations, parades, other events, and the use of the media, intended to inform the *electorate* of the platform of a particular candidate or political party and to gather support.

**Citizenship** – The status of being a citizen of a country, which is accompanied by a range of rights and obligations often defined in the constitution or a basic or organic law. Requirements for citizenship vary, and may include being born in a country, having one parent or both parents from that country, or *naturalization*.

**Closed list** – A form of *List proportional representation* (PR) in which *electors* are restricted to voting only for a party or political grouping, and cannot express a preference for any candidate within a party list. See also *Open list*.

**Communal roll** – A register of *elector*s for which the qualification for registration is a determinable criterion such as religion, ethnicity, language or gender. All *elector*s who meet the criterion may be entered in the communal roll automatically, or each such *elector* may be able to choose whether or not to be entered. This register is used for the election of representatives of the group defined by the criterion from *electoral districts* specified for that purpose.

**Diaspora** – Population of a country who have migrated abroad and keep strong identity ties with the homeland.

**Diplomatic mission** – A formal representation of a country in another country recognized under the Vienna Convention, for example an embassy, high commission or consulate.

**Distance voting** – See *Remote voting*.

**E-voting** – Short form for *electronic voting*. Any method of voting using electronic means. Examples include casting a vote through the Internet, by personal digital assistant (PDA), telephone or mobile phone, or digital television.

**Elector** – A person who is both qualified and registered to vote in an election.

**Electoral district** – One of the geographical areas into which a country, local authority or supranational institution may be divided for electoral purposes. An electoral district may elect one or more representatives to an elected body. See *Multi-member district* and *Single-member district*.

**Electoral law** – One or more pieces of legislation governing all aspects of the process for electing the political institutions defined in a country's constitution or institutional framework.

**Electoral management body (EMB)** – The organization tasked under the *electoral law* with responsibility for the conduct of elections. The EMB in most countries consists either of an independent commission appointed for the purpose or of part of a specified government department.

**Electoral register** – The list of persons registered as qualified to vote.

**Electoral regulations** – Rules subsidiary to legislation made, often by the *electoral management body*, under powers contained in the *electoral law* which govern aspects of the organization and administration of an election.

**Electoral system** – That part of the *electoral law* and *regulations* which determines how parties and candidates are elected to a representative body. Its three most significant components are the electoral formula, the ballot structure and the district magnitude.

**Electorate** – May have one of two distinct meanings: (a) the total number of *electors* registered to vote in an *electoral district*; and (b) a synonym for *electoral district* used predominantly in some anglophone countries. See *Electoral district*.

**Electronic voting** – See *e-voting*.

**Entitlement restrictions** – Provisions in the *electoral law* and *regulations* of a country which govern the practical requirements for an *elector* to cast his or her vote. They may be of two types, legal and administrative.

**External districts** – *Electoral districts* of which the *electorate* is made up of *external electors*, from which representatives are elected to *reserved seats*.

**External elector** – An *elector* who is registered as *resident* outside his or her country of *citizenship* or otherwise as being not present in his or her country of *citizenship*.

**External voting** – The inclusion in the *electoral law* and *regulations* of a country of provisions and procedures which enable some or all *electors* of a country who are temporarily or permanently outside the country to exercise their voting rights from outside the territory of the country.

**Fax voting** – A mechanism of voting in which an *elector* receives and returns the voting material by fax.

**Gerrymandering** – The deliberate manipulation of *electoral district* boundaries so as to advantage or disadvantage a particular political interest.

**Host country** – A country that allows *external voting* to take place on its territory by *electors* from another country.

**Immigrant** – A person who is accepted as a *resident* by a country other than that of his or her *citizenship*.

**Intention to return** – A specific commitment from a person living outside his or her country of *citizenship* to return to that country within a specified term, in order to ensure the exercise of defined rights.

**Internal voting** – Voting inside a country which is holding an election.

**Internally displaced person (IDP)** – A *refugee* within the borders of his or her own country.

**List proportional representation (List PR)** – An *electoral system* in which each participant party or grouping presents a list of candidates for an *electoral district*, voters vote for a party, and parties receive seats in proportion to their overall share of the vote. Winning candidates are taken from the lists. List PR systems include *Closed list* and *Open list*.

**Migrant worker** – A person who migrates abroad with the main purpose of obtaining a wage-earning job, often of a nature not requiring qualifications, and often for the purpose of sending remittances to relatives in the country of *citizenship*.

**Multi-member district** – An *electoral district* from which more than one representative is elected to a legislature or elected body. See also *Single-member district*.

**Multiple citizenship** – The possession by a person of the *citizenship*, and consequential political rights and obligations, of more than one country.

**Naturalization** – The acquisition by an *immigrant* of *citizenship* of the country in which he or she is now *resident*.

**Non-refoulement** – The principle in the 1951 Convention Relating to the Status of Refugees that 'No Contracting State shall expel or return ("refouler") a refugee in any manner whatsoever to the frontiers of territories where his life or freedom would be threatened on account of his race, religion, nationality, membership of a particular social group or political opinion'.

**Officer on duty abroad** – Any public servant carrying out duties abroad, for example representing his or her government or any regional or international official organization.

**Official external polling site** – A *diplomatic mission* or other official site of one country, which is holding an election, within another, the *host country*, where a *polling site* is set up.

**Open list** – A form of *List PR* in which voters can express a preference both for a party or grouping and for one, or sometimes more, candidates within that party or grouping. See also *Closed list*.

**Out-of-country voting** – See *External voting*.

**Permanent resident abroad** – A person who has established his or her permanent home in a country other than that of his/her *citizenship* in accordance with the laws of that country.

**Personal voting** – A mechanism for voting in which an *elector* attends at a *polling station* or *polling site* in person in order to cast his/her vote.

**Plurality/majority systems** – Plurality/majority *electoral system*s are based on the principle that a candidate(s) or party with a plurality of votes (i.e. more than any other) or a majority of votes (i.e. 50 per cent plus one—an absolute majority) is/are declared the winner(s). Such a system may use *single-member districts*—for example, First Past The Post, Alternative Vote or the Two-Round System—or *multi-member districts*—for example, the Block Vote and Party Block Vote.

**Preferential voting systems** – Electoral systems in which voters rank parties or candidates on the ballot paper in order of their choice.

**Political party** – A group of people who hold similar political aims and opinions who have organized, usually to contest elections so that they might form a government.

**Polling site** – A venue, for example a post office or a *diplomatic mission*, at which an *elector* exercising the right to *remote voting* attends to deposit his or her vote.

**Polling station** – A venue established for the purpose of polling and controlled by staff of the *electoral management body*.

**Postal voting** – A mechanism for voting in which an *elector* completes his or her ballot paper and returns it by post to an official designated to conduct the election.

**Proportional representation (PR)** – An *electoral system* family based on the principle of the conscious translation of the overall votes of a party or grouping into a corresponding proportion of seats in an elected body. For example, a party which wins 30 per cent of the votes will receive approximately 30 per cent of the seats. All PR systems require the use of *multi-member districts*. There are two major types of PR system, *List PR* and the Single Transferable Vote (STV).

**Proxy voting** – A mechanism for voting in which an *elector* who is qualified to vote formally appoints another person to vote on his or her behalf.

**Refugee** – A person who migrates from his or her home and country as a result of political, religious, ethnic, social or cultural conflicts which directly affect him or her.

**Remote voting** – A mechanism for voting by which voters are enabled to cast a vote which does not involve their attendance at a polling station on the day or days fixed for voting. Methods of remote voting include *postal voting*, *fax voting*, and *remote e-voting*.

**Remote e-voting** – A mechanism for voting in which an *elector* may cast his or her vote by means of an electronic device (for example a telephone or the Internet) at any place outside the *polling station* to which he or she is allocated.

**Reserved seats** – Seats in which a determinable criterion such as religion, ethnicity, language, gender or external registration is a requirement for nomination or election. See *External districts*.

**Resident** – A person who lives legally in a country on a long-term basis.

**Returnee** – An *internally displaced person* or *refugee* who has returned home but requires continued assistance for a period of time.

**Single-member district** – An *electoral district* from which only one member is elected to a legislature or elected body. See also *Multi-member district*.

**Special external polling station** – A public or private place located within a *host country* where the establishment of a *polling station* is permitted by that host country.

# Annex C

# References and further reading

### General and international agreements

African Charter on Human and People's Rights (Organization of African Unity, 1981, entered into force 1986)

American Convention on Human Rights (Organization of American States, 1969, entered into force 1978)

Convention Relating to the Status of Refugees (United Nations, 28 July 1951, entered into force April 1954) and Protocol Relating to the Status of Refugees (United Nations, 16 December 1966, entered into force October 1967)

European Convention on the Legal Status of Migrant Workers (Council of Europe, 1977, entered into force May 1983)

International Convention on the Protection of the Rights of All Migrant Workers and Members of Their Families, UN Document A/RES/45/158, 18 December 1990 (entered into force July 2003)

International Covenant on Civil and Political Rights, UN document A/6316, 16 December 1966 (entered into force 1976)

Universal Declaration of Human Rights (1948)

### Secondary literature

ACE Electoral Knowledge Network, 'Focus on E-Voting', <http://aceproject.org/ace-en/focus/e-voting/>

Alvarez, R. Michael and Hall, Thad E., *Point, Click and Vote: The Future of Internet Voting* (Washington, DC: Brookings Institution Press, 2004)

Bouchet-Saulnier, Françoise, *The Practical Guide to Humanitarian Law*, ed. and transl. by Laura Brav (Boulder, Colo., New York, Oxford and Lanham, Md.: Rowman & Littlefield, 2002)

Buchsbaum, Thomas, 'E-Voting: Lessons Learnt from Recent Pilots', Presentation at the International Conference on Electronic Voting and Electronic Democracy: Present and the Future, Seoul, March 2005, <http://www.hallym.ac.kr/~icat/e-voting2005/korean/81ppt/buchsbaum.doc>

Caarls, Susanne, 'Remote e-Voting in the Netherlands', Presentation at the 2nd Vienna Election Seminar, December 2004, <http://www.gv.at/view.php3?f_id=7466&LNG=de&version=>

Calderón Chelius, Leticia (ed.), *Votar en la distancia. La extensión de los derechos políticos a migrantes: Experiencias comparadas* [Remote voting. The extension of political rights to migrants: comparative experiences] (Mexico: Instituto Mora, 2003)

Carpizo, Jorge and Valadés, Diego, *El Voto de los Mexicanos en el Extranjero* [External voting for Mexicans], Serie E: Varios, no. 99 (Mexico: Universidad Nacional Autónoma de Mexico, Instituto de Investigaciones Jurídicas, 1998)

Council of Europe, Committee of Ministers, 'Recommendation on Legal and Operational Standards and Technical Requirements for e-Voting (Adopted by the Committee of Ministers in September 2004)', Rec (2004)11, 2004 and Explanatory Memorandum on Rec (2004)11, 2004, <https://wcd.coe.int/ViewDoc.jsp?id=778189&Lang=en>

Dahl, Robert A., *On Democracy* (New Haven, Conn.: Yale University Press, 1998)

Dundas, Carl W., *Organising Free and Fair Elections at Cost-Effective Levels* (London: Commonwealth Secretariat, June 1993)

Gallagher, Dennis and Schowengerdt, Anna, 'Refugees in Elections: A Separate Peace', Refugee Policy Group, October 1997

Gallagher, Dennis and Schowengerdt, Anna, 'Participation of Refugees in Postconflict Elections', in Krishna Kumar (ed.), *Postconflict Elections, Democratization, and International Assistance* (Boulder, Colo.: Lynne Rienner Publishers, 1998)

Grace, Jeremy, 'Challenging the Norms and Standards of Election Administration', in IFES, *Challenging the Norms and Standards of Election Administration*, 2007, pp. 35–58, <http://www.ifes.org/arc-project.html?projectid=electionstandards>

— 'The Electoral Rights of Conflict Forced Migrants: A Review of Relevant Legal Norms and Instruments', International Organization for Migration, Participatory Elections Project, Discussion Paper no. 1, 2003, <http://www.geneseo.edu/~iompress/>

— and Fischer, Jeff, 'Enfranchising Conflict Forced Migrants: Issues, Standards, and Best Practices', Discussion Paper no. 2, International Organization for Migration, Participatory Elections Project, September 2003, <http://www.geneseo.edu/~iompress/Archive/Outputs/Standards_Final.pdf>

Gritzalis, Dimitris A. (ed.), *Secure Electronic Voting* (Boston, Dordrecht and London: Kluwer, 2003)

Hupkes, Sebastiaan, 'Remote E-Voting in the Netherlands', Presentation at the International Conference on Electronic Voting and Electronic Democracy: Present and the Future, Seoul, March 2005, <http://www.hallym.ac.kr/~icat/e-voting2005/81ppt/Sebastiaan%20Hupkes.doc>

Independent Commission on Alternative Voting Methods, *Elections in the 21st Century: From Paper Ballot to E-Voting* (London: Electoral Reform Society, January 2002)

International Foundation for Election Systems (IFES) et al. (eds), 'Conferencia Trilateral: Canadá, Estados Unidos, Mexico. Sobre el voto en extranjero' [Trilateral conference: Canada, United States, Mexico. On external voting], Mexico, Tribunal Electoral del Poder Judicial de la Federación, 1998

International Institute for Democracy and Electoral Assistance (International IDEA) et al. (eds), 'Seminario International sobre el voto en el extranjero' [International seminar on voting from abroad], Mexico, Tribunal Electoral del Poder Judicial de la Federación, 1998

International Labour Organization, 'General Study on Migrant Workers', 1999

International Organization for Migration (IOM), 'Current Dynamics of International Labour Organization: Globalization and Regional Integration', 2002

— *International Migration Trends*, 2005

Jefferson, David, Rubin, Aviel D., Simons, Barbara and Wagner, David, 'A Security Analysis of the Secure Electronic Registration and Voting Experiment (SERVE)', 2004, <http://www.servesecurityreport.org>

Kersting, Norbert and Baldersheim, Harald (eds), *Electronic Voting and Democracy: A Comparative Analysis* (New York: Palgrave Macmillan, 2004)

Kilic, Mehmet, 'Das Wahlrecht der Auslandstürken' ['The electoral rights of the Turkish expatriate'], *Zeitschrift für Türkeistudien*, 9 (1996), pp. 207–25

Kumar, Krishna (ed.), *Postconflict Elections, Democratization, and International Assistance* (Boulder, Colo.: Lynne Rienner Publishers, 1998)

Navarro Fierro, Carlos, 'El voto en el extranjero' [External voting], in Dieter Nohlen et al. (eds), *Tratado de derecho electoral comparado de América Latina* [On the comparative election law of Latin America] (Mexico: Fondo de Cultura Económica, 2007)

Newland, Kathleen, 'Refugee Protection and Assistance', in P. J. Simmons and Chantal de Jonge Oudraat (eds), *Managing Global Issues: Lessons Learned* (Washington, DC: Carnegie Endowment for International Peace, 2001)

Nohlen, Dieter (ed.), *Elections in the Americas: A Data Handbook*, 2 vols (Oxford: Oxford University Press, 2005)

— and Kasapovic, Mirjana, *Wahlsysteme und Systemwechsel in Osteuropa* [Electoral systems and system change in Eastern Europe] (Opladen: Leske & Budrich, 1996)

—, Grotz, Florian and Hartmann, Christof (eds), *Elections in Asia and the Pacific: A Data Handbook*, 2 vols (Oxford: Oxford University Press, 2001)

—, Krennerich, Michael and Thibaut, Bernhard (eds), *Elections in Africa: A Data Handbook* (Oxford: Oxford University Press, 1999)

Pastor, Robert A., 'The Role of Electoral Administration in Democratic Transitions: Implications for Policy and Research', *Democratization*, 6/4 (winter 1999)

Pratchett, Lawrence et al., 'The Implementation of Electronic Voting in the UK', Local Government Association, London, 2002

Prosser, Alexander and Krimmer, Robert (eds), *Electronic Voting in Europe: Technology, Law, Politics and Society*, Lecture Notes in Informatics, P-47 (Bonn: Gesellschaft für Informatik, 2004)

Trechsel, Alexander H. and Mendez, Fernando (eds), *The European Union and e-Voting* (London/New York: Routledge, 2004)

Tumanjong, Emmanuel, 'Fallen Empire', *Africa Today*, November 1999, pp. 41–2

United Nations High Commissioner for Refugees (UNHCR), *2004 Global Refugee Trends*

## Individual countries and references in the case studies

### For all countries
ACE Electoral Knowledge Network website, <http://www.aceproject.org>

### Australia
Australian Electoral Commission (AEC), 'Can I Vote via the Internet?', <http://www.aec.gov.au/_content/What/enrolment/faq_os.htm>

<http://www.elections.act.gov.au/Elecvote.html>

### Austria
Federal Chancellery, 'e-Government in Österreich' [e-Government in Austria], 2003, <http://www.cio.gv.at/service/conferences/graz_2003/e-Gov_Broschuere.pdf>

### Bosnia and Herzegovina
Association of Election Officials of Bosnia and Herzegovina, 'Retrospective on Elections', 2003

Organization for Security and Co-operation in Europe (OSCE) Refugee Election Steering Group, 'The Relationship between Large-scale Forced Migration and the Electoral Process: The Case of Bosnia and Herzegovina', Vienna, International Centre for Migration Policy Development (ICMPD), June 1997

### Botswana
Independent Electoral Commission (IEC), *Report on the General Election* (Gaborone: Government Printer, 2004)

— *Report on the General Election* (Gaborone: Government Printer, 1999)

### Brazil
Regional Electoral Tribunal of the Federal District (TRE-DF), external voting legal resolutions for the 2006 presidential election: the Tribunal approved the implementation of electronic ballot boxes in some countries. Lei 22.155 y Resolução TRE-DF-5989, <http://www.tre-df.gov.br/eleicoes_exterior/legislacao.html>

On voting from abroad, explanation for traditional and electronic ballot boxes, <http://www.tre-df.gov.br/eleicoes2006/arquivos/cartilha_elei06_exterior.pdf>

On Brazilians voting from abroad electronically: USA, Portugal, Italy, etc., <http://www.senado.gov.br/agencia/internacional/es/not_76.aspx>

On the use of electronic ballot boxes by Brazilians residing in Ecuador: HOY-Noticias,

<http://www.hoy.com.ec/NoticiaNue.asp?row_id=249295:

On the presidential election results, October 2006: first round (TRE-DF), <http://www.tre-df.gov.br/eleicoes2006/resultados/Comparecimento_abstencao_validos_brancos_nulos_Exterior.pdf>, and <http://www.justicaeleitoral.gov.br/resultado/index.html>; second round: <http://www.justicaeleitoral.gov.br/resultado/>

On Brazilians living abroad, <http://www.tre-df.gov.br/eleicoes_exterior/legislacao.html>

### Colombia

Ley estatutaria por la que se expide el Código Electoral y se dictan otras disposiciones agosto de 2006: <http://www.cne.gov.co/noticias/BP_30_AGOSTO_2006.htm>

On the results of the 2006 elections, presidential, legislative and primary (Liberal Party and POLO): <http://www.registraduria.gov.co/reselec2006/0312/index.htm>;

<http://www.eluniverso.com/2006/10/03/0001/8/3F03FAE349C649F6B99C23DDF486E8A5.aspx>;

<http://www.alcaldiabogota.gov.co/sisjur//normas/Norma1.jsp?i=21837>;

<http://www.terra.com.co/elecciones_2006/reportaje/26-05-2006/nota286007.html>;

<http://www.elnuevodiario.com.ni/2006/05/29/internacionales/20538>;

<http://www.colombianosenelexterior.com/index.php?idcategoria=86&ts=d5fe3e800f7aac48ff1a42fa7f1b73ea&PHPSESSID=eca64e2d4253bf19a67713a3dd360a3d>; and

<http://es.wikipedia.org/wiki/Gustavo_Rojas_Pinilla>

### Cook Islands

Commission of Political Review, *Report*, 1998, Appendix: Draft Constitutional Amendments

Cook Islands News and ABC News, 18 September 2002, cited at <http://www.angelfire.com/wa3/hri/cook.html> on 22 March 2005

Crocombe, R. (ed.), *Cook Islands Politics: The Inside Story* (Auckland: Polynesian Press, 1979)

Ghai, Yash, 'Systems of Government I', in Y. Ghai (ed.), *Law, Government and Politics in the Pacific Island States* (Suva: University of the South Pacific, Institute of Pacific Studies, 1988), pp. 54–75

Hassall, G., 'Cook Islands', in Dieter Nohlen, Florian Grotz and Christof Hartmann (eds), *Elections in Asia and the Pacific: A Data Handbook* (Oxford: Oxford University Press, 2001)

Henry, G., *The Criminal Convictions of Albert Henry: Political Bribery, Corruption, Deception and Dishonour in the Cook Islands 1978–79* (Auckland: Sovereign Pacific Publishing Company, 2003)

**Dominican Republic**

On IDs and the electoral card: <http://www.ayudatotal.com/servicios_publicos/111206_ayuda_total_documentos.htm>

On new possibilities for the 2008 election: <http://www.jce.do/app/do/Voto%20en%20el%20Exterior.swf>

On the results of external voting in 2004:

<http://www.jce.do/stor/boletines/2004/Boletines2004/BExterior.asp>;

<http://www.pciudadana.com/Publicaciones/download/01.pe/(2000)01.Exp_Regionales_DE.pdf>;

<http://www.upd.oas.org/lab/MOE/2004/rca_dominicana/report_first_spa.pdf>; and

<http://www.elnuevodiario.com.do/app/article.aspx?id=40565>

**Estonia**

Kulu, H., 'The Estonian Diaspora', *TRAMES: A Journal of the Humanities and Social Sciences*, 1/3 (1997)

National Election Committee, 'E-voting Project', <http://www.vvk.ee/engindex.html>

— 'E-voting System: Overview', Tallinn, 2005, <http://www.vvk.ee/elektr/docs/Yldkirjeldus-eng.pdf>

**France**

Internet Rights Forum, 'Recommendation: What is the Future of Electronic Voting in France?', 26 September 2003, <http://www.foruminternet.org/telechargement/documents/reco-evote-en-20030926.pdf>

Ministry of Foreign Affairs (Ministère des Affaires Etrangères), 'Election de l'Assemblée des Français de l'étranger, le 18 juin 2006: Votez!' [Elections to the Assembly of French Citizens Abroad, 18 June 2006: vote!], 9 March 2006, <http://www.assemblee-afe.fr/IMG/File/Notice_generale.pdf>

— 'Election au Conseil Supérieur des Français de l'étranger' [Elections to the Council of French Citizens Abroad, results 2003], <http://www.assemblee-afe.fr/IMG/File/RESULTATS-2003.xls>

## Germany

Schreiber, Wolfgang, 'Novellierung des Bundestagswahlrechts' [The legislative reform of the electoral law to the Bundestag], *Neue Juristische Wochenschrift*, 25 (1985), pp. 1433–40

## Honduras

On external voting in the 2005 presidential election, 'Hondureños en el extranjero podrán votar' [Hondurans overseas will be able to vote], [no date], <http://www.terra.com.hn/noticias/elecciones/articulo/html/nac43121.htm>

On the failure of external voting in 2005, *La Prensa*, 18 December 2005, <http://www.laprensahn.com/pais_nota.php?id04962=2764&t=1134968400>; and *El Heraldo*, 19 December 2005, <http://www.elheraldo.hn/nota.php?nid=42759&sec=12&fecha=2005-12-19>

## Iraq

International Organisation for Migration, Iraq Out-of-Country Voting Program, Final Report, March 31, 2005

Independent Electoral Commission of Iraq (IECI), Final Report to Parliament (English version)

## Marshall Islands

Fraenkel, Jon, 'Strategic Registration from Metropolis to Periphery in the Republic of the Marshall Islands', *Journal of Pacific History*, 37(3), 2002

Ghai, Yash, 'Systems of Government I', in Y. Ghai (ed.), *Law, Government and Politics in the Pacific Island States* (Suva: University of the South Pacific, Institute of Pacific Studies, 1988), pp. 54–75

Office of Planning and Statistics, *1999 Census of Population and Housing: Final Report* (Majuro, 1999)

## Netherlands

Caarls, Susanne, 'Remote e-Voting in the Netherlands', Presentation at the 2nd Vienna Election Seminar, December 2004, <http://www.gv.at/view.php3?f_id=7466&LNG=de&version=>

Hupkes, Sebastiaan, 'Remote E-Voting in the Netherlands', Presentation at the

International Conference on Electronic Voting and Electronic Democracy: Present and the Future, Seoul, March 2005, <http://www.hallym.ac.kr/~icat/e-voting2005/81ppt/Sebastiaan%20Hupkes.doc>

**New Zealand**

Elections New Zealand, <http://www.elections.org.nz/voting/how_vote_overseas.html>

— 'How to Enrol from Overseas', <http://www.elections.org.nz/enrolment/how_to_enrol_overseas.html>

**Portugal**

Araújo, A., *A revisão Constitucional de 1997* [The constitutional revision of 1997], Coimbra Editora

National Electoral Commission (Comissão Nacional de Eleições (CNE), <http://www.cne.pt>

Technical Secretariat for Electoral Processes Matters (Secretariado Técnico dos Assuntos para o Processo Eleitoral, STAPE), <http://www.stape.pt>

**Switzerland**

'Botschaft des Bundesrates an die Bundesversammlung über die politischen Rechte der Auslandschweizer vom 3. März 1975' [Message of the Federal Assembly on the Political Rights of Swiss abroad, 3 March 1975], *Bundesblatt* (BBl) 1975 I 1285ss. The *Bundesblatt* (the official gazette) is available at <http://www.admin.ch/ch/d/ff/index.html> (in French, German and Italian)

'Botschaft über die Revision des Bundesgesetzes über die politischen Rechte der Auslandschweizer vom 15 August 1990' [Message on the revision of the Federal Law on the Political Rights of Swiss abroad, 15 August 1990], *Bundesblatt* 1990 III 445ss

*Bundesblatt* 1975 I 1292ss
*Bundesblatt* 1990 III 448 (change of practice)
Burckhardt, Walther, *Schweizerisches Bundesrecht*, Frauenfeld *1930–1931* [Public law of the Swiss Confederation], 1/23; 2/388

Federal Law of 19 December 1975 (SR 161.5) on the Political Rights of Swiss Citizens Resident or Staying Abroad, <http://www.admin.ch/ch/d/sr/c161_5.html> (in French, German and Italian)

Federal Chancellery, <http://www.bk.admin.ch/themen/pore/evoting/00776>

Federal Chancellery, 'Der Vote électronique in der Pilotphase' [E-voting in the pilot stage], Zwischenbericht, Bern, August 2004 (in German and French), <http://www.admin.ch/ch/d/egov/ve/dokumente/Zwischenbericht.pdf>

GfS Forschungsinstitut, *Internationale SchweizerInnen* [Final report of the study carried out for the Organisation of the Swiss Abroad (ASO) and swissinfo/Swiss Radio International on the voting behaviour of Swiss abroad], Bern, June 2003, <http://www.aso.ch/pdf/ASO-Bericht%20berdef.pdf>

Kaufmann, Bruno et al., *Guidebook to Direct Democracy in Switzerland and Beyond* (Amsterdam: Initiative & Referendum Institute Europe, 2005)

Linder, Wolf, *Swiss Democracy: Possible Solutions to Conflict in Multicultural Societies*, 2nd edn (New York: St Martin's Press, 1998)

Organisation of the Swiss Abroad (ASO), <http://www.aso.ch>

## Ukraine

Organization for Security and Co-operation in Europe (OSCE), Office for Democratic Institutions and Human Rights (ODIHR), 'Ukraine Presidential Election 31 October, 21 November and 26 December 2004: OSCE/ODIHR Election Observation Mission Final Report', Warsaw, 11 May 2005, ODIHR.GAL/33/05, <http://www.osce.org/documents/odihr/2005/05/14224_en.pdf>

## United Kingdom

British Electoral Commission, 'The Shape of Elections to Come: A Strategic Evaluation of the 2003 Electoral Pilot Schemes', London, 2003, <http://www.electoralcommission.org.uk/templates/search/document.cfm/8346>

Royal Borough of Kingston upon Thames (UK), 'Overseas Electors', <http://www.kingston.gov.uk/council_and_democracy/elections/overseas_electors.htm>

'Votes in the Bag', *The Economist*, 9 April 2005

## USA

US Embassy London, Consular Section, 'Absentee Voting for US Citizens', <http://www.usembassy.org.uk/cons_web/acs/scs/voting.htm>

# Annex D

# The cost of external voting: some examples

External voting processes involve logistical arrangements that often cost more per voter than elections organized in the home country. This section provides some examples of the costs associated with external voting in countries which have organized it. The figures shown are not complete or directly comparable, but they are presented to give an idea of how much external voting costs in some countries.

It is difficult to assess how much external voting costs, for several different reasons. The resources needed will depend partly on the procedures in place for external voting, so that some cost additional money while some involve using existing staff, premises or materials. Costs may also be paid for from different budgets, not all of them from that of the electoral management body (EMB), so that it is difficult to trace all the costs related to external voting at one election. For these reasons, it is equally difficult to compare costs between countries that organize external voting. For additional examples of the cost of external voting, see chapter 5.

Some of the data assembled here cover the costs of external voting for elections to the European Parliament, which is not dealt with further in this Handbook.

## Afghanistan

The voluntary donation project budget of the Afghanistan Reconstruction Trust Fund (ARTF) bears the expenses for voter registration and elections. The ARTF was set up in May 2002 to provide, among other things, support to Afghanistan in the area of recurrent costs of the government. Twenty-one donors, in addition to the United States, pledged altogether 430 million US dollars (USD). External election-specific fund-raising was coordinated by the United Nations Development Programme (UNDP), and 26.7 million USD were made available to the International Organization for Migration (IOM) on the basis of a cost estimate by the IOM as part of its proposal to the Joint Electoral Management Body (JEMB). The total costs of the programme amounted to

91 per cent of the initial estimate (24,289,322 USD), or approximately 20 USD per voter in Iran and 32 USD per voter in Pakistan (where advance registration increased the cost per voter). (See also the case study on Afghanistan.)

## Australia

At the 2004 election, there were around 16,000 registered overseas electors. In addition, people who were overseas temporarily as tourists were able to use overseas voting facilities without having registered as overseas electors. Altogether approximately 63,000 people voted from overseas at the 2004 election. The costs of external voting can be estimated at 1.21 million Australian dollars (AUD, or *c*. 891,000 USD in the exchange rate prevailing at the time), broken down as follows: 32,000 AUD for permanent staff costs, 730,000 AUD for freight transport of material to and from overseas posts; 81,000 AUD for printing (postal voting forms, ballot papers); 322,000 AUD for reimbursement of the Department of Foreign Affairs and trade costs at overseas posts, including overtime, temporary staff, advertising, security and in-country postage; and 45,000 AUD for distributing the returned material to the correct division (electoral district) in Australia. The cost of external voting is not seen as excessively high, given that it only forms a small part of overall election costs of 75 million AUD. The average cost of the election per elector inside the country in 2004 was 5.29 AUD, and the cost of external voting per voter was 19.21 AUD.

## Botswana

The Independent Electoral Commission (IEC) assesses the external voting in 1999 as well as in 2004 as too expensive when it is set against the very low turnout by external electors. In 1999, out of the 1,363 electors registered abroad, only 23.3 per cent voted, and in 2004, of 2,436 external electors registered, only 49.5 per cent voted. External travel expenses and the personnel costs of supervising elections abroad are among the main expenses that burden the general budget of the IEC. The IEC therefore claims that either the provisions relating to external voting should be reviewed in order to cut down the costly logistical preparations or additional funds should be made available. In the 2004 election the cost of external travel was 647,950 pula (BWP—*c*. 161,460 USD) excluding the costs of salaries, administration and supplies. The overall cost of the elections is estimated at 19 million BWP in 1999 and 21 million BWP in 2004. (See also the case study.)

## Canada

External voting is done exclusively by post and is only possible with the use of a voting 'kit' that is sent to the nearest consular office, Canadian embassy or high commission. There are no polling sites established outside the country. In the 2004 general election a total of 13,830 ballot papers were mailed out to electors, of which 8,127 were sent back by citizens who were residing outside Canada and 1,368 by electors who were resident in Canada but were temporarily out of the country on voting day. The total costs of the external voting programme for the 2004 elections amounted to 274,024 Canadian dollars (CAD, or *c.* 211,000 USD), of which 76,000 CAD was disbursed for initiatives and material costs between voting events and 198,024 CAD for expenses during an event. The latter included 115,000 CAD for human resource costs, 3,024 CAD for postage and around 80,000 CAD expenses for courier services from each embassy.

## Estonia

It is difficult to separate the costs of external voting from the total election budget since different authorities are concerned and the amount of money involved is rather small. The electoral register is managed by the Ministry of the Interior and the ministry is not able to separate the costs for external voting from the total costs of elections. All printed materials for elections come from the National Election Committee, but since the amount of external voting materials is so small the costs are not counted separately. A large part of the work for external voting (staffing, transport of materials, postage etc.) is done by the Ministry of Foreign Affairs. As an example, for the European Parliament elections in 2004, the National Electoral Committee allocated 450,000 Estonian crowns (EEK; *c.* 29,000 euros (EUR) or 35,000 USD) to the ministry. This money covered most of the costs of implementing external voting.

## Finland

An estimate of the cost of external voting for elections to the European Parliament in 2004 was about 110,000 EUR (*c.* 137,500 USD at the exchange rate prevailing then). About 9,000 external electors voted. (The total Finnish electorate inside and outside Finland is about 4.1 million.) The cost per external voter was therefore roughly 12 EUR (15 USD). However, what this cost includes or excludes is not described in further detail.

## France

According to the French EMB, the costs related to external voting in France are considered to be too high. As an example, in the referendum in May 2005, external voters represented only 1.09 per cent of all French voters, but more than 1.36 per cent of the total cost of the referendum. In particular, the cost of dispatching information for the electors to French consulates and diplomatic missions (705,786 EUR, or *c.* 1.4 million USD) contributed to the high expenses. The estimated costs related to the organization of external voting for the referendum (additional to the cost of dispatching information for the voters) are: 9,000 EUR for ballot boxes and polling booths; 678,000 EUR for postage; 86,000 EUR for voting by proxy facilities; 8,800 EUR for the diplomatic bag; 66,000 EUR for stationery; and 78,000 EUR for staffing. The total costs of external voting for the referendum were therefore around 1,631,000 EUR. Considering the low turnout by external electors in the referendum (the abstention rate was *c.* 67 per cent), external voting is seen as very costly in France.

## Germany

The overall costs of external voting activities cannot be identified separately in Germany. Voting from abroad is only possible by postal voting and only for those who have applied to be included on the electoral register of the electoral district where they were formerly resident. They have to pay for the postage of their ballot papers themselves. The only costs that arise for the federal government in relation to external voting are therefore expenses for material and postage to foreign countries. Around 55,000 German citizens living temporarily or permanently abroad registered for postal voting in the 2005 elections for the Bundestag. No figures for turnout by external voters are available.

## Greece

The table below shows the costs associated with external voting for the elections to the European Parliament in 2004. The Greek EMB estimates the costs of organizing external voting for those elections at approximately 1,108,985 EUR (c. 1,347,000 USD), although the costs are fairly difficult to assess. The number of external electors who voted was 25,546 and the cost per external voter was approximately 43 EUR. Turnout among registered Greek external voters at those elections was 74.9 per cent.

Table: Principal expenses for external voting in Greece in the European Parliament elections, 2004

| Purpose of the expenditure | Cost (EUR) |
| --- | --- |
| Reimbursements of returning officers, supervisors and secretaries | 383,070 |
| Reimbursements of officials of the Ministry of the Interior | 367,200 |
| Procurement of consulates | 260,000 |
| Creation of software for the online handling of applications of voters abroad | 31,270 |
| National Printing House | 353 |
| Reimbursements of officials of other state services | 44,100 |

EUR = euro.

## Iraq

External voting was organised for Iraqis abroad in the January and December 2005 elections. January was the first occasion ever in which external voting took place, designed and implemented with the assistance of international partners (see Iraq case study). The cost reached a high of 92 USD -the most expensive external voting programme in history. Twenty five percent of that related to security costs, and 35% to personnel costs. The December election was organised mainly by the IECI and Iraqi partners and servants, reaching a cost of 17 million USD. Detailed information can be found in the final report of the January election by the IOM and the report of the December election by the IECI (see Annex C).

## Mexico

For the preliminary arrangements and the initial setting up of the external voting mechanism, the Federal Electoral Institute (Instituto Federal Electoral, IFE) invested approximately 119.3 million pesos (MXN—c. 10.8 million USD at the prevailing exchange rate) during 2005. For the implementation phase throughout 2006, it devoted another 186 million MXN (16.9 million USD), making an estimated overall cost of 305 million MXN (c. 27.7 million USD).

## Sweden

Around 115,000 Swedish citizens are entitled to vote from abroad in national elections. Turnout is low among external electors: in the 2002 general elections only 27.7 per cent of external electors voted. The costs of external voting—for example, for the 2004 European Parliament elections—have been significantly lower than estimated due to the low turnout. This applies mainly to the expenses for postal voting. For the 2004 European Parliament elections, 47,776 people were registered as external electors, but only 12,787 external votes were cast, including postal voting and personal voting. Another reason for the low costs is that some of the voting materials bought for the 2002 and 2003 referendums but never used could be used in 2004. The costs for external voting are mainly borne by the Swedish missions and authorities abroad, which are authorized to organize the external voting and which bear the costs of sending ballot papers back to Sweden. For postal voting from abroad, the voter bears the costs. The only data available about the costs of external voting for the Swedish EMB are data about the material costs for posting ballot papers to around 300 missions and authorities abroad.

## Switzerland

No specific data are available on the costs of external voting in Switzerland, but the cost of postal voting can be estimated on the basis of the following information. There are around 110,000 external electors, of whom about 88,000 live inside Europe and 22,000 outside Europe. The costs for external votes from inside Europe are based on data about postal charges for priority mail within Europe, and are estimated at 381,300 EUR. External votes from outside Europe cost around 129,000 EUR. An amount of 146,700 EUR for personnel costs for the packing and advance posting of voting material has to be added. The overall expenses add up to 657,000 EUR.

# Annex E

# About the contributors

**Luis Arias Núñez** is the president of the Plenary of the Central Electoral Board in the Dominican Republic and a former judge. He has had a long career as a professor and researcher, and has published several books and more than 400 articles in the fields of law and international politics in national and international specialist journals, as well as in newspapers of the Dominican Republic. He has a PhD in jurisprudence from the University of Warsaw, and a Master's degree in international affairs and a PhD in law from the Autonomous University of Santo Domingo.

**Reginald Austin** has extensive experience of election management. During the 1960s and 1970s he was actively involved with the political and armed struggle of the Zimbabwean nationalist movement in the then Southern Rhodesia. He was a legal adviser to PF-ZAPU (Patriotic Front-Zimbabwe African People's Union) during the constitutional and ceasefire negotiations in 1976–9, and in the Election Council and Ceasefire Commission during the 1980 independence election. From 1982 to 1992 he served on the Zimbabwean Electoral Delimitation Commission, on the Zimbabwe Red Cross and at the Zimbabwe Legal Resources Centre. During the 1980s he worked with the Council for Namibia, the Commonwealth Secretariat and the Southern African Research and Documentation Centre (SARDC), advising on transition and post-conflict multiparty elections in Mozambique and Angola. In 1992 he worked in the United Nations on drafting an electoral law for the transition in Cambodia, and was appointed chief election officer (CEO) of the UN Transitional Authority in Cambodia (UNTAC). In 1994 he headed the UN Observer Mission in South Africa (UNOMSA) electoral operation in South Africa, and in 2003–4 he undertook the same task with the UN Assistance Mission in Afghanistan (UNAMA) for the presidential election there. Between 1994 and 1998 he was director of the Constitutional and Legal Division of the Commonwealth Secretariat, and from 1998 to 2003 a director of International IDEA. Since 2005 he has undertaken independent consultancy work.

**Nadja Braun** is currently working as a legal adviser in the Political Rights Section of the Swiss Federal Chancellery (the Swiss federal electoral management body). She has wide experience in the field of e-voting and direct democracy. She was the Swiss legal expert in the Council of Europe's group of experts on e-voting, and her other assignments include membership of the IDEA group of experts on direct democracy. She completed her PhD in law at Bern University. Her recent publications include *Stimmgeheimnis* [The secrecy of the vote] (Reihe: Abhandlungen zum schweizerischen Recht 708, Bern, 2005), based on her doctoral dissertation; *Guidebook to Direct Democracy in Switzerland and Beyond* (co-edited with Bruno Kaufmann, Rolf Büchi and Paul Carline, 2005 edn); and 'E-Voting: Switzerland's Projects and their Legal Framework in a European Context', in Alexander Prosser and Robert Krimmer (eds), *Electronic Voting in Europe: Technology, Law, Politics and Society* (2004), pp. 43–52.

**Leticia Calderón-Chelius** is a researcher and professor at the José María Mora Institute in Mexico City and a member of the National Researchers System in Mexico. She was the coordinator of *Voto en la distancia: Extensión de derechos politicos a migrantes, experiencias comparadas* [Voting at a distance: the extension of political rights to migrants, comparative experiences] (2004) and co-author (with Jesús Martínez) of *La dimensión política de la migración mexicana* [The political dimension of Mexican migration] (2003). She has a PhD in social sciences from the Facultad Latinoamericana de Ciencias Sociales (FLACSO), Mexico.

**Manuel Carrillo** has been chief of staff for international affairs at the Federal Electoral Institute of Mexico (Instituto Federal Electoral, IFE) since 1993. He has worked on the public officials' training programme at the National Institute of Public Administration, as well as several agencies of the Mexican Government, and has participated in several electoral observation missions and technical assistance projects on the organization of elections in other countries; and he has written several articles on electoral issues. He has a BA in political science and public administration from the Faculty of Social and Political Science of the National Autonomous University of Mexico, and a Master's degree in political science from the Center of International Studies of the Colegio de México.

**Arlinda Chantre** joined the Portuguese Directorate General for Electoral Management in 2003. She works mainly on the legal bases of voter registration and elections, providing legal advice to both political parties and electoral enrolment commissions, and on the administration of voter registration and electoral administration. She has a law degree from the Universidade Católica Portuguesa, and was a postgraduate student at the Instituto Superior de Ciências Politicas e Sociais (in international relations) and the University of Lisbon Law Faculty (in political and international studies).

**Linda Edgeworth** has been a consultant specializing in international election law and administration for 16 years and is associated with such organizations as IFES (formerly called the International Foundation for Election Systems), the Organization for Security and Co-operation in Europe (OSCE) Office of Democratic Institutions and Human Rights (ODIHR), and the UN. In that time she has served in 31 countries including many in the

Caucasus, the Balkans, Central Asia, Central and Eastern Europe, and Africa, as well as in Bangladesh, Yemen and the Philippines. From 1997 to 1999 she was the OSCE director of elections in Bosnia and Herzegovina, where she developed and implemented the first voter registration programme after the war, conducted elections at all levels of government, and initiated programmes to ensure a smooth transition of electoral functions from international to domestic control. In 2001 she designed the polling-station, vote-counting and auditing procedures for Kosovo. She has also been involved in projects related to the advancement of women in political life and leadership, and the development of international standards for the conduct of democratic elections. Most recently, she has consulted with several states in the United States regarding election reform and implementation of the Help America Vote Act. Prior to her international work Ms Edgeworth was an election administrator for the US state of Alaska.

**Andrew Ellis** is currently the Director of Operations at International IDEA in Stockholm. Between 2003 and 2006 he was the head of the Electoral Processes Team. He has wide experience as a technical adviser on electoral and institutional matters in democratic transitions. He acted as senior adviser for the National Democratic Institute (NDI) in Indonesia from 1999 to 2003, working with members of the Indonesian legislature on constitutional amendment and reform of the electoral and political laws, and with non-governmental organizations (NGOs) and political commentators. His other recent assignments include acting as chief technical adviser to the Palestinian Election Commission under the European Commission's support for all aspects of the preparation of the first Palestinian elections in 1996, and design and planning for the commission's electoral assistance programme in Cambodia for the 1998 elections.

**Jeff Fischer** is the team leader for Elections and Political Process programming at Creative Associates International, Inc. where he leads initiatives to establish and conduct programmes to develop democratic processes and culture. He has held three internationally appointed posts in post-conflict electoral transitions. In 1996, he was appointed by the OSCE to serve as director general of elections for the first post-conflict elections in Bosnia and Herzegovina. In 1999, he was appointed by the UN as chief electoral officer for the Popular Consultation for East Timor, and in 2000 he received a joint appointment from the UN and OSCE to head the Joint Registration Taskforce in Kosovo and served as the OSCE's director of election operations in Kosovo. Additionally, Mr Fischer served as a senior adviser to the United Nations and the Independent Electoral Commission of Iraq during the 2005 election cycle. Since 1987, he has conducted electoral assistance and observation or provided conference services in over 50 countries and territories in the Americas, Europe, the Middle East, Africa and Asia. In the United States he has been an election official, as a commissioner on both the Kansas City (Missouri) Election Board (1985–9) and the Missouri Campaign Finance Review Board (1990–2). Mr Fischer has published numerous articles on electoral processes, and in the autumn term of 2006 he was a visiting lecturer in international affairs at the Woodrow Wilson School of Princeton University teaching a course on Managing Elections in Fragile States, and a lecturer at the Scuola Superiore Sant'Anna in Pisa, Italy.

**Jon Fraenkel** is a senior research fellow in governance at the Pacific Institute of Advanced Studies in Development and Governance (PIAS-DG) at the University of the South Pacific. He is the author of *The Manipulation of Custom: From Uprising to Intervention in the Solomon Islands* (2004). His research and publications focus on the economic history of Oceania, electoral systems and contemporary Pacific politics, and he regularly covers Pacific issues for international press and radio outlets.

**Maria Gratschew** joined International IDEA in 1999 as project manager responsible for the Voter Turnout Project (<http://www.idea.int/turnout>) and works mainly on voter turnout and civic education, election administration, external voting and compulsory voting issues in International IDEA's Design of Democratic Institutions and Processes Programme (formerly the Elections Team). She is a graduate of the University of Uppsala. Together with Rafael López Pintor she served as lead writer and editor for International IDEA's *Voter Turnout since 1945: A Global Report* (2002), *Voter Turnout in Western Europe: A Regional Report* (2004) and *Engaging the Electorate: Initiatives to Promote Voter Turnout from Around the World* (2006).

**Phil Green** has been the electoral commissioner for the Australian Capital Territory (ACT) since 1994, having previously worked for the Australian Electoral Commission from 1982 to 1992 in a variety of roles, including director for information and director for legislation and research. He specializes in the Hare-Clark Single Transferable Vote system, which is used in the ACT, and has used technology extensively for ACT elections. Most notably, he was responsible for the first use of computers for electronic voting for a legislative election in Australia, using computers at the October 2001 and October 2004 ACT Legislative Assembly elections to take votes and distribute preferences (see <http://www.elections.act.gov.au>). He was the lead writer for the Elections and Technology topic area of the Administration and Cost of Elections (ACE) Project (see <http://www.aceproject.org>).

**Florian Grotz** is adjunct professor ("Privatdozent") for political science at the Free University of Berlin. His research has focused on German politics, political institutions in Europe and electoral systems in comparative perspective. His books include *Political Institutions and Post-Socialist Party Systems in East Central Europe* (2000), *Elections in Asia and the Pacific* (2 vols, 2001, co-edited with Dieter Nohlen and Christof Hartmann), *Professionalising Europe: Order of Competencies and Institutional Reform within the EU* (2005, with J. J. Hesse), *Europeanisation and National State Organisation: Institutional Politics in Federal and Unitary EU States* (2007) and *Comprehensive Encyclopedia of Political Science* (4th ed. 2007, co-edited with Dieter Nohlen).

**Nada Hadzimehic** has been involved in the conduct of elections since 1996 when she was employed by the OSCE Mission to Bosnia and Herzegovina for the country's first post-war elections. In 1998 she became the first Bosnian national to be made a division director within the OSCE Election Department, where she was directly responsible for supervising the registration of all political parties and candidates for elections at all levels of government. Following the adoption of the Election Law of Bosnia and Herzegovina and the transfer of election responsibilities to the Central Election Commission, Ms Hadzimehic continued to provide these services for the Election Commission Secretariat. She also served as project manager for the Association of Election Officials of Bosnia and Herzegovina. Since she left the Secretariat, her involvement in elections has extended more broadly in the international arena. She was the project manager for the Money and Politics Project organized by IFES. Most recently she has worked with the International Organization for Migration (IOM) on the out-of-country voting programmes for the elections in Afghanistan and Iraq.

**Graham Hassall** is professor of governance at the Pacific Institute for Advanced Studies in Development and Governance, University of the South Pacific. He attended the University of Sydney (BA Hons), the University of New South Wales (B.ED), and the Australian National University (PhD in Pacific and Asian history) before teaching at the University of Melbourne and the University of Papua New Guinea. He has published on electoral systems, parliamentary affairs, conflict resolution and civil society. His recent publications include *Asia Pacific Constitutional Systems* (2002) and his current projects include coordination of the *Third Pacific Human Development Report*.

**Jacobo Hernández Cruz** is a lawyer and notary from the Universidad Autónoma de Honduras. He is a magistrate of the Supreme Electoral Court of Honduras, which he previously chaired, and a member of the Honduran Bar Association. He was a professor at the Instituto de Investigaciones Jurídicas at the Facultad de Ciencias Jurídicas y Sociales in the Universidad Autónoma de Honduras and has held different public offices, including as a deputy to the National Constituent Assembly, a deputy to the National Congress, and one of three elected vice-presidents of the Republic. As a magistrate he has represented the Supreme Electoral Court in different electoral observation missions in countries such as El Salvador, Colombia and Spain.

**Brett Lacy** has served since 2006 as a programme officer at the National Democratic Institute for International Affairs in the United States, where she contributes to democracy and governance programmes in Central and West Africa. Previously, she served as senior long-term observer and then deputy director of the Carter Center's International Election Observation Program in Liberia, where she organized long-term observation and reporting on that country's post-war presidential and legislative elections in 2005. She has also worked as an assistant project coordinator with the Carter Center's Democracy Program, contributing to election observation, civil society and rule-of-law programmes in East Timor, Zambia, Nicaragua, Guyana and Indonesia. In 2004 Brett was the Hybl Democracy Studies Fellow at IFES, where she produced a policy paper examining issues surrounding refugees, the internally displaced, and the right to political participation. Her BA degree (in political science) is from Duke University, in 1999, and her MA degree in international administration with a focus on human rights is from the Graduate School of International Studies of the University of Denver.

**Stina Larserud** joined International IDEA in 2003 and has acted as project manager for the Electoral System Design Project, primarily with *Electoral System Design: The New International IDEA Handbook* (2005). As a member of International IDEA's Elections Team, she worked on issues relating to electoral legislation and electoral administration with a focus on electoral systems and participation. Since late 2006 she has been one of the network facilitators for the ACE Knowledge Network. She holds a Master's degree in political science from the University of Uppsala in comparative politics and institutional design.

**Marina Costa Lobo** is a political scientist researcher at the Instituto de Ciências Sociais at the University of Lisbon, where she co-directs a project on Portuguese electoral behaviour and political attitudes. Her research interests centre on Portuguese electoral behaviour, political parties, and political attitudes towards Europe. She has published on these topics in international journals including *Party Politics,* the *European Journal of Political Research* and *South European Society and Politics,* as well as in Portuguese. She is co-author of *Portugal at the Polls* (forthcoming 2007). Her DPhil is from Oxford University (2001).

**Pasquale Lupoli** is the head of the Operations Support Department of the IOM.

**Epp Maaten** is a councillor at the Elections Department of the Chancellery of the Estonian Parliament, the Riigikogu. The main task of the department is to provide operational support to the Estonian National Electoral Committee. She is responsible for the technical and practical arrangement of elections, in particular for electoral information technology (IT) systems. Her recent assignments include working on the Estonian e-voting project and the preparation of pilots. She has prepared reports on the Estonian electoral arrangements for international institutions and has been an election observer for the OSCE.

**Patrick Molutsi** is currently the executive secretary of Botswana Tertiary Education. He was formerly head of the Political Participation and Democracy Assessment Methodology Programme at International IDEA. From 1996 to 1999 he was dean of the Faculty of Social Science at the University of Botswana, and before joining IDEA in 1999 he was senior research fellow at the Southern African Regional Institute for Policy Studies/Southern African Political Economy Series (SARIPS/SAPES), responsible for a regional report on governance and human development in Southern Africa. He has written and consulted actively on democracy, civil society, governance and political party issues in Botswana and Southern Africa. He has a BA from the University of Botswana, a post-graduate Diploma in Population Studies from the University of Ghana, and an MPhil and PhD in sociology from the University of Oxford.

**Isabel Morales** joined the International Affairs Unit of the IFE in Mexico in 2002, working initially with the Department of International Liaison and Political Affairs. She currently works for the International Electoral Studies Department, mainly on comparative studies of electoral management bodies and systems, as well as being an editorial assistant. One of her main contributions there has been collaboration with the EPIC (Election Process Information Collection) Project and with the edition of the Spanish version of the IDEA *Handbook of Electoral System Design.* She has also worked for the Electoral Institute of the Federal District in Mexico City, with the logistics team responsible for organizing local electoral processes. She has a BA in international relations from the Political and Social Sciences Faculty at the National Autonomous University of Mexico, graduating with a thesis entitled 'The Revaluation of Democracy in the New World Order and the International Activities of the Federal Electoral Institute of Mexico, 1993–2003'.

**Simon-Pierre Nanitelamio**, an electoral expert from the Republic of the Congo (Congo-Brazzaville), is currently the chief technical adviser of the United Nations Development Programme (UNDP) technical assistance project for the electoral process in Mozambique. Since the UN-conducted elections in Cambodia in 1992, he has acquired wide experience as a technical adviser on electoral matters in democratic transitions in Africa (Mozambique, Malawi, the Central African Republic, Guinea-Bissau, Côte d'Ivoire, Chad, and São Tomé and Principe), Asia (Cambodia and East Timor) and Europe (Bosnia and Herzegovina). His other recent assignments include participation in the UN Electoral Assistance Division (UNEAD) electoral advisory mission in Angola (March 2005) and electoral needs assessment missions in Côte d'Ivoire (March 2000) and Chad (October 2000). An accredited facilitator for IDEA's BRIDGE (Building Resources in Democracy, Governance and Elections) programme, he has also conducted electoral administration courses in Mozambique (2002) and Burkina Faso (2003) for International IDEA. He has acted regularly as a technical adviser to the Mozambican electoral management bodies (in 1994–5, 1997–8 and 2003–5).

**Carlos Navarro Fierro** has been an official of the IFE since 1993 and is currently director of electoral studies and political affairs at the IFE's International Department. He has authored publications prepared by the IFE for the international community, as well as various international comparative studies on political and electoral issues. He has a BA in international relations and is a candidate for a Master's degree in Latin American studies from the Faculty of Political and Social Science at the National Autonomous University of Mexico.

**Dieter Nohlen** is professor emeritus of political science at the University of Heidelberg and a well-known expert on electoral systems, political development and democratization, with a focus on Latin America. He received the Max Planck prize for internationally outstanding research in 1991, the University of Augsburg prize for research on Spain and Latin America in 2000, and the Medal of the University of Heidelberg in 2005. His numerous books include *Wahlsysteme der Welt* [Electoral systems of the world] (1978; Spanish edn 1981), *Elections and Electoral Systems* (1996), *Wahlrecht und Parteiensystem* [Electoral law and party systems] (4th edn 2004), and *Sistemas electorales y partidos políticos* [Electoral systems and party politics] (3rd edn 2004). He is the editor of a seven-volume encyclopedia *Lexikon der Politik* [Lexicon of politics] (1992–8), and co-editor of *Tratado de Derecho Electoral Comparado de América Latina* [Comparative electoral laws of Latin America] (1998; 2nd edn 2005), as well as of an eight-volume *Handbook of the Third World* (3rd edn 1991–4) and a two-volume encyclopedia of political science, *Lexikon der Politikwissenschaft* [Lexicon of political science] (3rd edn. 2005, Spanish edn. 2005). Currently he is working on *Elections in Europe*, the last volume of the Elections Worldwide series, three volumes of which have already been published—*Elections in Africa* (1999), *Elections in Asia and the Pacific* (2001), and *Elections in the Americas* (2005).

**Nydia Restrepo de Acosta** is a magistrate and former president of the National Electoral Council in Colombia. She has had a wide-ranging career in legal positions within the public service in Colombia and has been a professor at the University of the Guajira. She graduated from the Law School at the University of Antioquia and she has a Master's degree in political studies from the University Javieriana of Bogota.

**Nuias Silva** is currently the general director of electoral administration in Cape Verde, and since 2004 has been a member of the Board of Directors of the Imprensa Nacional de Cabo Verde, SA, being in charge of the Department of New Technologies. He has a Master's degree on information systems management from the Instituto Superior Economia e Gestão of the University of Lisbon, a postgraduate degree on systems and technology of information from the Instituto Superior Economia e Gestão, and a degree in engineering and industrial management from the University of Aveiro, Portugal. Previously, he worked at the Sociedade Interbancaria e Sistemas de Pagamentos, SA.

**Catinca Slavu** is an electoral consultant who carried out an assignment with IFES as deputy director of the Out-of-Country Voting Program for Iraq's 2005 Transitional National Assembly election, conducted by the IOM. Prior to this, she was the senior adviser to the out-of-country registration and voting programme for Afghanistan's 2004 presidential election, also conducted by the IOM. She began electoral work in 1992, when she joined a human rights NGO monitoring Romanian elections, with which she continued until 2000. Meanwhile, she joined the OSCE election supervision missions in Bosnia and Herzegovina (1997–2000) and in July 2000 she moved to Kosovo to work with the OSCE on the organization of two municipal elections (2000 and 2002) and one Assembly election (2001). During her time in Kosovo, she specialized in the administration of electoral registers and managed two special-needs voting programmes. After the 2002 election, she coordinated the technical transfer of responsibility from the OSCE to the Kosovo electoral management body. She continued her capacity-building work as technical adviser for Georgia's post-Shevardnadze presidential and legislative elections of 2004, also with the OSCE. Also in Georgia, in 2004, Catinca began to collaborate with IDEA as a BRIDGE curriculum developer (ACCESS module) and as a consultant on the regionalization of the BRIDGE curriculum for the South Caucasus.

**Judy Thompson** is a former deputy chief electoral officer for Manitoba, Canada. She served on a national committee to develop voter education programmes for first-time voters, including new Canadians, and is currently working as an election consultant internationally. Her assignments have included election administration, external voting and training as well as democracy and voter education—most recently in Kosovo, Sierra Leone and Lesotho, and she has also been an observer for the Commonwealth Secretariat.

**Ozias Tungwarara** is currently deputy director of AfriMAP, a programme of the Open Society Institute that seeks to strengthen civil society capacity to monitor and advocate for African governments' compliance with human rights and governance commitments. A human rights lawyer by training, he has wide-ranging experience of implementing human rights, democracy and governance programmes and was previously senior programme officer at IDEA responsible for cross-cutting issues such as democracy assessment, analysis and evaluations. He has also headed a USAID-funded Southern Africa Regional Democracy Fund that aimed to strengthen democratic processes in the Southern African Development Community (SADC) region and has been executive director of ZimRights, a leading Zimbabwean human rights NGO.

**Richard Vengroff**, PhD is a professor of political science at the University of Connecticut specializing in development management, comparative politics (Africa and Canada/Quebec) and comparative electoral systems. He is an experienced administrator, most recently having been the founding dean of international affairs at the University of Connecticut, a position he held for six years. He is the author or editor of seven books, more than 75 articles and chapters in scholarly journals and edited volumes, and a series of training materials in project management. His current research is devoted to issues of electoral reform, municipal organization and reform, democratic governance and decentralization.

**Kåre Vollan** is a private consultant combining management consulting work with advisory services on electoral systems and electoral processes. He has advised on electoral systems in a number of countries and territories, including Nepal, Iraq, Palestine, and Bosnia and Herzegovina, and was head of the Norwegian election observation mission to Zimbabwe in March 2002. From May 1999 to November 2000 he was deputy head of the OSCE Mission to Bosnia and Herzegovina responsible for organizing the two elections held in 2000. In 1999 he advised on electoral and citizenship issues for the OSCE Mission to Croatia. During the period 1996–8 he was head of ten OSCE/ODIHR election observation missions and in 1995–6 he led the Norwegian observation mission for the Palestinian elections. Between 2002 and 2006 he participated in a number of missions to Palestine and he has published a comprehensive report together with Nils Butenschøn on the electoral processes in Palestine during that period. Since 2003 he has issued opinions on election laws for the Council of Europe Venice Commission covering Moldova, Ukraine, Albania and Macedonia. He is a mathematician by profession.

**Alan Wall** is an electoral consultant. From 2000 to 2004 he was manager of IFES' Indonesian activities, encompassing programmes assisting electoral, legal, media, parliamentary reform and civil society development. Prior to this posting he managed IFES' democracy assistance projects for the 1999 local government elections in Azerbaijan. Other recent postings include as the United Nations' chief technical adviser to the Nigerian election commission in 1998, as deputy chief electoral officer for the United Nations Transitional Administration for Eastern Slavonia in 1996, and as an adviser to the South African Government for the local government elections in 1995. He was one of the initial lead writers for the ACE Project (<http://www.aceproject.org>), the electronic textbook of electoral matters developed jointly by the United Nations, the IFES and International IDEA, and a lead writer for *Electoral Management Design: The International IDEA Handbook* (2006).

# About International IDEA

The International Institute for Democracy and Electoral Assistance—International IDEA—is an intergovernmental organization that supports sustainable democracy worldwide. Its objective is to strengthen democratic institutions and processes.

## What does International IDEA do?

International IDEA acts as a catalyst for democracy building by providing knowledge resources and policy proposals or by supporting democratic reforms in response to specific national requests. It works together with policy makers, governments, UN agencies and regional organizations engaged in the field of democracy building.

International IDEA provides:

- **assistance with democratic reforms** in response to specific national requests;
- **knowledge resources**, in the form of handbooks, databases, websites and expert networks; and
- **policy proposals** to provoke debate and action on democracy issues.

## Areas of work

International IDEA's key areas of expertise are:

- *Electoral processes*. The design and management of elections has a strong impact on the wider political system. International IDEA seeks to ensure the professional management and independence of elections, the best design of electoral systems, and public confidence in the electoral process.

- *Political parties*. Polls taken across the world show that voters have little confidence in political parties even though they provide the essential link between the electorate and government. International IDEA analyses how political parties involve their members, how they represent their constituencies, and their public funding arrangements, management and relationship with the public.

- *Constitution-building processes.* A constitutional process can lay the foundations for peace and development or plant seeds of conflict. International IDEA provides knowledge and makes policy proposals for constitution building that is genuinely nationally owned, sensitive to gender and conflict-prevention dimensions, and responds effectively to national priorities.

- *Democracy and gender.* If democracies are to be truly representative, then women— who make up over half of the world's population—must be able to participate on equal terms with men. International IDEA develops comparative analyses and tools to advance the participation and representation of women in political life.

- *Democracy assessments.* Democratization needs to be nationally driven. The *State of Democracy methodology* developed by International IDEA allows people to assess their own democracy instead of relying on externally produced indicators or rankings of democracies.

## Where does International IDEA work?

International IDEA works worldwide. It is based in Stockholm, Sweden, and has offices in Latin America, Africa and Asia.

## Which are International IDEA's member states?

International IDEA's member states are all democracies and provide both political and financial support to the work of the institute. They are: Australia, Barbados, Belgium, Botswana, Canada, Cape Verde, Chile, Costa Rica, Denmark, Finland, Germany, India, Mauritius, Mexico, Namibia, the Netherlands, Norway, Peru, Portugal, South Africa, Spain, Sweden, Switzerland and Uruguay. Japan has observer status.

# About the Federal Electoral Institute of Mexico

The Federal Electoral Institute (Instituto Federal Electoral, IFE) is a permanent autonomous public body, independent in its decisions and its functioning, responsible for organizing federal elections in Mexico—those for president and for the deputies and senators of the Congress. The IFE was created in October 1990 by constitutional mandate, and must observe five main principles—certainty, legality, independence, impartiality and objectivity—in its operations. Its highest steering body is the General Council, made up of nine members who may speak and vote (the president of the Council and eight electoral councillors, who are elected for a seven-year term by the Chamber of Deputies) as well as councillors of the Legislative Branch, representatives of the national political parties, and the executive secretary, all of whom may contribute to its deliberations but not vote.

As of 1993, through its specialist International Department, the IFE has established systematic networking, exchange and cooperation with institutions and organizations of the international community that are involved with or specialize in the promotion of democracy and electoral technical assistance. Since then, officers and experts from the IFE have participated in over 50 missions of technical assistance in 26 countries throughout the world.

Since 1998 the IFE has maintained fruitful collaboration with International IDEA.

> Federal Electoral Institute
> Viaducto Tlalpan No. 100, Arenal Tepepan
> 14610 Mexico City, Mexico
> Telephone: (5255) 5449 0450
> Fax: (5255) 5449 0457
> Website: <http://www.ife.org.mx>